Nigerian Women in Development:
A Research Bibliography

Catherine M. Coles and Barbara Entwisle

P
E
S
S
CROSSROADS

NIGERIAN WOMEN IN DEVELOPMENT: A RESEARCH BIBLIOGRAPHY

By

Catherine M. Coles and Barbara Entwisle
With the Assistance of Margaret Hardner

November 1985

ISBN 0-918456-58-4

Crossroads Press
255 Kinsey Hall
University of California-Los Angeles
Los Angeles, California 90024

(Crossroads Press is a subsidiary
of the African Studies Association)

Printed in the United States of America

TABLE OF CONTENTS

Acknowledgements

There are many persons whose individual and combined efforts made the completion of this document possible. A grant from the Rockefeller Center for the Social Sciences at Dartmouth College provided funding for the project. Dr. James Wright, Associate Dean of the Social Sciences, was especially supportive of our efforts, as was the chair of the African and Afro-American Studies Program, Professor Richard Joseph. The Department of Sociology provided on-going clerical and secretarial assistance, augmented by the Department of Anthropology and Program in African and Afro-American Studies. In particular Vera Kidder, Brenda LeBlanc, Evelyn Johnson and Debbie Hodges for their clerical help. Our special thanks go also to Jo Steele for her help in preparation of the final manuscript.

Of crucial importance to our efforts were the library and computing systems at Dartmouth. At Baker Library, Fran Oscadal, Patsy Carter and Lois Krieger gave freely of their time, as did Elaine Bent at Dana Library. We also thank Jo Steele and Emily Bryant, who assisted us at Kiewit Computer Center, and Dartmouth College for time on the college's computing system.

Many colleages around the world responded generously to our request for advice and information, for which we are grateful. We thank especially G. T. Acsadi, Gwendolyn Johnson-Acsadi, Hilary Page, Ron Lesthaeghe, David Lucas, Nadine Horenstein, Karen White, Michael Armer, Bolanle Awe, Paul Beckett, Jerome Barkow, Sandra Barnes, Sara Berry, John C. Caldwell, Paul Campbell, Alan Frishman, Michael Horowitz, Sidney Kasfir, Lillian Trager, Patricia Kuntz, Paul Lovejoy, Beverly Mack, Paulina Makinwa-Adebusoye, David Norman, Philip Olusanya, Christine Oppong, Margaret Peil, Robert Stock, Constance Sutton, Helen Tartaro, and Helen Ware.

Finally we wish to thank especially two individuals who provided enthusiastic support and continuous assistance throughout the entire project: Robin Wagner-Birkner, formerly a reference librarian at Baker Library, and Margaret Hardner, our able research assistant, who conducted much of the literature search.

The production of this document has been a genuinely mutual endeavor to which we have contributed equally: as such, the form of authorship represents only an alphabetical listing of names.

Catherine M. Coles
Dartmouth College
Hanover, New Hampshire

Barbara Entwisle
University of North Carolina
Chapel Hill

November 6, 1985

Chapter 1
Introduction

Researchers and policy-makers alike increasingly acknowledge the crucial nature of roles played by women in Third World development. As Brown (1979) and others have noted, no country can afford to exclude half of its population from development processes. Yet the impact of social and economic transformation on women, and conversely the particular contributions women make to these changes, are not well understood. Because of its prominence in subSaharan Africa and the Third World, its variegated and complex social and economic system, and its melange of different cultures and religions, Nigeria represents an important case for the study of women in development.

This bibliography assembles for the first time a wide range of materials relevant to the participation of women in development processes in Nigeria. These materials include books, articles, chapters, conference papers, theses, unpublished papers and manuscripts, and reports of varying origins. The bibliography draws principally on the literature in the social sciences: demography; anthropology; sociology; economics; women's studies. In addition, and where relevant, it selects from the medical, legal, and administrative literatures. Titles are organized according to topic: roughly half of the chapters involve various roles of women; the other half focus on particular issues of development.

References were obtained from a variety of sources. First, we searched *Abstracts in Anthropology, A Current Bibliography on African Affairs, Dissertation Abstracts International, Economic Abstracts International, Economic Literature Index, International African Bibliography, the Peabody Collection, Population Bibliography, Population Index, PopLine, Sociological Abstracts, Social Sciences Citation Index*, and *Women's Studies Abstracts*. For the most part, these indexes yielded titles appearing between 1968 and 1983. Recent issues of key journals (e.g., *The African Studies Review, Rural Africana*) were hand-searched to bring coverage as up to date as possible, usually from mid-1984 to early 1985. Second, we consulted recently compiled bibliographies on related topics. Three proved particularly helpful: Lucas et al., *An Annotated Bibliography of the Nigerian Fertility and Family Planning Literature* (1985); Kisekka, *Women and Development in Nigeria; An Annotated Bibliography* (1981); and Aguolu, *Nigeria: A Comprehensive Bibliography in the Humanities and Social Sciences, 1900-1971* (1973). Third, we benefitted from the help and advice of numerous colleagues, to whom our thanks are directed specifically in the Acknowledgements above.

The titles contained in the bibliography vary in their availability. Some are easily accessible; others are not. For references falling in the former category, the accuracy of the entry could be verified. For less accessible references, we provide bibliographic information as reported by our sources, and cannot vouch for its complete accuracy. Certain issues of African journals (e.g., *Savannah*), documents of national and state governments in Nigeria, conference proceedings, and unpublished papers written at Nigerian universities proved particularly difficult to locate. Nevertheless, these materials appear in the bibliography since others may have better access to them.

This bibliography is the outgrowth of a project to study the feasibility of conducting joint anthropological and sociological research on Nigerian women in development. As such it reflects the particular interests of the authors, and we do not claim that it is comprehensive in its coverage of literature on Nigerian women generally. For example, we did not investigate written sources on political roles and activities of Nigerian women (see Westfall 1974). Our motivation for disseminating this bibliography to a wide audience is to encourage and facilitate research on various roles of women in Nigeria, connections between these roles and the course that development is taking there, and related topics. We therefore take this opportunity not only to share bibliographic information but also to comment broadly on problems and potentialities in the study of Nigerian women and development. The remainder of this introductory chapter is devoted to: (1) approaches to the conceptualization and measurement of development; (2) the kinds of data available on Nigerian women, and the weaknesses of these data; (3) the need for improved conceptual

1

frameworks to guide further data collection and analysis; (4) the utility of a role category framework; and (5) the application of this framework as an organizing principle in the current bibliography.

Few would dispute the desirability of societal development, but this consensus does not imply agreement on what the concept entails or how to measure it. Relatively narrow definitions were used by early modernization theorists (e.g. Levy 1966) and are still applied by some economists today. For example, in the Harrod-Domar model development is identified with a sustained increase in economic production. Broader approaches are used in varying forms by proponents as diverse as developmentalists and marxists. They tend to include the reduction of poverty, inequality, and unemployment along with economic growth in the concept of development (Todaro 1977:60-61; Frank 1972). Typical indicators of the narrower concept of development are per capita income and growth in national product, whereas the broader conceptions might be defined operationally in terms of infant mortality, literacy, and adequacy of diet (Morris 1979).

Choice of particular concept and indicator have important consequences for assessing the apparent improvement, stagnation, or retrogression of a country's standing, as is readily demonstrated for Nigeria. According to estimates prepared by the World Bank (1984), GNP per capita in 1982 equalled $860, placing Nigeria in the category of middle-income economies and close to the top of subSaharan African countries. The average annual growth rate in gross domestic product between 1970 and 1982 was 3.8 percent, which, while not unusual for Third World countries during this period, did exceed the growth experienced by a majority of subSaharan economies (World Bank 1984:220). Thus, measures based upon a narrow conception of development show clear advances in the Nigerian situation.

Yet increases in aggregate income and product do not necessarily transform the lives of the persons who live in a country. Nigeria's ranking according to such indicators as life expectancy at birth, infant mortality, and calorie supply falls short of its ranking on per capita income and growth in product. The former measures, used within the context of a broader conception of development, are more sensitive to the distribution of wealth than the latter ones. They indicate that the benefits of recent economic growth have not been felt equally by all segments of the Nigerian population. Furthermore, while confirmatory data are sparse, women appear to be one of the groups to have benefitted relatively little (Anker 1978). It is even possible that the position of women has deteriorated (Afonja 1981), although not all investigators would agree (Standing and Sheehan 1978).

Significantly, the shift to a broader needs-based, welfare concept of development coincides with an increased recognition of women as both participants in and beneficiaries of the process. This is seen immediately in the kinds of social indicators which become relevant. Consider, for example, adequacy of nutrition. The social reality underlying this indicator involves women as key actors. In the case of Nigeria, women play a central role in agricultural production and food processing, as well as having responsibility for preparation of food within the family (Adeyokunnu 1981; Norman, Simmons, and Hays 1982; Women in Nigeria 1985). Other indicators related to health and mortality, and to some extent education, similarly reflect aspects of the productive and reproductive roles of women and place them at a point central to development processes.

The centrality of women in development becomes readily apparent when taking a broad approach to conceptualization and measurement, but it does not depend crucially on such an approach. For example, the poor performance of Nigerian agriculture has been a matter of concern to all, regardless of approach. Unlike many countries with a lagging agricultural sector, "...the size of the country and its varieties of climate and soil give Nigeria the potential to become a leading agricultural nation" (McWilliam 1982:471). This potential has not been realized; in fact, food production per capita has declined in recent years (World Bank 1984:228). Since Nigerian women are responsible in large part for the subsistence of the entire population, recognition of the crucial roles played by them in agriculture, and a reorientation of programs and policies to address the interests and needs of female farmers, may be the key to a reversal of this trend. Thus, however one defines and measures development, the activities of women must be taken into consideration.

2

Data pertinent to the participation of women in development processes in Nigeria might be generously described as sparse. This is part and parcel of the general paucity of social and economic information for Nigeria. Take a datum as basic as population size. According to official figures, the population of Nigeria consisted of 85 million inhabitants in 1980 (McWilliam 1982). This figure is in considerable dispute, however. Other sources peg population size at about 77 million in that year (e.g., United Nations 1984). The difference is not trivial. Using the official count, the World Bank (1982) estimates a GNP per capita in 1980 at $1010. If the alternative count were substituted, GNP per capita would instead equal $1111 in that year.[1]

Given disagreement on the statistical totals, the lack of disaggregated data comes as no surprise. Recently, the USAID Women in Development Office sponsored an effort to assemble and make available statistics on education, health, households, income and employment separately for men and women in 120 countries. The resulting collection of data for Nigeria (USAID 1983) is notable less for what it contains than for what is absent. The USAID report shows table titles and stubs regardless of data availability. The thirty-one pages of this publication consist largely of tables with blank interiors. The information is either unavailable, too restricted in coverage, or of unacceptable quality.

Although few data pertinent to the activities and roles of Nigerian women are available centrally, information of varying quantity and quality can be found in other sources. International statistical compendia sometimes report useful details. For example, the *World Development Report 1982* indicates a ratio of male to female literacy of 2.0 for Nigeria in 1980 (World Bank 1982:198). Similar types of data are also available in *Africa South of the Sahara* (numerous editions); *Women of the World: Sub-Saharan Africa* (Newman 1984); and *Africa: Nigeria--Selected Statistical Data by Sex* (USAID 1983; Newman 1984). Statistics presented in such sources must be used with caution, however, as there are serious problems associated with reliability and recording of the data (Pittin 1982; USAID 1983).

Many of the specifically quantitative data available on women come from surveys conducted in Nigeria. For example, the sex-specific infant mortality rates which represent one of the few items to appear in the AID report referenced above, come from the National Family and Family Planning Survey 1971-73 (Acsadi, Igun and Johnson 1972). Although survey data vary in quality, are not national in coverage, and are not always available for the purposes of secondary analysis, they nevertheless represent an important source of data on women and one which has not been fully exploited (Entwisle and Coles 1985). Surveys have been undertaken for a wide variety of purposes in Nigeria. Those relevant to women in development, at least potentially, include surveys of the family and family relationships (Okedeji, F.O. et al. 1976), surveys of contraceptive knowledge, attitudes, and practice (Acsadi, Igun and Johnson 1972; Rehan 1984), surveys of childbearing (Lesthaeghe et al. 1981), and surveys of migration experience (Lacey 1981).

Qualitative data from travel accounts, reports of missionaries and colonial officials, ethnographies, and field studies also yield information on Nigerian women and changes in their roles and activities. Travel and mission records dating generally from the nineteenth century (such as Clapperton 1829; Barth 1857-58; Denham and Clapperton 1826; Johnson 1921) provide some of the earliest accounts. Colonial records, historical works, and ethnographic studies, some commissioned by colonial authorities, soon followed (e.g. Tremearne 1913; Meek 1931; Buchanan and Pugh 1955). Unfortunately, these and subsequent ethnographic materials tend neither to document fully the activities of women nor to represent their perspectives. Nevertheless, when used with care and discretion, they do offer valuable information, especially of an historical nature.

There are important exceptions, of course. A few intensive studies of women predated the recent upsurge of interest in women in development, including D. A. Talbot's *Woman's Mysteries of a Primitive People* (1915, on Ibibio women), Leith-Ross's *African Women* (1939, on Ibo women), Mary Smith's *Baba of Karo* (1954, on Hausa women), and Gloria Marshall's (now Niara Sudarkasa) dissertation 'Women, Trade and the Yoruba Family' (1964). Within the last fifteen years, increasing numbers of scholars have studied the roles and activities of Nigerian women within particular contexts--political (Awe 1979; Okonjo 1976; Van Allen 1972, 1976; Mba 1982); economic (Sudarkasa 1973; Longhurst 1982; Lucas 1976; Ottenberg 1959); ritual and religion

(Drewal and Drewal 1983; Barkow 1972; Hoch-Smith 1978), and others.

As this brief review indicates, the details available on the roles of Nigerian women in development are sketchy, in many cases arising from studies designed for other purposes. Clearly, there is a need for more information, and we are not the first to issue this call (Nelson 1981; Pittin 1984). However, we do not recommend a blind extension of previous data collection efforts. The concepts used to guide data collection and analysis are themselves in need of revision, first, to recognize and give appropriate weight to the activities of women and, secondly, to document accurately the linkages between these activities and the contexts of their occurrence.

Standard approaches to the collection of social and economic data, particularly at the aggregate level, have tended to focus disproportionately on the activities of men. Probably the most glaring example is the concept of the economically active population or of labor force participation. Typically, the latter is defined and measured in terms of cash-remunerated employment in the formal sector of the economy. Work in the informal sector is frequently overlooked, with the result that the productive contribution made by women is understated (Pittin 1982; USAID 1983). In Nigeria, the extensive participation of women in subsistence agriculture may pass unnoticed if only statistics on the formal labor force are examined. Self-employed women and women whose labor is expended primarily within the domestic setting may also be missed because these occupations do not fall within the wage labor system.

A more balanced picture requires that the work performed by women in the informal sector of the economy, in familial settings, in the absence of monetary compensation, and in conjunction with childcare and other domestic tasks be taken into account. To this end, however, analysts may have over-corrected for previous bias through the creation of artificial distinctions between male and female domains. This is seen in conceptual dichotomies such as formal/informal, public/private, and productive/reproductive which set off female activities and spheres of influence as distinct from and in opposition to those of males (Pittin 1984). While it is beyond the scope of this document to assess fully the range of conceptual and analytical categories applied in contemporary studies of African and Third World women and development, it may be useful to consider the shortcomings of a few of the more widely used dichotomous classifications as a precautionary guide in the construction of a more fruitful approach (Beneria 1981; Newman 1984; Pittin 1982; Tiano 1981).[2]

One dichotomy of which extensive use has been made is that between public and private (or domestic) domains of activity and influence. Rosaldo describes this dichotomy as follows:

"Domestic," as used here, refers to those minimal institutions and modes of activity that are organized immediately around one or more mothers and their children; "public" refers to activities, institutions, and forms of association that link, rank, organize, or subsume particular mother-child groups (1974:23).

Scholars working within this paradigm have documented, in many areas for the first time, the actual activities, behavior and perceptions of women. Insights have also been gained through the application of this framework to investigate patterns of power and influence exercised through informal means in society, usually by females, as opposed to formal authority structures most often controlled by males. Unfortunately, however, use of the public/domestic framework has led too often to the portrayal of women only in relation to households and families assumed to comprise the private sphere, neglecting the study of linkages between the public and private arenas and of significant roles which do not confine females to the household domain (Bujra 1979; Nelson 1974).

A related point concerns difficulties arising from the use of the household as a unit of analysis within which women's activities and labor are studied. Among the most significant of these are the lack of uniformity in meaning as the term, household, is used (Guyer, 1981). Household composition may depend on whether households are considered as units of production, consumption, kinship or residence. Moreover, their membership for any single purpose may be fluid over time (see Arnould 1984). The labor of women within households, and the degree to which women may serve as household heads, varies accordingly. Finally, we note an imperfect congruence between the household and the private or domestic domain. As Nelson (1974) has pointed out for Middle Eastern women, households and families have a profound significance in the public domain. This holds true throughout Nigeria.

Dichotomies have been applied by proponents of modernization theory and developmentalism, as well as marxism, to generalize about the relative participation of males and females in particular spheres of the economy (Tiano 1981). For example, the concepts of productive and reproductive labor have been used to characterize the majority of male and female work, respectively (see Bujra 1979); and the occupations of women have been described as falling primarily within the informal as opposed to formal sector of the economy. The central problem in applying these concepts and constructs to the study of women in development lies in the lack of fit between the models of society they represent and the actual behavior and activities of women themselves.

Indeed, Nigerian women defy many of the dichotomies and constructs developed to analyze their behavior. They participate in public as well as private domains, and may also act as links between the two (Okonjo 1983). For example, in northern Nigeria, Jackson (1978) has described rural Muslim Hausa women on strike to obtain higher wages in bean harvesting, Pittin (1979) has pointed out the political activities and involvement of Hausa prostitutes in Katsina, and Coles (1983) has shown the implications of the occupations of older Hausa women in Kaduna for high levels of prestige and wealth in the public community. Women are involved in both formal and informal sectors of the economy (E. Fapohunda 1978, 1983). Nigerian women are active within and sometimes as heads of various types of households, yet they are also tied to kin and social groups outside their immediate households (Van Allen 1976). When accurately recognized, their labor often includes both productive and reproductive aspects.

If the actual and potential participation of Nigerian women in the development process is to be assessed accurately and addressed seriously, a framework is needed for the collection and analysis of data on the activities and behaviors of women. We would propose that such a framework be based on the many roles in which women engage. We prefer a focus on roles rather than the overall "status" of women, because the latter obscures the different aspects of the economic power, political influence, and social prestige held by women and therefore varies in its application from one context to another (Mason 1984; Oppong 1980). Furthermore, the totality of women's interrelated roles is emphasized rather than isolation of a single aspect of women's activities identified by topic or arena (such as 'political', 'domestic', or 'public').

Roles may be defined for present purposes as those patterns of behavior and expectations associated with particular differentiated social positions occupied by members of society in specific social contexts (see Biddle 1979:58ff).[3] Role analysis allows the analyst to begin at the grassroots level with the individual woman and her ideas, attitudes, and behaviors. It is then possible to consider the social, political, and economic context within which these roles are situated. In the case of Nigeria, such structural conditions include a highly skewed distribution of income and resources; the conspicuous wealth of those at the top end of the continuum; a recent recession accompanied by severe inflation and unemployment; increasing job competition between men and women within the informal sector as a result of the recession; the introduction within the last ten years of universal primary education; the even more recent burgeoning of Arabic schools in the North; laws which do not guarantee women's position in divorce, custody of children, and child support; and the thoroughly multicultural nature of the society. Our approach is explicitly multilevel in that it attempts to link the actual activities of individual women with characteristics of the local, national, and international culture and environment. It is also able to draw on quantitative and qualitative data and methods of analysis, gaining insights from both.

In our judgement, the most useful conceptual and methodological framework for the study of women's roles is that proposed by Oppong (1980). Oppong delineates seven role categories: parental; occupational; conjugal; domestic; kin; community; and individual. These role constructs are sufficiently inclusive to cover virtually all aspects of women's activities and behavior, and provide a minimal framework which will allow for comparative cross-cultural analyses. Yet they can be 'filled in' with data from categories developed by actors in specific societies, and are not so restrictive nor isolated from each other as to force the data into artificial and inappropriate 'boxes'. Furthermore, Oppong's framework directs attention to various aspects of roles, all of which are significant: ideal role behavior, expected role behavior, perceptions of role behavior, and actual role behavior.

Oppong's role framework provides an excellent starting point for data collection and analysis in studies related to women and development in Nigeria. Indeed, it provides an organizing principle for our collection of references on this topic. Two adjustments seem useful and appropriate in the Nigerian context, however.

The first modification that we propose concerns the categories of 'domestic role' and 'occupational role.' Distinctions drawn according to the location or arena of labor, as opposed to the type of labor carried out (i.e. productive or reproductive) or the relationships between people resulting from this labor, may lead to the same artificial separation inherent in the public/domestic framework (Tiano 1981:13). An example of the dilemma posed by this dichotomy can be found in the food processing industry, in which many Nigerian women are engaged. Foodstuffs may be bought by women in public markets; they are then processed and partially prepared within the home; and finally may be cooked and sold in a public location, such as a streetcorner (Coles 1984). While these activities take place in different settings, they are part of a complex yet single directed process of productive labor, and are initiated primarily for the purpose of securing income. Not only are women's work in the home and outside frequently integrated; so also are relationships in which a woman is involved within the domestic setting, for they are derived not only from that residential base, which might be considered a subset of community roles, but from her conjugal, maternal, and kinship roles. Rather than separating types of work and relationships on the basis of locational context, thereby creating occupational and domestic roles, we suggest the use of a single category to include all women's work activities. Including all work within a single conceptual category allows one to eliminate many of the problematic distinctions posed by application of dichotomies such as productive and reproductive labor, or income-earning as opposed to non-remunerated work. In the Nigerian case, the closely integrated nature of women's different work activities, and the significance of each, can then be recognized.

A second change to the Oppong framework, intended to better adapt it to the Nigerian context, is the delimitation of a religious or ritual role. Oppong classifies activities associated with this domain as part of the individual and/or community roles. However, since religious and ritual activities are not undertaken purely for individual ends in Nigeria, and are subject to considerable peer pressure, to incorporate them in the individual role category seems inappropriate. Yet, these activities may be conducted privately, or within a kin setting, and so do not fall cleanly within the community role category either. As an example, Muslim women in various parts of Nigeria engage in a variety of activities that cross-cut the individual and community roles: they make the hajj to Mecca, attend Arabic schools, and engage in private prayer several times a day. We therefore add a religious/ritual role to the other role categories in Oppong's framework.

Both proposed changes are organizational. The elimination of distinctions among the productive activities of women, and the subsetting of religious and ritual activities, do not alter any fundamental aspects of the role framework. Of course, the application of this framework to a particular research situation may require further reorganization of the role categories.

To maximize the utility of the role framework for future data collection and analysis, we thought it would be helpful to organize the existing literature on Nigerian women and development in terms of role categories. If pertinent references are viewed as a kind of data, then the attempt to do so represents an initial empirical application of the framework. Unfortunately, some distinctions which are conceptually desirable in the analysis of roles provide little leverage in the classification of articles, papers, reports, monographs, theses, and books relevant to women in Nigeria. This is not surprising given the recency of interest in females roles as a focus of study in Nigeria. Nevertheless, it means that for the purposes of the bibliography we must condense the role framework into four categories: economic, conjugal, ritual/religious, and family/household. Each category corresponds to a subsequent chapter of this document.

Chapter Two groups references on the work of women, whatever its characteristics and purposes may be, under the heading of economic roles. The primary work activities of Nigerian women appear to consist of domestic maintenance and childcare, cooking, and farming, with trading, food processing, and the sale of prepared foods highest on the list of income-earning activities practised (see for example, Hill 1972; Sudarkasa 1973). Although the particular activities of women vary across urban and rural sectors, and only a relatively small proportion of women are wage laborers, economic roles comprise a major portion of the daily activities of Nigerian women.

Chapter Three brings together references on the roles of women in marriage and divorce (i.e., conjugal roles). Because marriage patterns and practices are widely diverse, conjugal roles of Nigerian women may reflect monogamous or polygynous marriages. Many do not have rights of custody over children after divorce, nor can they expect continued support from a former husband. For Nigerian women, marriage does not necessarily imply financial support by the husband, and many women contribute substantial amounts to their own and their children's subsistence.

Chapter Four assembles references on the roles of women in the household and family. In the family and household, women's roles may arise out of kin relationships if they are living in kin- based residences; yet increasingly in urban centers women find themselves in rented housing, sharing compounds with Nigerians from various ethnic, cultural and religious backgrounds. Here the family and household take on new forms: neighbors may be treated as fictive kin, and a large compound housing a hundred people or more may constitute the smallest community in which a woman participates. Thus, we group references involving kinship and residential community roles with those addressing the roles of women in the family and household.

Chapter Five draws together references on the religious and ritual roles of women in Nigeria. These roles vary, as women may be adherents of Islam, Christianity, indigenous ritual religous systems, or various combinations of these. Religious roles frequently have implications for the roles of women in kin groups, in marriage, and in the community. Indeed, all roles in which women engage are mutually reinforcing to some degree.

The application of this condensed version of the role framework reveals that much can be learned on roles of women from currently available sources in the published and unpublished literature. However, it is not possible to classify all existing references according to role categories. We therefore use a second axis of organization for the bibliography, this one based on issues of development especially germane to the Nigerian setting. These issues represent a long-standing and common orientation for commentary and research. Particular interest attaches to issues and problems in which women figure prominently. Thus, chapters on family planning, fertility, health and nutrition, female associations and networks, education, and migration and development are included. In addition, a final chapter lists ethnographies and other general works which take up many of the different roles and issues that we have identified.

NOTES

[1]The collapse of oil prices and the ensuing recession of 1980-82 accounts for most of the difference between these figures and those reported earlier for 1982; the difference in reference years during which time currency values vary accounts for the remainder. See above, p. 2.

[2]Numerous critiques of contemporary conceptual and analytical approaches to women and development exist: see for example Tiano 1981; Newman 1984; Pittin 1982; Beneria 1981.

[3]Role theory has developed an extensive record in both sociology and anthropology, with sources too numerous to report here. See for example Banton 1961, 1965; Linton 1936; Merton 1949, 1957; Southall 1959, 1973; and Turner 1966.

References Cited

Acsadi, Gyorgy T.; Igun, Adenola A.; and Johnson, Gwendolyn Z. 1972. Surveys of Fertility, Family, and Family Planning in Nigeria. Institute of Population and Manpower Studies (IPMS), Publication No.2. University of Ife. Ile-Ife.

Adeyokunnu, Tomilayo. 1981. *Women and Agriculture in Nigeria*. Addis Ababa: ATRCW, UNECA.

Afonja, Simi. 1981. Changing Modes of Production and the Sexual Division of Labour Among the Yoruba. *Signs* 7(2):299-313.

Aguolu, Christian Chukwunedu. 1973. *Nigeria: A Comprehensive Bibliography in the Humanities and Social Sciences, 1900-1971*. Boston: G.K. Hall and Co.

Anker, Richard. 1978. Demographic Change and the Role of Women: A Research Programme in Developing Countries. Population and Employment Working Paper No. 69. World Employment Programme Research. ILO. Geneva.

Arnould, Eric J. 1984. Marketing and Social Reproduction in Zinder, Niger Republic. In *Households: Comparative and Historical Studies of the Domestic Group*, ed. Robert McC. Netting, Richard R. Wilk and Eric J. Arnould, pp. 130-162. Berkeley: University of California Press.

Awe, Bolanle. 1979. The Iyalode in the Traditional Yoruba Political System. In *Sexual Stratification: A Cross Cultural Perspective*, ed. Alice Schlegel, pp. 144-195. New York: Columbia University Press.

Banton, Michael. 1961. The Restructuring of Social Relationships. In *Social Change in Modern Africa*, ed. Aidan Southall, pp. 113-125. London: Oxford University Press.

----. 1965. *Roles: An Introduction to the Study of Social Relations*. New York: Basic Books.

Barkow, Jerome H. 1972. Hausa Women and Islam. *Canadian Journal of African Studies* 6:317-328.

Barth, H. 1857. *Travels and Discoveries in North and Central Africa. 5 vols. 2nd ed.*

Beneria, Lourdes. 1981. Conceptualizing the Labor Force: The Underestimation of Women's Economic Activities. In *African Women in the Development Process*, ed. Nici Nelson, pp. 10-28. London: Frank Cass.

Berry, S. 1975. *Cocoa, Custom and Socio-Economic Change in Rural Western Nigeria*. Oxford: Clarendon Press.

8

Biddle, B. J. 1979. *Role Theory: Expectations, Identities and Behavior*. London: Academic Press.

Brown, C. K. 1979. The Participation of Women in Rural Development in Kaduna State of Nigeria. Centre for Social and Economic Research. Ahmadu Bello University. Zaria.

Buchanan, K. M., and Pugh, J. C. 1955. *Land and People in Nigeria*. London.

Bujra, Janet M. 1979. Introductory: Female Solidarity and the Sexual Division of Labour. In *Women United, Women Divided*, ed. Patricia Caplan and Janet M. Bujra, pp. 13-45. Bloomington: Indian University Press.

Clapperton, H. 1829. *Journal of a Second Expedition into the Interior of Africa*. London.

Coles, Catherine M. 1983. The Old Woman in Hausa Society: Formal and Informal Power and Authority in Northern Nigeria. Paper presented at the annual meeting of the African Studies Association. Boston, MA.

----. 1984. Hausa Women in the Urban Economy: Productive and Reproductive Roles of Kaduna Women. Presented at the Annual Meeting of the African Studies Association. Los Angeles.

Denham, D., and Clapperton, H. 1826. *Narrative of Travels and Discoveries in Northern and Central Africa*. London.

Drewal, Henry J., and Drewal, Margaret T. 1983. *Gelede: Art and Female Power Among the Yoruba*. Bloomington: Indiana University Press.

Entwisle, Barbara, and Coles, Catherine. 1985. Methodology in the Study of Female Roles: Demographic Surveys and Nigerian Women. Presented at the Annual Meeting of the African Studies Association. New Orleans.

Fapohunda, Eleanor R. 1978. Women at Work in Nigeria: Factors Affecting Modern Sector Employment. In *Human Resources and African Development*, ed. U.G. Damachi and V.P. Diejomaoh, pp. 220-241. New York/London: Praeger.

----. 1983. Female and Male Work Profiles. In *Female and Male in West Africa*, ed. C. Oppong, pp. 32-53. London: George Allen and Unwin.

Frank, A. G. 1972. Sociology of Development and Underdevelopment of Sociology. In *Dependence and Underdevelopment*, ed. J.D. Cockcroft, A.G. Frank and D.L. Johnson, pp. 321-397. Garden City, New York: Anchor Books.

Guyer, Jane I. 1981. Household and Community in African Studies. *The African Studies Review XXIV (2/3):* 87-137.

Hill, Polly. 1972. *Rural Hausa: A Village and a Setting.* London: Cambridge University Press.

Hoch-Smith, J. 1978. Radical Yoruba Female Sexuality. In *Women in Ritual and Symbolic Roles,* ed. J. Hoch-Smith and A. Spring, pp. 245-267. New York: Plenum Press.

Jackson, Sam. 1978. Hausa Women on Strike. *Review of African Political Economy* 13:21-36.

Johnson, Reverend Samuel. 1921. *The History of the Yorubas.* London: Routledge and Kegan Paul Ltd.

Kisekka, Mere Nakateregga. 1981. *Women and Development in Nigeria: An Annotated Bibliography.* Addis Abada: Economic Commission for Africa, United Nations.

Lacey, Linda. 1981. Urban Migration in Developing Countries: A Case Study of Three Cities in Nigeria. Ph.D. Dissertation. Cornell University. Ithaca.

Leith-Ross, Sylvia. 1939. *African Women: A Study of the Ibo of Nigeria.* London: Faber and Faber.

Lesthaeghe, R.; Page, H. J.; and Adegbola, O. 1981. Child-spacing and Fertility in Lagos. In *Child-spacing in Tropical Africa: Traditions and Change,* ed. H.J. Page and R. Lesthaeghe, pp. 147-179. New York: Academic Press.

Levy, M. J., Jr. 1966. *Modernization and the Structure of Societies.* Princeton: Princeton University Press.

Linton, Ralph. 1936. *The Study of Man.* New York: D. Appleton-Century Company.

Longhurst, Richard. 1982. Resource Allocation and the Sexual Division of Labor: A Case Study of a Moslem Hausa Village in Northern Nigeria. In *Women and Development,* ed. L. Beneria, pp. 95-117. New York: Praeger.

Lucas, David. 1976. Participation of Women in the Nigerian Labour Force Since the 1950's with Particular Reference to Lagos. Ph.D. Dissertation. Dept. of Economics. University of London. London.

Lucas, David; Sherlaimoff, Tania; Waddell-Wood, Peter; and Higman, Merle. 1985. *An Annotated Bibliography of the Nigerian Fertility and Family Planning Literature.* Canberra: Dept. of Demography, Australian National University.

McWilliam, J. A. 1982. Nigeria. In *International Encyclopedia of Population. Vol.2*, ed. J.A. Ross, pp. 471-476. New York: Free Press.

Marshall, Gloria Albertha. 1964. Women, Trade, and the Yoruba Family. Ph.D. Dissertation. Columbia University. New York.

Mason, Karen. 1984. The Status of Women, Fertility and Mortality: A Review of the Interrelationships. Research Reports No. 84-58. Population Studies Center. University of Michigan. Ann Arbor.

Mba, Nina Emma. 1982. *Nigerian Women Mobilized*. Berkeley: Institute of International Studies, University of California.

Meek, Charles Kingsley. 1931. *Tribal Studies in Northern Nigeria*. London: Oxford University Press.

Merton, Robert K. 1949. *On Theoretical Sociology*. New York: The Free Press.

----. 1957. The role-set: problems in sociological theory. *British Journal of Sociology* 8:106-120.

Morris, M. D. 1979. *Measuring the Conditions of the World's Poor*. New York: Pergamon Press.

Nelson, Cynthia. 1974. Public and Private Politics: Women in the Middle Eastern World. *American Ethnologist* 1(3):551-563.

Nelson, Nici. 1981. Introduction. In *African Women in the Development Process*, ed. Nici Nelson, pp. 1-9. London: Frank Cass.

Newman, Jeanne S. 1984. *Women of the World: Sub-Saharan Africa*. Washington, D.C.: WID-USAID and U.S. Department of Commerce, Bureau of the Census.

Norman, David W.; Simmons, E. B; and Hays, Henry M. 1982. *Farming Systems in the Nigerian Savanna: Research and Strategies for Development*. Boulder, CO.: Westview Press.

Okediji, Francis Olu; Caldwell, John C.; Caldwell, Pat; and Ware, Helen. 1976. The Changing African Family Project: A Report With Special Reference to the Nigeria Segment. *Studies in Family Planning* 7(5):126-136.

Okonjo, Isabel Kamene. 1976. The Dual-Sex Political System in Operation: Igbo Women and Community Politics in Midwestern Nigeria. In *Women in Africa: Studies in Social and Economic Change*, ed. N.J. Hafkin and ed.a Bay, pp. 45-58. Stanford: Stanford University Press.

Okonjo, Kamene. 1983. Sex Roles in Nigerian Politics. In *Female and Male in West Africa*, ed. Cristine Oppong, pp. 211-222. London: George Allen and Unwin.

Oppong, Christine. 1980. A Synopsis of Seven Roles and the Status of Women: An Outline of A Conceptual and Methodological Approach. Population and Labour Policies Programme Working Paper No. 94. World Employment Programme Research. ILO. Geneva.

Ottenberg, Phoebe. 1959. The Changing Economic Position of Women Among the Afikpo Ibo. In *Continuity and Change in African Cultures*, ed. W. Bascom and M.J. Herskovits, pp. 205-303. Chicago: The University of Chicago Press, Phoenix Books.

Pittin, Renee. 1979. Marriage and Alternative Strategies: Career Patterns of Hausa Women in Katsina City. Ph.D. Dissertation. The School of Oriental and African Studies, University of London. London.

----. 1982. Documentation of Women's Work in Nigeria: Problems and Solutions. Population and Labour Policies Program Working Paper No. 125. World Employment Programme Research. ILO. Geneva.

Rehan, N. 1984. Knowledge, Attitude and Practice of Family Planning of Hausa Women. *Social Science and Medicine* 18:839-844.

Rosaldo, Michelle Zimbalist. 1974. Woman, Culture, and Society: A Theoretical Overview. In *Woman, Culture and Society*, ed. M.Z. Rosaldo and L. Lamphere, pp. 17-42. Stanford: Stanford Unversity Press.

Simmons, E. B. 1975. The Small-Scale Rural Food Processing Industry in Northern Nigeria. *Food Research Institute Studies* 14:147-161.

----. 1976. Economic Research on Women in Rural Development in Northern Nigeria. American Council on ed.cation, Paper 10. Overseas Liaison Committtee. Washington, D.C.

Smith, Mary F. 1954. *Baba of Karo*. London: Faber and Faber.

Southall, Aidan. 1959. An Operational Theory of Role. *Human Relations* 12:17-34.

----. 1973. The Density of Role-Relationships as a Universal Index of Urbanization. In *Urban Anthropology*, ed. Aidan Southall, pp. 71-106. London: Oxford University Press.

Standing, G., and Sheehan, G. 1978. Economic Activity of Women in Nigeria: Case Study No.8. In *Labour Force Participation in Low-Income Countries*, ed. G. Standing and G. Sheehan, pp. 129-36. Geneva: International Labour Organization.

Sudarkasa, Niara. 1973. *Where Women Work: A Study of the Yoruba in the Market Place and in the Home.* Ann Arbor, University of Michigan.

Talbot, D. Amaury. 1915. *Woman's Mysteries of A Primitive People.* London: Frank Cass and Co. Ltd. Reprinted 1968.

Tiano, Susan. 1981. The Separation of Women's Remunerated and Household Work: Theorectical Perspectives on "Women in Development". Women in International Development Working Paper No. 2. East Lansing: Michigan State University.

Todaro, Michael P. 1977. *Economic Development in the Third World.* New York: Longman.

Tremearne, A. J. H. 1913. *Hausa Superstitions and Customs.* London.

Turner, Ralph. 1966. Role-Taking, Role Standpoint, and Reference-Group Behavior. In *Role Theory: Concepts and Research,* ed. Bruce J. Biddle and ed.in J. Thomas, pp. 151-159. New York: John Wiley and Sons.

United Nations. 1984. *Demographic Yearbook 1981.* New York: UNFPA.

USAID. 1983. *Africa: Nigeria--Selected Statistical Data by Sex.* Washington D.C.: US Bureau of the Census, AID.

Van Allen, J. 1972. "Sitting on a Man": Colonialism and the Lost Political Institutions of Igbo Women. *Canadian Journal of African Studies* 6(2):165-181.

----. 1976. 'Aba Riots' or Igbo 'Women's War'? Ideology, Stratification, and the Invisibility of Women. In *Women in Africa: Studies in Social and Economic Change,* ed. N.J. Hafkin and E. Bay, pp. 59-86. Stanford: Stanford University Press.

Westfall, G. D. 1974. Nigerian Women: A Bibliographical Essay. *Africana Journal* 5:99-138.

Women In Nigeria. 1985. The Conditions of Women in Nigeria and Policy Recommendations up to 2000 A.D. Presented at the NGO Forum, UN Conference on Women, Nairobi, Kenya. Zaria, Nigeria.

World Bank. 1982. *World Development Report 1982.* New York: Oxford University Press.

----. 1984. *World Development Report 1984.* New York: Oxford University Press.

Chapter Two
Economic Roles of Women

1 Abbott, Joan. 1974. The Employment of Women and the Reduction of Fertility: Implications for Development. *World Development* 2:23-26.

2 Abdu, L. J. 1973. Female Labour in the Modern Economy of Kano. B.Sc. Essay. Dept. of Sociology. Ahmadu Bello University. Zaria.

3 Abell, H. 1962. The Role of Rural Women in Farm and Home Life. Report to the Government of Nigeria (Northern Region) on the Home Economics Aspects of the F.A.O. Socioeconomic Survey of Peasant Agriculture in Northern Nigeria. FAO. Rome.

4 Aboyade, B. 1976. Barriers to Participation of Nigerian Women in Modern Labour Force. Conference on Nigerian Women and Development. University of Ibadan. Ibadan.

5 Adamu, Ladi. 1978. Women and Farming. *African Women* 23:44.

6 Adekanye, Tomilayo O. 1984. The Ownership of Agricultural Products: Some Considerations for Integrating Women Into Rural Development in Africa. Presented at the Workshop on Women in Agriculture in West Africa, May 1984. International Livestock Centre for Africa. ITTA. Ibadan.

7 Adeokun, Lawrence A.; Adepoju, Aderanti; Ilori, Felicia; Adewuyi, A. A.; and Ebigbola, J. A. 1984. The Ife Labour Market: A Nigerian Case Study. Population and Labour Policies Programme, Working Paper No.144. ILO. Geneva.

8 Adepoju, Aderanti. 1976. Population Growth in Nigeria and Its Impact on the Labor Force. International Educational Materials Exchange, No.3114. International Institute for Labour Studies. Geneva.

9 Adewuyi, Alfred A. 1980. Childcare and Female Employment in a Nigerian Metropolis. *Nigerian Journal of Economic and Social Studies* 22(2):197-218.

10 ----. 1981. Estimation of Labour Supply for the 1980's in Nigeria. In *Population and Economic Development in Nigeria in the 1980's*, ed. Helena Chojnacka, P.O. Olusanya and F. Ojo, pp. 103-117. New York: United Nations Dept. of Technical Co-operation for Development.

11 Adeyokunnu, Tomilayo. 1970. The Markets for Foodstuffs in Western Nigeria. *Odu* 3:71-86.

12 ----. 1981. *Women and Agriculture in Nigeria*. Addis Ababa: ATRCW, UNECA.

13   Affrifah, S. F. 1965. Some Aspects of Hausa Economy. Master's Thesis. University of Ghana. Legon.

14   Afonja, Simi. 1974. Participation of Nigerian Women in Industry. *Ife African Studies* 1:39-44.

15   ----. 1977. Female Marginality in the Nigerian Labour Force. Paper presented at the Workshop on the Economic Marginalization of Women. Meetings of the African and Latin American Studies Associations. Houston, TX.

16   ----. 1981. Changing Modes of Production and the Sexual Division of Labour Among the Yoruba. *Signs* 7(2):299-313.

17   ----. 1984. Status of Women in West Africa. *African Women* 1(3):63-66.

18   Akande, J. O. 1979. Law and the Status of Women in Nigeria. Economic Commision for Africa. (ECA/ATRCW/RE801/79). Addis Ababa: ATRCW.

19   ----. 1979. Women in the Labour Force: Socio-legal Analysis. Presented at the Symposium on Women in Industry. Nigeria, Federal Ministry of Labour.

20   Akeredolu-Ale, E. A. 1975. *The Underdevelopment of Indigenous Entrepreneurship in Nigeria.* Ibadan: Ibadan University Press.

21   Amon-Nikoi, Gloria. 1978. Women and Work in Africa. In *Human Resources and African Development*, ed. U.G. Damachi and U.P. Diejomaoh, pp. 188-219. New York: Praeger.

22   Anaza, J. A. 1975. The Labour Market Implications of UPE. Paper presented to the Conference on Economic Development and Employment Generation in Nigeria. NISER. University of Ibadan. Ibadan.

23   Ardener, Shirley. 1977. *Perceiving Women.* London: Dent.

24   Arinola, O. A. N. 1978. The Implications of Female Labour Force Participation on the Family: A Case Study of Some Factory Workers. B.Sc. Essay. Department of Sociology. University of Ibadan. Ibadan.

25   Aronson, D. R. 1978. *The City is Our Farm: Seven Migrant Ijebu Yoruba Families.* Boston, MA.: Schenkman.

26   Arowolo, Oladele O. 1977. Fertility of Urban Yoruba Working Women: A Case Study of Ibadan City. *Nigerian Journal of Economic and Social Sciences* 19:37-66.

15

27   ----. 1978. *Female Labour Force Participation and Fertility: The Case of Ibadan City in the Western State of Nigeria.* Canberra: Australian National University. Changing African Family Project Monograph Series, No. 4, Vol.2.

28   Awe, Bolanle. 1975. The Economic Role of Women in a Traditional African Society: the Yoruba Example. La Civilization de la Femme Dans la Tradition Africaine. *Presence Africaine. pp.* 259-274.

29   Awosika, Keziah. 1976. Nigerian Women in the Informal Labour Market: Planning for Effective Participation. Paper presented at the Conference on Women and Development. Wellesley College. Wellesley, MA.

30   ----. 1976. Nigerian Women in the Labour Force: Implications for National Economic Planning. Paper presented at the National Conference on Women and Development in Relation to Changing Family Structure. University of Ibadan. Ibadan.

31   ----. 1977. Nigerian Women in the Labour Force-Implications for Manpower Planning in Nigeria. Paper presented at the Nigerian Economic Society Conference on Urbanisation and Nigerian Development. Kaduna.

32   ----. 1981. Women's Education and Participation in the Labour Force: The Case of Nigeria. In *Women, Power and Political Systems,* ed. M. Rendel, pp. 81-93. London: Croomhelm.

33   Axinn, Nancy W. 1969. An African Village in Transition: Research into Behavior Patterns. *Journal of Modern African Studies* 7(3):527-534.

34   Baker, Tanya. 1954. The Social Organization of the Birom People. Ph.D. Dissertation. University of London. London.

35   Barkow, Jerome H. 1971. The Institution of Courtesanship in the Northern States of Nigeria. *Africa* 10:58-73.

36   Barrett, S. R. 1974. *Two Villages on Stilts: Economic and Family Change in Nigeria.* New York/London: Chandler.

37   Bashir, M. K. 1972. The Economic Activities of Secluded Married Women in Kurawa and Lallokin Lemu, Kano City. B.Sc. Essay. Dept of Sociology. Ahmadu Bello University. Zaria.

38   Beier, H. 1955. The Position of Yoruba Women. *Presence Africaine* 1(2):39-46.

39   Benson, Susan, and Duffield, Mark. 1979. Women's Work and Economic Change: The Hausa in Sudan and in Nigeria. *Institute of Development Studies Bulletin* 10(9):13-19.

40   Berry, S. 1975. *Cocoa, Custom and Socio-Economic Change in Rural Western Nigeria*. Oxford: Clarendon Press.

41   ----. 1983. Work, Migration, and Class in Western Nigeria: A Reinterpretation. In *Struggle for the City: Migrant Labour, Capital, and the State in Urban Africa*, ed. Frederick Cooper, pp. 247-273. Beverly Hills: Sage.

42   Bohannan, Paul. 1951. The Political and Economic Aspects of Land Tenure and Settlement Patterns Among the Tiv of Central Nigeria. Ph.D. Dissertation. Oxford University. Oxford.

43   ----. 1954. *Tiv Farm and Settlement*. London: H.M. Stationery Office.

44   Bohannan, Paul, and Bohannan, Laura. 1968. *Tiv Economy*. Evanston, IL.: Northwestern University Press.

45   Bohannan, Paul, and Dalton, George. 1965. *Markets in Africa*. Garden City, NY.: The Natural History Library, Anchor Books, Doubleday and Co.,Inc.

46   Boserup, Esther. 1970. *Woman's Roles in Economic Development*. London: George Allen and Unwin, Ltd.

47   Boulding, E. 1976. *Handbook of International Data on Women*. New York: Wiley.

48   Brown, C. K. 1979. The Participation of Women in Rural Development in Kaduna State of Nigeria. Centre for Social and Economic Research. Ahmadu Bello University. Zaria.

49   Buntjer, B. J. 1970. The Changing Structure of Gandu. In *Zaria and Its Region*, ed. M.J. Mortimore, pp. 1957-1969. Zaria: Ahmadu Bello University, Dept. of Geography.

50   Caldwell, John C. 1975. *Population Growth and Socioeconomic Change in West Africa*. New York/London: Columbia University Press.

51   Caldwell, John C.; Netting, Robert; Norman, D. W.; Hill, Polly; Weil, Peter; and Johnson, Robert. 1969. Population and Rural Development Research in West Africa. *Rural Africana* 8:5-60.

52   Carew, Jay Gleason. 1981. A Note on Women and Agricultural Technology in the Third World. *Labour and Society* 6(3):279-285.

53   Chubb, L. T. 1961. *Ibo Land Tenure*. Ibadan: Ibadan University Press.

54   Clarke, R. J. M. 1979. Agricultural Production in a Rural Yoruba Community. Ph.D. Dissertation. University of London. London.

55   Cohen, Abner. 1969. *Custom and Politics in Urban Africa: A Study of Hausa Migrants in Yoruba Towns.* Berkeley: University of California Press.

56   Coles, Catherine M. 1982. Urban Muslim Women and Social Change in Northern Nigeria. Working Papers on Women in International Development, No.19. Michigan State University. East Lansing.

57   ----. 1983. The Old Woman in Hausa Society: Formal and Informal Power and Authority in Northern Nigeria. Paper presented at the annual meeting of the African Studies Association. Boston, MA.

58   ----. 1984. Hausa Women in the Urban Economy: Productive and Reproductive Roles of Kaduna Women. Presented at the Annual Meeting of the African Studies Association. Los Angeles.

59   Di Domenico, Catherine M. 1973. Nigerian Industrial Recruits: A Case Study of New Workers at the Nigerian Tobacco Factory at Ibadan. Ph.D. Dissertation. University of Ibadan. Ibadan.

60   ----. 1980. Women in Development: A Case Study of Their Labor Force Participation in Ibadan and Its Implications for Differential Role Performance. CenSCER Conference. University of Ibadan. Ibadan.

61   ----. 1983. Male and Female Factory Workers in Ibadan. In *Female and Male in West Africa,* ed. C. Oppong, pp. 256-265. London: George Allen and Unwin.

62   Di Domenico, Catherine M.; Asuni, Judy; and Scott, Jacqueline. 1977. Changing Status of African Women: An Exploratory Study of Working Mothers in Ibadan, Nigeria. In *Family Welfare and Development in Africa,* ed. F.T. Sai, pp. 283-284. London.

63   Di Domenico, Catherine M., and Lacey-Mojuetan, L. 1977. Occupational Status of Women in Nigeria: A Comparison of Two Urban Centers. *Africana Marburgensia* 10:62-79.

64   Drew, Catherine F. 1975. Economic Roles of Women in an Expanding Market Town: A Case Study in Mangu, Benue-Plateau State, Nigeria. M.Sc. Thesis. Ahmadu Bello University. Zaria.

65   Driesen, V. I. H. 1972. Some Observations on the Family Unit, Religion and the Practice of Polygamy in the Ife Division of Western Nigeria. *Africa* 42(1):44-56.

66   Due, Jean M. 1982. Constraints to Women and Development in Africa. *Journal of Modern African Studies* 20(1):155-166.

67   Ejiogu, C. N. 1968. African Rural-Urban Migrants in the Main Migrant Areas of the Lagos Federal Territory. In *The Population of Tropical Africa*, ed. J.C. Caldwell and C. Okonjo, pp. 320-330. New York: Columbia University Press.

68   Essang, S. M. 1970. The Distribution of Earnings in the Cocoa Economy of Western Nigeria. Ph.D. Dissertation. Michigan State University. East Lansing.

69   Fadayomi, Theophilus O. 1977. The Role of Working Mothers in Early Childhood Education: A Nigerian Case Study. Final report to UNESCO submitted through the Federal Ministry of Education.

70   Fagbemi, S. O. 1978. Occupational and Familial Role Conflicts of Working Women: A Case Study of the Lafia Canning Factory, Ibadan. B.Sc. Essay. Dept. of Sociology. University of Ibadan. Ibadan.

71   Famolu, M. A. F. 1973. Petty Trading in Isanlu, Kabba Division, Kwara State. Research essay. Ahmadu Bello University. Zaria.

72   Fapohunda, Eleanor R. 1978. Characteristics of Women Workers in Lagos. *Labour and Society* 3:158-171.

73   ----. 1978. Women at Work in Nigeria: Factors Affecting Modern Sector Employment. In *Human Resources and African Development*, ed. U.G. Damachi and V.P. Diejomaoh, pp. 220-241. New York/London: Praeger.

74   ----. 1983. Female and Male Work Profiles. In *Female and Male in West Africa*, ed. C. Oppong, pp. 32-53. London: George Allen and Unwin.

75   Fapohunda, O. J. 1978. Characteristics of the Informal Sector of Lagos. *Human Resources Research Bulletin* 78(1).

76   ----. 1978. The Informal Sector in Lagos: An Inquiry into Urban Poverty and Employment. Report to the I.L.O. Lagos.

77   ----. 1981. Human Resources and the Lagos Informal Sector. In *The Urban Informal Sector in Developing Countries*, ed. S.V. Sethuraman, pp. 70-82. Geneva: International Labour Office.

78   Fapohunda, O. J.; Adegbola, O.; and Sada, P. O. 1977. *Population, Employment and Living Conditions in Lagos*. Lagos: Human Resources Research Unit, University of Lagos.

79   Filani, M. O., and Richards, P. 1976. Periodic Market Systems and Rural Development: The Ibarapa Case Study, Nigeria. *Savanna* 5:149-162.

80   Galletti, R.; Baldwin, K. D. S.; and Dina, I. O. 1956. *Nigerian Cocoa Farmers: An Economic Survey of Yoruba Cocoa Farming Families*. London: Oxford University Press.

81   Gana, J. A. 1976. The Locational Pattern and Functions of Periodic Markets in Zaria Division, Nigeria. *Savanna* 5(2):163-175.

82   Grant, B., and Anthonio, Q. B. O. 1973. Women's Cooperatives in the Western State of Nigeria. *Bulletin of Rural Economics and Sociology* 8:7-35.

83   Green, M. 1941. *Land Tenure in an Ibo Village in South-Eastern Nigeria*. London: Lund Humphries.

84   Gugler, Josef, and Flanagan, William. 1978. *Urbanization and Social Change in West Africa*. Cambridge, England: Cambridge University Press.

85   Guyer, Jane I. 1978. Women's Work in the Food Economy of the Cocoa Belt: A Comparison. Working Paper No.7. African Studies Center. Boston University. Brookline, MA.

86   Hafkin, Nancy J., and Bay, E. G. 1976. *Women in Africa: Studies in Social and Economic Change*. Stanford: Stanford University Press.

87   Harrington, Judith A. 1983. Nutritional Stress and Economic Responsibility: A Study of Nigerian Women. In *Women and Poverty in the Third World*, ed. M. Buvinic, pp. 130-156. Baltimore: Johns Hopkins University Press.

88   Harris, J.; Umoh, U. J.; and Van Heer, N. 1983. Nigerian Agriculture. *New African* 18(9):49.

89   Harris, Jack S. 1943. Papers on the Economic Aspect of Life Among the Ozuitem Ibo. *Africa* 14(1):12-23.

90   ----. 1944. Some Aspects of the Economics of Sixteen Ibo Individuals. *Africa* 14(6):302-305.

91   Hay, Margaret Jean, and Stichter, Sharon. 1984. *African Women South of the Sahara*. London, New York: Longman.

92   Hays, H. M. 1976. Agricultural Marketing in Northern Nigeria. *Savanna* 5(2):139-149.

93   Hibler, Michelle. 1980. On Women and Children. *Agenda* 10-11.

94   Hill, Polly. 1969. Aspects of Socio-Economic Life in an Hausa Village in Northern Nigeria. *Rural Africana* 8:25-36.

95   ----. 1969. Hidden Trade in Hausaland. *Man* 4(3):392-409.

96   ----. 1971. Two Types of West African House Trade. In *The Development of Indigenous Trade and Markets in West Africa*, ed. C. Meillassoux, pp. 303-318. London: Oxford University Press.

97   ----. 1972. *Rural Hausa: A Village and a Setting*. London: Cambridge University Press.

98   ----. 1975. Some Socio-Economic Consequences of the High Population Density in Rural Areas Near Kano City. In *The Population Factor in African Studies*, ed. R.P. Moss and R.J.A.R. Rathbone. London: University of London Press.

99   ----. 1977. *Population, Prosperity and Poverty: Rural Kano 1900 and 1970*. Cambridge: Cambridge University Press.

100   ----. 1982. *Dry Grain Farming Families: Hausaland (Nigeria) and Karnataka (India) Compared*. Cambridge: Cambridge University Press.

101   Hodder, B. W. 1961. Rural Periodic Day Markets in Parts of Yorubaland. *Institute of British Geographers Transactions and Papers* 29:149-159.

102   ----. 1962. The Yoruba Rural Market. In *Markets in Africa*, ed. P. Bohannan and G. Dalton, pp. 103-117. Evanston, IL.: Northwestern University Press.

103   Hodder, B. W., and Ukwu, U. I. 1969. *Markets in West Africa: Studies of Markets and Trade Among the Yoruba and the Ibo*. Ibadan: University of Ibadan Press.

104   Huff, Richard. 1974. Economic Change and the Status of Women Among the Tiv. Senior Honors Thesis. Department of Anthropology. Harvard University. Cambridge, MA.

105   Ijomah, B. I. C. The Prostitutes of Nsukka. In *The Social Structure of Contemporary Society*, ed. A. Akiwowo. New York: Macmillan Press.

106   Ilori, Felicia Adedoyin. 1978. The Effect of Female Labour Force Participation on Fertility Behavior and Family Welfare in South Western Nigeria. Paper presented at the National Workshop on the Introduction of Population Concepts into the Curricula of Agricultural Rural Development Training Institutions. University of Ife. Ile-Ife.

107   ----. 1978. Urbanization and Fertility: A Case Study of Western Nigeria. Paper presented at the International Seminar on the Integration of Theory and Policy in Population Studies, 2-5 January, 1978. University of Ghana. Legon.

108   Imam, Ayesha, and Pittin, Renee. 1984. The Identification of Successful Women's Projects: Kaduna State, Nigeria. ILO Report. Geneva.

109   Iro, M. I. 1976. The Main Features of a Working Life Table of the Female Labour Force in Nigeria, 1965. *Journal of the Royal Statistical Society, Series A* 139:258-264.

110   Jackson, A. C. 1981. Change and Rural Hausa Women: A Study in Kura and Kano Districts, Northern Nigeria. Ph.D. Dissertation. Wye College, University of London. London.

111   Jackson, Sam. 1978. Hausa Women on Strike. *Review of African Political Economy* 13:21-36.

112   Jahn, Jahneinz. 1968. A Yoruba Market-Woman's Life. In *Every Man His Way: Readings in Cultural Anthropology*, ed. A. Dundes, pp. 226-237. New Jersey: Englewood Cliffs.

113   Janelid, Ingrid. The Role of Women in Nigerian Agriculture. Monograph based on a paper presented at the National Seminar on Home Economics Development Planning held at the International Institute of Tropical Agriculture, Ibadan, 8-14, December 1974. FAO. Rome.

114   ----. 1974. *Social Characteristics of Nigerian Agriculture and the Role of Women*. Rome: FAO, Human Resources Institutions and Agrarian Reform Division.

115   ----. 1974. Study of Small Farm Households in Different Agrarian Structures. Paper presented at the National Seminar on Home Economics Development Planning held at the International Institute of Tropical Agriculture, 8-14 December 1974. Ibadan.

116   Johnson, E. J. 1973. Market Women and Capitalist Adaptation: A Case Study in Rural Benin, Nigeria. Ph.D. Dissertation. Michigan State University. East Lansing.

117   Jones, G. I., and Lucas, David. 1979. Some Sociocultural Factors Affecting Female Labour Force Participation in Jakarta and Lagos. *Labour, Capital, and Society* 12:19-49.

118   Karanja-Diejomaoh, W. M., and Scott, J. 1976. Social Structure, Economic Independence and the Status of Nigerian Women: The Dialectics of Power. Paper presented at the National Conference on Nigerian Women and Development in Relation to Changing Family Structure. University of Ibadan. Ibadan.

119   Kisekka, Mere Nakateregga. 1981. The Role of Women in Socioeconomic Development: Indicators as Instruments of Social Analysis--The Case of Nigeria and Uganda. In *Women and Development*, pp. 33-47. Paris: UNESCO.

120 Koll, M. 1969. *Crafts and Cooperation in Western Nigeria: A Sociological Contribution to Indigenous Economics*. Groiberg: Arnold-Bergstraesser-Institut.

121 Konan, M. M. 1975. Occupations and Family Patterns Among the Hausa in Northern Nigeria. Samaru Miscellaneous Paper 52. Institute for Agricultural Research. Ahmadu Bello University. Zaria.

122 Kungwai, N. N. 1976. Land Tenure and Social Structure in Three Zaria Suburbs. Research paper. Ahmadu Bello University. Zaria.

123 Kuoh, T. 1971. Women's Place in the World, Not in the Home: Interviews. *Atlas* 20:39.

124 Ladipo, P. A. 1981. Developing Women's Cooperatives: An Experiment in Rural Nigeria. *Journal of Development Studies* 17(3):123-136.

125 Leis, Nancy Boric. 1964. Economic Independence and Ijaw Women: A Comparative Study of Two Communities in the Niger Delta. Ph.D. Dissertation. Northwestern University. Evanston.

126 Leith-Ross, Sylvia. 1938. Women of Affairs. *Journal of the Royal African Society* 37(149):477-482.

127 ----. 1956. The Rise of the New Elite Amongst Women of Nigeria. *International Social Science Bulletin* 8(3):481-488.

128 ----. 1965. The Rise of a New Elite Amongst the Women of Nigeria. In *Africa: Social Problems of Change and Conflict*, ed. P. Van den Berghe, pp. 221-229. San Fransico: Chandler.

129 LeVine, Robert. 1966. Sex Roles and Economic Change in Africa. *Ethnology* 5(2):186-193.

130 Little, Kenneth. 1973. *African Women in Towns*. London: Cambridge University Press.

131 Lock, Max. 1974. Women in Maiduguri: Some Aspects of Their Lives. In *Maiduguri: Surveys and Planning Reports*. pp. 7.6.1-7.6.34 UK: Warminster Press for Max Lock Group Ltd.

132 Longhurst, Richard. 1982. Resource Allocation and the Sexual Division of Labor: A Case Study of a Moslem Hausa Village in Northern Nigeria. In *Women and Development*, ed. L. Beneria, pp. 95-117. New York: Praeger.

133 Lucas, David. 1971. Women in the Nigerian Labour Force. Paper presented at the African Population Conference, Accra, Ghana, December 9-18, 1971. Accra.

134   ----. 1973. Nigerian Women and Family Resources. Paper presented at the Family Research Seminar of the Institute of African Studies, University of Ghana. Accra.

135   ----. 1974. Demographic Class Project 1971-1972: Occupation and Family Size of Lagos Wives. *Lagos Notes and Records* 5:68-69.

136   ----. 1974. Female Employment in Lagos. *Manpower and Unemployment Research in Africa: A Newsletter* 7:37-41.

137   ----. 1974. Occupation, Marriage and Fertility Among Nigerian Women in Lagos. Human Resources Research Unit. Research Bulletin No.3/001. University of Lagos. Lagos.

138   ----. 1976. Participation of Women in the Nigerian Labour Force Since the 1950's with Particular Reference to Lagos. Ph.D. Dissertation. Dept. of Economics. University of London. London.

139   ----. 1977. Demographic Aspects of Women's Employment in Africa. *Manpower and Unemployment Research* 10(1):31-38.

140   Mabogunje, A. L. 1959. Yoruba Market Women. *Ibadan* 9.

141   ----. 1961. The Market Woman. *Ibadan* 11:14-17.

142   ----. 1967. The Ijebu. In *The City of Ibadan*, ed. P.C. Lloyd, A.L. Mabogunje and B. Awe, pp. 85-95. London: Cambridge University Press.

143   ----. 1977. The Urban Situation in Nigeria. In *Patterns of Urbanization: Comparative Country Studies*, ed. S. Goldstein and D.F. Sly, pp. 569-641. Dolhain: Ordina Editions.

144   Mabogunje, A. L., and Filani, M. O. 1981. The Informal Sector in a Small City: The Case of Kano. In *The Urban Informal Sector in Developing Countries*, ed. S.V. Sethuraman, pp. 83-89. Geneva: International Labour Office.

145   McDowell, D. W. 1971. Education and Occupational and Residential Mobility in an Urban Nigerian Community. Ph.D. Dissertation. Columbia University. New York.

146   Marshall, Gloria Albertha. 1964. Women, Trade, and the Yoruba Family. Ph.D. Dissertation. Columbia University. New York.

147   ----. 1963. The Marketing of Farm Produce: Some Patterns of Trade Among Women of Western Nigeria. In *Proceedings of the 1962 NISER Conference at the University of Ibadan*, pp. 88-99. Ibadan, Nigeria.

148   Martin, Carol. 1981. Women Job Seekers in Bauchi State, Nigeria: Policy Options for Employment Training. Ed.D. Dissertation. University of Massachusetts. Amherst.

149   ----. 1983. Skill-Building or Unskilled Labour For Female Youth: A Bauchi Case. In *Female and Male in West Africa*, ed. C. Oppong, pp. 223-235. London: George Allen and Unwin.

150   Masha, G. I. 1979. Occupational Preferences, Cognative and Affective Factors in Female Students in Nigeria: A Comparative Study. Ph.D. Dissertation. University of Wales.

151   Mere, Ada, and Anikpo, Mark. The Impact of Wage-Employment of Women on Fertility in an Urban Town in Nigeria. Paper presented at CenSCER Conference, September 1980. CenSCER. University of Benin. Benin.

152   Miner, Horace. 1972. The Zaria Hausa in a Rural Ecosystem. Paper presented at the African Studies Association Meeting. Philadelphia.

153   Mintz, S. W. 1971. Men, Women and Trade. *Comparative Studies in Society and History* 13(3):247-269.

154   Mohammed, A. 1975. Prostitution as a Social Problem in the North-Western State: Sabon Garin Sokoto Case Study. B.Sc. Essay. Ahmadu Bello University. Zaria.

155   ----. 1980. Home Outside the Home (A Sociological Concept of Prostitution Among the Hausa). Seminar paper. Department of Sociology. Bayero University. Kano.

156   Moore, J. Aduke. 1960. The Sphere and Influence of Women in Africa. *Journal of Human Relations* 8(3-4):709-717.

157   Mormoni, Z. L. 1976. The Effect of the 1972/73 Drought on the Economic Role of Women in Hurumi Hamlet, Kausani, Kano State, Nigeria. Research paper. Ahmadu Bello University. Zaria.

158   Mortimore, M. J. 1970. *Zaria and Its Region: A Nigerian Savanna City and Its Environs.* Zaria: Dept. of Geography, Ahmadu Bello Univeristy.

159   Moude, H. N. 1973. The Causes and Consequences of Rural-Urban Migration in Kwoi. Research essay. Ahmadu Bello University. Zaria.

160   Netting, Robert. 1964. Beer as a Locus of Value Among the West African Kofyar. *American Anthropologist* 66:375-385.

161   ----. 1969. Marital Relations in the Jos Plateau of Nigeria, Women's Weapons: The Politics of Domesticity Among the Kofyar. *American Anthropologist* 71(6):1037-1076.

162   Newman, Jeanne S. 1984. *Women of the World: Sub-Saharan Africa.* Washington, D.C.: WID-USAID and U.S. Department of Commerce, Bureau of the Census.

163   Nigeria. Federal Government. 1971. *Survey of Working Women with Family Responsibilities.* Federal Ministry of Labour.

164   Nigeria. Federal Ministry of Labour. 1971. Report on the Survey of Working Women with Family Responsibilities. Lagos.

165   Norman, David W.; Simmons, E. B; and Hays, Henry M. 1982. *Farming Systems in the Nigerian Savanna: Research and Strategies for Development.* Boulder, CO.: Westview Press.

166   Norman, David W. Et. Al.; Fine, J. C.; Goddard, A. D.; Kroeker, W. J.; and Pryor, D. H. 1971. A Socio-Economic Study of Three Villages in the Sokoto Close-Settled Zone. Samaru Miscellaneous Paper No.33. Ahmadu Bello University. Zaria.

167   Ntiri, Daphne Williams. 1983. *The African Woman in a Transitional Society.* Troy, MI.: Bedford Publishers, Inc.

168   Odita, Florence Chinyere. 1972. Differences in Pay, Promotion, Job Title and Other Related Factors Between Employed Male and Female College Graduates as Indicators of Sex Discrimination. Ph.D. Dissertation. Ohio State University.

169   Ogunnika, Olo. 1973. Fertility of Lagos Market Women. *Unilag Sociologist* 1(1):14-17.

170   Ogunsheye, F. A. 1960. The Women of Nigeria. *Presence Africaine* 4(32):33-49.

171   Oguntoye, O. A. 1968. Occupational Survey of Old Bussa. Nigerian Institute of Social and Economic Research. Ibadan.

172   Ojo, G. J. Afolabi. 1966. *Yoruba Culture.* Ibadan: The Caxton Press (West Africa) Ltd.

173   Okali, C. 1979. The Changing Economic Position in Rural Communities in West Africa. *Africana Marburgensia* 12(1/2):59-93.

174   Okali, C., and Sumberg, J. E. 1984. Sheep and Goats, Men and Women: Household Relations and Small Ruminant Development in Southwest Nigeria. Unpub. paper. Small Ruminant Programme, International Livestock Centre for Africa. Ibadan.

175   Okere, L. C. 1983. *The Anthropology of Food in Rural Igboland, Nigeria.* New York: University Press of America.

176   Okonjo, Isabel Kamene. 1976. The Dual-Sex Political System in Operation: Igbo Women and Community Politics in Midwestern Nigeria. In *Women in Africa: Studies in Social and Economic Change,* ed. N.J. Hafkin and Edna Bay, pp. 45-58. Stanford: Stanford University Press.

26

177   ----. 1976. The Role of Women in Social Change Among the Igbo of Southeastern Nigeria Living West of the River Niger. Ph.D. Dissertation. Boston University. Boston.

178   Okono, F. J. 1974. Handicrafts and Small Industries Policy in Nigeria. Paper presented to the Workshop on Participation of Women in Handicrafts and Small Industries. Kitwe, Zambia.

179   Olatunbosun, Dupe. 1975. *Nigeria's Neglected Rural Majority*. Ibadan: Oxford University Press.

180   Olowolaiyemo, Michael. Urban Petty Producers in Nigeria and Programmes for Assisting Them. Vol. V. Center for Developmental Studies. University College of Swansea. Swansea.

181   Olusanya, P. O. 1975. In-Migration and the Development of Absentee Farming in the Forest Zone of South-West Nigeria. Paper presented at the Internal Migration Conference. Ile-Ife.

182   Olusanya, Philip O. 1981. *Nursemaids and the Pill: A Study of Household Structure, Female Employment and the Small Family Ideal in a Nigerian Metropolis*. Legon: University of Ghana. Ghana Population Series No. 9.

183   Oluwasanni, H. A. Et. Al. 1966. *Uboma, A Socio-economic and National Survey of of a Rural Community in Eastern Nigeria.*. The World Land Use Survey Occasional Papers No. 6. Berkhamsted, United Kingdom: Geographical Publications, Ltd.

184   Onah, J. Onuora, and Iwuji, E. C. 1976. Urban Poverty in Nigeria. *South African Journal of Economics* 44(2):185-193.

185   Onyemelukwe, Josiah O. C. 1971. Staple Food Trade in Onitsha Market: An Example of Urban Market Distribution Function. Ph.D. Dissertation. University of Ibadan. Ibadan.

186   Oppong, C. 1979. Family Structure and Women's Reproductive and Productive Roles: Some Conceptual and Methodological Issues. Population and Labour Policies Programme Working Paper No. 79. World Employment Programme Research. ILO. Geneva.

187   ----. 1983. *Female and Male in West Africa*. London: George Allen and Unwin.

188   Osunade, M. A. 1978. A Descriptive Profile of the Non-farm Factor: A Case Study of Ipetu Ijesa, Oyo State, Nigeria. *South African Journal of African Affairs* 8(1):44-52.

189   Ottenberg, Phoebe. 1959. The Changing Economic Position of Women Among the Afikpo Ibo. In *Continuity and Change in African Cultures*, ed. W. Bascom and M.J. Herskovits, pp. 205-303. Chicago: The University of Chicago Press, Phoenix Books.

190 Oyekanmi, Felicia Durojaiye. 1985. Women and the Modern Sector Labour Force in Nigeria. Presented at the Conference on the Contribution of Women to National Development, Nigerian Association of University Women, June 1985. Lagos.

191 Park, E. 1965. *Careers for Nigerian Girls*. Cambridge: Cambridge University Press.

192 Peil, Margaret. 1975. Female Roles in West African Towns. In *Changing Social Structure in Ghana*, ed. J. Goody, pp. 73-90. London: International African Institute.

193 ----. 1975. Migration and Labour Force Participation: A Study of Four Towns. Paper presented at the Internal Migration Conference. Ile-Ife.

194 ----. 1981. *Cities and Suburbs: Urban Life in West Africa*. New York: Africana Publishing Corp.

195 Pittin, Renee. 1976. Social Status and Economic Opportunity in Urban Hausa Society. Paper presented at the National Conference on Women and Development in Relation to Changing Family Structure, 26-30 April. University of Ibadan. Ibadan.

196 ----. 1979. Marriage and Alternative Strategies: Career Patterns of Hausa Women in Katsina City. Ph.D. Dissertation. The School of Oriental and African Studies, University of London. London.

197 ----. 1982. Documentation of Women's Work in Nigeria: Problems and Solutions. Population and Labour Policies Program Working Paper No. 125. World Employment Programme Research. ILO. Geneva.

198 ----. 1983. Houses of Women: A Focus on Alternative Life-Styles in Katsina City. In *Female and Male in West Africa*, ed. C. Oppong, pp. 291-302. London: George Allen and Unwin.

199 ----. 1984. Documentation and Analysis of the Invisible Work of Invisible Women: A Nigerian Case-Study. *International Labour Review* 123(4):473-490.

200 Raza, M. Rafique. 1983. Men and Women At Work: Theoretical Perspectives on Division of Labour in Developing Societies. Presented at Second Annual Women in Nigeria Conference: Women and the Family, April 1983. Ahmadu Bello University. Zaria.

201 Raza, M. Rafique, and Adi, N. D. Ngur. 1984. Role of Women in Agricultural Product Marketing: An Urban Perspective. Presented at the Workshop on Women in Agriculture in West Africa, May 1984. International Livestock Centre for Africa. IITA. Ibadan.

202   Remy, Dorothy. 1973. Adaptive Strategies of Men and Women in Zaria, Nigeria: Industrial Workers and Their Wives. Ph.D. Dissertation. University of Michigan. Ann Arbor.

203   ----. 1974. Social Networks and Patron-Client Relations: Ibadan Market Women. Dept. of Urban Studies. Federal City College. Washington, D.C.

204   ----. 1975. Underdevelopment and the Experience of Women: A Nigerian Case Study. In *Toward an Anthropology of Women*, ed. R.R. Reiter, pp. 358-71. New York, London: Monthly Review Press.

205   ----. 1982. Formal and Informal Sectors of the Zaria, Nigeria Economy: An Analytic Framework with Empirical Content. In *Towards a Political Economy of Urbanization in Third World Countries*, ed. H.I. Safa, pp. 233-246. Delhi: Oxford University Press.

206   Rendel, Margherita. 1981. *Women, Power, and Political Systems*. London: Croomhelm.

207   Romalis, Coleman, and Romalis, Shelly. 1983. Sexism, Racism, and Technological Change: Two Cases of Minority Protest. *International Journal of Women's Studies* 6:270-287.

208   Sada, P. O., and McNulty, M. L. 1974. Traditional Markets in Lagos: A Study of the Changing Administrative Processes and Marketing Transactions. *Quarterly Journal of Administration* 8:149-165.

209   ----. 1978. The Market Traders in the City of Lagos. In *Urbanization Processes and Problems in Nigeria*, ed. P.O. Sada and J.S. Oguntoyinbo, pp. 63-80. Ibadan: Ibadan University Press.

210   Sandra, A. O. 1978. Career Aspirations and Opportunities in Nigeria. *African Social Research* 25:429-437.

211   Saunders, Margaret Overholt. 1978. Marriage and Divorce in a Muslim Hausa Town (Mirria, Niger Republic). Ph.D. Dissertation. Indiana University. Bloomington.

212   Schildkrout, Enid. 1978. Thoughts on Child Labor, Education and Marriage in Kano City. Paper presented at the African Studies Association Meeting. Baltimore.

213   ----. 1979. Women's Work and Children's Work: Variations Among Moslems in Kano. In *Social Anthropology of Work*, ed. S. Wallman, pp. 69-85. London: Academic Press.

214   ----. 1980. Children's Work Reconsidered. *International Social Science Journal* 32:479-489.

29

215   ----. 1981. The Employment of Children in Kano, Nigeria. In *Participation or Exploitation? The Economic Roles of Children in Low-Income Countries*, ed. G. Rogers and G. Standing, pp. 81-112. Geneva: ILO.

216   ----. 1981. Young Traders of Northern Nigeria. *Natural History* 90(1):44-53.

217   ----. 1983. Dependence and Autonomy: The Economic Activities of Secluded Hausa Women in Kano. In *Female and Male in West Africa*, ed. C. Oppong, pp. 107-126. London: George Allen and Unwin.

218   Schubert, P.; Iroh, E.; and Moroney, S. 1983. Nigerian Survey. *African Business* 59:29.

219   Sethuraman, S. V. 1981. *The Urban Informal Sector in Developing Countries*. Geneva: International Labour Organization.

220   Sheehan, Glen, and Standing, Guy. 1978. A Note on the Economic Activity of the Women in Nigeria. *Pakistan Development Review* 17(2):253-261.

221   Shehu, D. M. 1973. Tangale Women and Marketing in Kaltungo. Research essay. Ahmadu Bello University. Zaria.

222   Simmons, E. B. 1975. The Small-Scale Rural Food Processing Industry in Northern Nigeria. *Food Research Institute Studies* 14:147-161.

223   ----. 1976. Economic Research on Women in Rural Development in Northern Nigeria. American Council on Education, Paper 10. Overseas Liaison Committtee. Washington, D.C.

224   Smith, M. G. 1952. A Study of Hausa Domestic Economy in Northern Zaria. *Africa* 22:333-347.

225   ----. 1955. *The Economy of Hausa Communities of Zaria, Colonial Research Studies No. 16*. London: H.M. Stationery Office.

226   ----. 1962. Exchange and Marketing Among the Hausa. In *Markets in Africa*, ed. P. Bohannan and G. Dalton, pp. 299-334. Evanston: Northwesten University Press.

227   Smith, Mary F. 1954. *Baba of Karo*. London: Faber and Faber.

228   Southall, Aidan W. 1961. The Position of Women and the Stability of Marriage. In *Social Change in Modern Africa*, ed. A.W. Southall. London: Oxford University Press.

229   Spiro, Heather M. 1980. The Role of Women in Farming in Oyo State, Nigeria; A Case Study of Two Rural Communities. Agricultural Economics Discussion Paper No. 7. International Institute of Tropical Agriculture. Ibadan.

230 Standing, G., and Sheehan, G. 1978. Economic Activity of Women in Nigeria: Case Study No.8. In *Labour Force Participation in Low-Income Countries*, ed. G. Standing and G. Sheehan, pp. 129-36. Geneva: International Labour Organization.

231 Starns, William W., Jr. 1974. *Land Tenure Among the Rural Hausa*. Madison: Land Tenure Center, University of Wisconsin.

232 Sudarkasa, Niara. 1973. *Where Women Work: A Study of the Yoruba in the Market Place and in the Home*. Ann Arbor, University of Michigan.

233 ----. 1976. Where Women Work - Study of Yoruba Women in the Market Place and in the Home. *Africa* 46(3):295.

234 Sutter, John William. 1982. Peasants, Merchant Capital and Rural Differentiation: A Nigerian Hausa Case Study. Ph.D. Dissertation. Cornell University. Ithaca.

235 Tiffany, Sharon. 1982. *Women, Work and Motherhood: The Anthropological Perspective on Working Women*. New York: Prentice-Hall Spectrum Books.

236 Trager, Lillian. 1976. New Economic Structures and Women's Trade Activities: Ilesha, Nigeria. Paper presented at the African Studies Association Meeting. Boston.

237 ----. 1976. Market Women in the Urban Economy: The Role of Yoruba Intermediaries in a Medium Sized City. *African Urban Notes* 2(3):1-10.

238 ----. 1976. Yoruba Markets and Trade: Analysis of Spatial Structure and Social Organization in the Ijesaland Marketing System. Ph.D. Dissertation. University of Washington. Seattle.

239 ----. 1977. Role of Women Traders in Urban and Regional Economy of Ilesha, Nigeria. *Urban Anthropology* 6:183.

240 ----. 1981. Customers and Creditors: Variations in Economic Personalism in a Nigerian Marketing System. *Ethnology* 20:133-146.

241 Uchendu, Patrick Kenechukwu. 1981. The Changing Cultural Role of Igbo Women in Nigeria 1914-1975. Ph.D. Dissertation. New York University. New York.

242 Ukwu, I. U. 1965. Markets in Iboland, Eastern Nigeria. Ph.D. Dissertation. Cambridge University. Cambridge.

243 UN. 1962. The Employment and Conditions of Work of African Women. ILO. Tananarive.

244   ----. 1975. Participation of Women in Handicrafts and Small Industries. Report on the ILO/ECA/ YMCA/SIDA Workshop held in Kitwe, 9-20 December 1974. ILO. Geneva.

245   UNECA. 1973. Nigerian Country Report. Economic Commission for Africa. Addis Ababa.

246   Upton, M. 1970. Agriculture in South-Western Nigeria. Development Studies Series. Reading University.

247   USAID. 1983. *Africa: Nigeria--Selected Statistical Data by Sex*. Washington D.C.: US Bureau of the Census, AID.

248   US Dept. of Commerce. Bureau of the Census. 1980. Social Statistics in Nigeria. Federal Office of Statistics. Washington, D.C.

249   Usman, A. 1976. The Farmer in an Agrarian Hausa Community. Research paper. Ahmadu Bello University. Zaria.

250   Usoro, Eno J. 1961. The Place of Women in Nigerian Society. *African Women* 4(2):27-30.

251   Uyanga, Joseph. 1977. Family Size, Family Income and Working Mothers in the Jos Plateau Area. *Savanna* 6:25-29.

252   Uzoma, Adoaha C. 1971. The Changing Postion of Married Women of One Ibo Community in Township and Village: A Socioeconomic Analysis. *Der Ostblock and die Entwicklungslander* 44:113-150.

253   Van Allen, J. 1972. "Sitting on a Man": Colonialism and the Lost Political Institutions of Igbo Women. *Canadian Journal of African Studies* 6(2):165-181.

254   ----. 1976. 'Aba Riots' or Igbo 'Women's War'? Ideology, Stratification, and the Invisibility of Women. In *Women in Africa: Studies in Social and Economic Change*, ed. N.J. Hafkin and E. Bay, pp. 59-86. Stanford: Stanford University Press.

255   Walker, Kathryn, and Hanck, Hazel. 1964. Women's Work in Changing Villages. *Journal of Home Economics* 56(4):233-238.

256   Ware, Helen. 1975. The Relevance of Changes in Women's Roles to Fertility Behavior: The African Experience. Paper presented at the Population Association of America Meeting. Seattle, WA.

257   ----. 1976. Security in the City: The Role of the Family in Urban West Africa. The Economic and Social Supports for High Fertility: Proceedings of the Conference held on Family and Fertility Change, November 16-18, 1976, pp. 385-408. Canberra: Austrailian National University. Dept. of Demography.

258   ----. 1977. Women's Work and Fertility in Africa. In *The Fertility of Working Women: A Synthesis of International Research*, ed. Stanley Kupinsky, pp. 1-34. New York: Praeger.

259   ----. 1981. *Women, Education and Modernization of the Family in West Africa*. Canberra: Australian National University, Dept. of Demography. Changing African Family Project Series Monograph No.7.

260   Waters-Bayer, Ann. 1984. Women As Decision-Makers in Dairying. Presented at the Workshop on Women in Agriculture in West Africa, May 1984. International Livestock Centre for Africa. IITA. Ibadan.

261   Westfall, G. D. 1974. Nigerian Women: A Bibliographical Essay. *Africana Journal* 5:99-138.

262   Young, Kate; Wolkowitz, Carol; and McCullagh, Roslyn. 1981. *Of Marriage and the Market: Women's Subordination in International Perspective*. London: CSE Books.

263   Youssef, Nadia. 1974. *Women and Work in Developing Societies*. Berkeley: University of California, Institute of International Studies. Population Monograph Series No.15.

264   ----. 1976. Women in Development: Urban Life and Labour. In *Women and World Development*, ed. Irene Tinker and Michele Bo Bramsen, pp. 70-77. Washington, D.C.: Overseas Development Council.

265   Zollner, Joy. 1971. African Conference on the Role of Women in National Development. *International Labour Review* 104:555-557.

266   ----. 1972. African Seminar on the Participation of Women in Economic Life. *International Labour Review* 105:175-177.

Chapter Three
Women in the Family and Household

1   Abba, Isa A. 1980. Kulle (Purdah) Among the Muslims in the Northern States of Nigeria: Some Clarifications. *Kano Studies* 2:45-50.

2   Abell, H. 1962. The Role of Rural Women in Farm and Home Life. Report to the Government of Nigeria (Northern Region) on the Home Economics Aspects of the F.A.O. Socioeconomic Survey of Peasant Agriculture in Northern Nigeria. FAO. Rome.

3   Achike, Okay. 1974. Problems of Creation and Dissolution of Customary Marriages and Legitimation of Children under Customary Law in Nigeria. Paper presented at the seminar New Directions in African Family Law. Leiden.

4   Adamu, P. 1976. Child Socialisation Among the Gwari. Research paper. Ahmadu Bello University. Zaria.

5   Adeokun, Lawrence A.; Adepoju, Aderanti; Ilori, Felicia; Adewuyi, A. A.; and Ebigbola, J. A. 1984. The Ife Labour Market: A Nigerian Case Study. Population and Labour Policies Programme, Working Paper No.144. ILO. Geneva.

6   Adewoye, O. 1973. Law and Social Change in Nigeria. *Journal of the Historical Society of Nigeria* 7(1):149-158.

7   Adewuyi, Alfred A. 1980. Childcare and Female Employment in a Nigerian Metropolis. *Nigerian Journal of Economic and Social Studies* 22(2):197-218.

8   Afonja, Simi. 1980. Current Explanations of Sex Roles and Inequality: A Reconsideration. *Nigerian Journal of Economic and Social Studies* 22(1):85-108.

9   African Women. 1958. Growing up in Nigeria. *African Women* 2(4):73-79.

10   Aig-Ojehomon-Ketting, R. 1975. Modern Marriage in Benin City: A Power Struggle Between Men and Women. *Kroniek von Afrika* 4:60-71.

11   Akande, J. O. 1968. Women's Rights in Property. L.L.M. Thesis. University of Lagos. Lagos.

12   ----. 1976. Constitutional Infringement of Women's Rights. In *The Great Debate*, ed. Daily Times. Lagos: Daily Times.

13   ----. 1978. Law, Status of Women and Family Welfare: Matrimonial Causes Decree 1970. Paper read at the International Planned Parenthood Federation Regional Conference. Nairobi.

14   ----. 1979. Law and the Status of Women in Nigeria. Economic Commision for Africa. (ECA/ATRCW/RE801/79). Addis Ababa: ATRCW.

15   Akande, S. 1971. *Marriage and Homemaking in Nigerian Society*. Ibadan: Daystar Press.

16   Aldous, Joan. 1962. Urbanization, The Extended Family and Kinship Ties in West Africa. *Social Forces* 41(1):6-12.

17   Aluko, Timothy. 1950. Polygamy and the Surplus of Women. *The West African Review* 21(270):259-260.

18   Amechi, E. E. A. 1979. The Legal Status of Nigerian Women. Ph.D. Dissertation. Institute of Oriental and African Studies. University of London. London.

19   Anderson, J. N. D. 1967. *Family Law in Asia and Africa*. New York: Praeger.

20   ----. 1970. *Islamic Law in Africa*. London: Frank Cass.

21   ----. 1976. *Law Reform in the Muslim World*. London: The Athlone Press. University of London Legal Series XI.

22   Andreski, Iris. *Old Wives' Tales: Life Histories From Iboland*. London: Routledge and Kegan Paul.

23   Anker, R.; Buvinic, M.; and Youssef, N. H. 1982. *Women's Roles and Population Trends in the Third World*. London: Croomhelm.

24   Arinola, O. A. N. 1978. The Implications of Female Labour Force Participation on the Family: A Case Study of Some Factory Workers. B.Sc. Essay. Department of Sociology. University of Ibadan. Ibadan.

25   Ariwoola, Olagoke. 1965. *The African Wife*. London: The Author (35 Linthorpe Rd., No. 16).

26   Aronson, D. R. 1978. *The City is Our Farm: Seven Migrant Ijebu Yoruba Families*. Boston, MA.: Schenkman.

27   Axinn, Nancy W. 1969. An African Village in Transition: Research into Behavior Patterns. *Journal of Modern African Studies* 7(3):527-534.

28   Ayodele, Stephen Arate. 1983. The Impact of the Process of Modernization and Stability in the Yoruba Family. Ph.D. Dissertation. Howard University. Washington, D.C.

29   Ayonrinde, Akolawole. 1976. Marriage, Family Planning and Mental Health Status of Nigerian Women. Paper presented to the National Conference on Nigerian Women and Development in Relation to Changing Family Structure. University of Ibadan. Ibadan.

30   Babotunde, S. O. 1973. Changes in Yoruba Marriage and Family. B.Sc. Essay. University of Ibadan. Ibadan.

31   Baker, Tanya. 1954. The Social Organization of the Birom People. Ph.D. Dissertation. University of London. London.

32   Baker, Tanya, and Bird, Mary. 1959. Urbanization and the Position of Women. *The Sociological Review* 7(1):99-122.

33   Balogun, I. A. B. 1972. Islam, Polygamy and Family Planning in Nigeria. *Birthright* 7(1):35-42.

34   ----. 1976. Teachings and Practices of Islam and the Status of Nigerian Muslim Women. Paper presented at the National Conference on Nigerian Women and Development in Relation to Changing Family Structure. University of Ibadan. Ibadan.

35   Barkow, Jerome H. 1971. The Institution of Courtesanship in the Northern States of Nigeria. *Africa* 10:58-73.

36   ----. 1972. Hausa Women and Islam. *Canadian Journal of African Studies* 6:317-328.

37   ----. 1973. Muslims and Maguzawa in the North Central State of Nigeria. *Canadian Journal of African Studies* 2(1):59-76.

38   Barrett, S. R. 1974. *Two Villages on Stilts: Economic and Family Change in Nigeria.* New York/London: Chandler.

39   Bascom, William. 1942. The Principle of Seniority in the Social Structure of the Yoruba. *American Anthropologist* 44:37-46.

40   Beier, H. 1955. The Position of Yoruba Women. *Presence Africaine* 1(2):39-46.

41   Bird, Mary. 1958. Social Change in Kinship and Marriage Among the Yoruba in Nigeria. Ph.D. Dissertation. University of Edinburgh. Edinburgh.

42   ----. 1963. Urbanization, Family and Marriage in Western Nigeria. In *Proceedings of the Inaugural Seminar, Centre of African Studies*, pp. 59-74. Edinburgh: University of Edinburgh.

43   Bohannan, Paul. 1954. *Tiv Farm and Settlement.* London: H.M. Stationery Office.

44   Buntjer, B. J. 1970. The Changing Structure of Gandu. In *Zaria and Its Region*, ed. M.J. Mortimore, pp. 1957-1969. Zaria: Ahmadu Bello University, Dept. of Geography.

45   Burfisher, Mary, and Horenstein, Nadine. 1983. *Sex Roles in the Nigerian Tiv Farm Household and the Differential Impacts of Development Projects*. New York: Population Council.

46   Buvinic, Mayra et al. 1978. Women-Headed Households: The Ignored Factor in Development Planning. Report Submitted to AID/WID. International Center for Research on Women. Washington, D.C.

47   Caldwell, John C. 1968. *Population Growth and Family Change in Africa*. Canberra: Australian National University Press.

48   ----. 1976. Fertility and the Household Economy in Nigeria. *Journal of Comparative Family Studies* 7(2):193-253.

49   ----. 1976. Marriage, the Family and Fertility in Sub-Saharan Africa With Special Reference to Research Programmes in Ghana and Nigeria. In *Family and Marriage in Some African and Asiatic Countries*, ed. S.A. Huzayyin and G.T. Acsadi, pp. 359-371. Cairo: Cairo Demographic Centre.

50   ----. 1979. Variations in the Incidence of Sexual Abstinence and the Duration of Postnatal Abstinence Among the Yoruba of Nigeria. In *Natural Fertility: Patterns and Determinants of Natural Fertility*, ed. H. Leridon and J. Menken, pp. 397-407. Liege: Ordina Editions.

51   Callaway, Barbara J. 1984. Ambiguous Consequences of the Socialisation and Seclusion of Hausa Women. *The Journal of Modern African Studies* 22(3):429-450.

52   Callaway, Barbara J., and Kleeman, Katherine E. 1985. Women in Nigeria--Three Women of Kano: Modern Women and Traditional Life. *Africa Report* 30(2):26-29.

53   Chalifoux, Jean-Jacques. 1980. Secondary Marriage and Levels of Seniority Among the Abisi(Piti), Nigeria. *Journal of Comparative Family Studies* 11(3):325-334.

54   Changing African Family Project. 1974. *The Value of Children*. Canberra: Australian National University, Department of Demography. Changing African Family Project Series, No. 2.

55   Chojnacka, Helena. 1980. Polygamy and the Rate of Population Growth. *Population Studies* 34:91-107.

56   Chubb, L. T. 1961. *Ibo Land Tenure*. Ibadan: Ibadan University Press.

57   Clarke, Julian. 1981. Households and Political Economy of Small-Scale Cash Crop Production in S.W. Nigeria. *Africa* 51:807-823.

58   Clignet, R. 1970. *Many Wives, Many Powers: Authority and Power in Polygynous Families.* Evanston, IL.: Northwestern University Press.

59   Cohen, Abner. 1969. *Custom and Politics in Urban Africa: A Study of Hausa Migrants in Yoruba Towns.* Berkeley: University of California Press.

60   Cohen, Ronald. 1967. Family Life in Bornu. *Anthropologica* 9(1):21-42.

61   Coker, G. B. A. 1966. *Family Property Among the Yoruba.* London: Sweet and Maxwell.

62   Coles, Catherine M. 1982. Urban Muslim Women and Social Change in Northern Nigeria. Working Papers on Women in International Development, No.19. Michigan State University. East Lansing.

63   ----. 1983. Muslim Women in Town: Social Change Among the Hausa of Northern Nigeria. Ph.D. Dissertation. University of Wisconsin. Madison.

64   ----. 1983. The Old Woman in Hausa Society: Formal and Informal Power and Authority in Northern Nigeria. Paper presented at the annual meeting of the African Studies Association. Boston, MA.

65   Comhaire-Sylvain, Suzanne. 1949. The Status of Women in Lagos, Nigeria. *Phi Lambda Theta Journal* 27(3):158-163.

66   Cross, C., and Ibru, C. 1978. A Portrait of Foster Care: Private Fostering among Two Generations of Nigerians. *West African Journal of Sociology and Political Science* 1:285-308.

67   Damachi, U. G. 1972. *Nigerian Modernization.* New York: The Third Press.

68   Dangiwa, A. M. 1971. The Changing Role and Status of the Hausa Woman of Northern Nigeria. Dissertation for Diploma in Development Studies. Ruskin College. Oxford University. Oxford.

69   Dennis, Carolyne. 1975. Research and Policy on Family Patterns. Paper presented at the Conference on Social Research and National Development in Nigeria. University of Ibadan. Ibadan.

70   Derrette, J. M. 1965. *Studies in the Laws of Succession in Nigeria.* London: Oxford University Press.

71   Doi, A. Rahman I., and Parratt, J. I. 1968. Polygamy in Yoruba Society: A Religious or Sociological Issue. *African Quarterly* 8(1):52-58.

72   Donnerreichle, C. 1979. Role of Women in Africa - Marriage, Birth and Disease in the Lives of the Hausa Women in Nigeria. *Argument* 21:766-768.

73   Dorjahn, Vernon. 1954. The Demographic Aspects of African Polygamy. Ph.D. Dissertation. Northwestern University. Evanston.

74   ----. 1959. The Factor of Polygamy in African Demography. In *Continuity and Change in African Cultures*, ed. M. Herskovitz and W. Bascom, pp. 87-112. Chicago: University of Chicago Press.

75   Driesen, V. I. H. 1972. Some Observations on the Family Unit, Religion and the Practice of Polygamy in the Ife Division of Western Nigeria. *Africa* 42(1):44-56.

76   Dry, D. P. L. 1950. The Family Organization of the Hausa of Northern Nigeria. B.Sc. Essay. Oxford University. Oxford.

77   ----. 1956. The Social Development of the Hausa Child. In *Proceedings of the Third International West African Conference, held at Ibadan, Nigeria, December 12-21, 1949*, pp. 164-70. Lagos: Nigerian Museum.

78   ----. 1956. Some Aspects of Hausa Family Structure. In *Proceedings of the Third International West African Conference, held at Ibadan, Nigeria. December 12-21, 1949*, pp. 158-163. Lagos: Nigerian Museum.

79   Duru, Mary Steimel. 1980. Socialization Among the Igbo: An Intergenerational Study of Cultural Patterns, Familial Roles and Child Rearing Practices. Ph.D. Dissertation. University of Maryland. College Park.

80   Egboh, E. O. 1973. The Place of Women in the Ibo Society of South-Eastern Nigeria From the Earliest Times to the Present. *Civilisations* 23/24:305-316.

81   Eghareuba, J. 1946. *Benin Laws and Customs*. Benin: Service Press Ltd.

82   Ekechi, F. K. 1976. African Polygamy and Western Christian Ethnocentrism. *Journal of African Studies* 3(3):329-349.

83   Ekpere, J. A.; Oyedipe, F. P. A.; and Adegboye, R. O. 1978. *Family Role Differentiation Within the Kwara Nomadic Fulani*. Canberra: Australian National University, Dept. of Demography. Changing African Family Project Monograph Series, No.4, Vol.1.

84   Elias, Taslim Olawale. 1962. *Nigerian Land Law and Custom*. London: Routledge and Kegan Paul.

85   ----. 1971. *Nigerian Land Law*. London: Sweet and Maxwell.

86   Ema, Udo A. J. 1940. Fattening Girls in Oron, Calabar Province. *Nigeria* 21:386-389.

87   Ezeani, A. O. N. 1965. Legal Effect of Religious Marriages. *Nigerian Law Journal* 1:1-227.

88   Fadayomi, Theophilus O. 1977. The Role of Working Mothers in Early Childhood Education: A Nigerian Case Study. Final report to UNESCO submitted through the Federal Ministry of Education.

89   Fadipe, N. A.; Okediji, Francis; and Oladejo, O. 1970. *The Sociology of the Yoruba*. Ibadan: University Press.

90   Fagbemi, S. O. 1978. Occupational and Familial Role Conflicts of Working Women: A Case Study of the Lafia Canning Factory, Ibadan. B.Sc. Essay. Dept. of Sociology. University of Ibadan. Ibadan.

91   Farooq, Ghazi M. 1979. Household Fertility Decision-Making in Nigeria. World Employment Programme. Population and Employment Project, Working Paper No.75. ILO. Geneva.

92   Fleischer, L. M. 1974. Crises of Life and How They are Handled: A Case Study Among Hausa Women in Jos, Nigeria. M.Phil. Thesis. University of Edinburgh. Edinburgh.

93   Forde, Daryll. 1941. *Marriage and the Family Among the Yako of Southeastern Nigeria*. London: Lund Humphries.

94   ----. 1950. Double Descent Among the Yako. In *African Systems of Kinship and Marriage*, ed. A.R. Radcliffe-Brown and Daryll Forde, pp. 285-332. London: Oxford University Press.

95   Frantz, Charles. 1978. Ecology and Social Organization Among Nigerian Fulbe. In *The Nomadic Alternative: Modes and Models of Interaction in the African-Asian Deserts and Steppes*, ed. Wolfgang Weissleder, pp. 97-118. The Hague: Mouton.

96   George, Sister Aguin O'Connor. 1960. The Status of Women in Selected Societies of West Africa: A Study of the Concept in Law and Practice. Ph.D. Dissertation. New York University. New York City.

97   Goddard, A. D. 1969. Are Hausa-Fulani Family Structures Breaking Up?. *Samaru Agricultural Newsletter* 11(3):34-48.

98   ----. 1973. Changing Family Structures Among the Rural Hausa. *Africa* 43(3):207-218.

99   Goody, Ester. 1983. *Parenthood and Social Reproduction*. Cambridge: Cambridge University Press.

100   Goody, Esther. 1978. *Some Theoretical and Empirical Aspects of Parenthood in West Africa*. Canberra: Australian National University, Dept. of Demography. Changing African Family Project Monograph Series, No.4, Vol.1.

101   Goody, John Rankine. 1959. The Mother's Bretheren and Sister's Son in West Africa. *Journal of the Royal Anthropological Institute* LXXXIX:61-86.

102   Grayshon, M. C., and Olanlokun, J. O. 1966. Authority Patterns in the Yoruba Family. *West African Journal of Education* 10:113-118.

103   Green, M. 1941. *Land Tenure in an Ibo Village in South-Eastern Nigeria*. London: Lund Humphries.

104   Grossbard, Amyra S. 1976. An Economic Analysis of Polygyny: The Case of Maiduguri. *Current Anthropology* 17(4):701-707.

105   ----. 1980. The Economics of Polygamy. In *Research in Population Economics, Vol.2*, ed. Julian L. Simon and Julie DaVanzo, pp. 321-350. Greenwich, CT.: JAI Press, Inc.

106   Gugler, Josef, and Flanagan, William. 1978. *Urbanization and Social Change in West Africa*. Cambridge, England: Cambridge University Press.

107   Hafkin, Nancy J., and Bay, E. G. 1976. *Women in Africa: Studies in Social and Economic Change*. Stanford: Stanford University Press.

108   Hake, I. E. 1972. *Child-Rearing Practices in Northern Nigeria*. Ibadan: University Press.

109   Harrington, Judith A. 1978. Some Micro-Socioeconomics of Female Status in Nigeria. Paper presented at the Conference on Women in Poverty: What Do We Know?. International Centre for Research on Women. Washington, D.C.

110   Harris, Jack S. 1940. The Position of Women in Nigerian Society. *Transactions of the New York Academy of Sciences, Series 2*, 2(5):141-148.

111   ----. 1943. Papers on the Economic Aspect of Life Among the Ozuitem Ibo. *Africa* 14(1):12-23.

112   Hay, Margaret Jean, and Stichter, Sharon. 1984. *African Women South of the Sahara*. London, New York: Longman.

113   Henderson, Helen Kreider. 1969. Ritual Roles of Women in Onitsha Ibo Society. Ph.D. Dissertation. University of California. Berkeley.

114   Henderson, Richard. 1966. *An Outline of Traditional Onitsha Ibo Socialization.* Ibadan: University of Ibadan. Institute of Education.

115   ----. 1966. *Socialisation Among the Onitsha Ibo.* Ibadan: University of Ibadan, Institute of Education.

116   Hibler, Michelle. 1980. On Women and Children. *Agenda* 10-11.

117   Hill, Polly. 1972. *Rural Hausa: A Village and a Setting.* London: Cambridge University Press.

118   Ibanibo, I. 1974. The Impact of Westernisation on the Puberty of Girls in Okirika. B.Sc. Thesis. Dept. of Sociology/Anthropology. University of Nigeria. Nsukka.

119   Ighodaro, Irene E. B. 1969. Changing Patterns of Marriage and Family Life in West African Society. *Ibadan* 26:36-38.

120   Ijomah, B. I. C. The Prostitutes of Nsukka. In *The Social Structure of Contemporary Society,* ed. A. Akiwowo. New York: Macmillan Press.

121   ----. 1974. The Role of Women in Nigerian Society. *Conch* 6:47-59.

122   Imoagene, S. O. 1970. The Marriage System of the Weppa-Wano (Midwestern Nigeria). *African Studies* 29:207-218.

123   Isichei, P. A. C. 1973. Sex in Traditional Asaba. *Cahiers d'Etudes Africanes* 13(52):682-699.

124   Isiugo-Abanihe, Uche C. 1983. Child Fostering in West Africa: Prevalence, Determinants and Demographic Consequences. Ph.D. Dissertation. University of Pennsylvania. Philadelphia.

125   Iyalla, B. S. 1968. Womanhood in the Kalabari. *Nigeria Magazine* 98:216-224.

126   Izzet, A. 1961. Family Life Among the Yoruba in Lagos, Nigeria. In *Social Change in Modern Africa,* ed. A. Southall, pp. 305-315. London: Oxford University Press.

127   Jackson, A. C. 1981. Change and Rural Hausa Women: A Study in Kura and Kano Districts, Northern Nigeria. Ph.D. Dissertation. Wye College, University of London. London.

128   Jeffreys, M. D. W. 1950. Age Groups Among the Ika and Kindred People. *African Studies* 9(4):157-166.

129   ----. 1969. Some Notes on the Igbo Female. *Afrika und Ubersee* 53(1):37-44.

130   Jones, G. I. 1961. Ecology and Social Structure Among the North-Eastern Ibo. *Africa* 31(2):117-134.

131   ----. 1962. Ibo Age Organisation with Special Reference to the Cross River and North-Eastern Ibo. *Journal of the Royal Anthropological Institute* 92:191-211.

132   Kanam, Yahaya. 1968. The Effect of Custom on Certain Apsects of Maliki Law in the Northern States of Nigeria. *Journal of Islamic and Comparative Law* 2:79-87.

133   Karanja-Diejomaoh, W. M. 1978. Disposition of Incomes by Husbands and Wives: An Exploratory Study of Families in Lagos. In *Marriage, Fertility and Parenthood in West Africa*, ed. C. Oppong, G. Adaba, M. Bekombo-Priso and J. Mogey, pp. 407-432. Canberra: Australian National University, Dept. of Demography. Changing African Family Project Monograph Series, No. 4, Vol.2.

134   ----. 1983. Conjugal Decision-Making: Some Data From Lagos. In *Female and Male in West Africa*, ed. C. Oppong, pp. 236-241. London: George Allen and Unwin.

135   Kasunmu, Alfred B. 1964. Principle of Acknowledgement or Recognition of Paternity Under Customary Law in Nigeria. *International Comparative Law Quarterly* 13:1093-1104.

136   Kasunmu, Alfred B., and Salacuse, Jeswald B. 1966. *Nigerian Family Law*. London: Butterworth African Law Series (No.12).

137   Khalil, K. H. 1976. Some Notes on Marriage and Family Relations in Senegal and Nigeria. Paper presented at the Seminar on Marriage and Family in Some Arab and African Countries. Cairo Demographic Center. Cairo.

138   Kirk-Green, A. H. M. 1957. A Lala Initiation Ceremony. *Man* 57(5):9-11.

139   Kisekka, Mere Nakateregga. 1975. Sex and Marital Differences in Sexism Among Zaria Residents. Presented at the Nigerian Psychological Society Conference. Ahmadu Bello University. Zaria.

140   ----. 1976. Aspects of Family Structure Among Zaria Residents. Presented at the National Conference on Nigerian Women and Development in Relation to Changing Family Structure. University of Ibadan. Ibadan.

141   ----. 1976. Polygyny and the Status of African Women. Paper presented at the National Conference on Nigerian Women and Development in Relation to Changing Family Structure. University of Ibadan. Ibadan.

142   ----. 1980. Marital and Familial Patterns in Zaria, Nigeria. *Africana Marburgensia* 13:43-50.

143   ----. 1981. The Role of Women in Socioeconomic Development: Indicators as Instruments of Social Analysis--The Case of Nigeria and Uganda. In *Women and Development*, pp. 33-47. Paris: UNESCO.

144   Konan, M. M. 1975. Occupations and Family Patterns Among the Hausa in Northern Nigeria. Samaru Miscellaneous Paper 52. Institute for Agricultural Research. Ahmadu Bello University. Zaria.

145   Kumo, S. 1977. The Applications of Islamic Law in Northern Nigeria: Problems and Prospects. *Journal of Islamic and Comparative Law* 7:21-30.

146   Kungwai, N. N. 1976. Land Tenure and Social Structure in Three Zaria Suburbs. Research paper. Ahmadu Bello University. Zaria.

147   Kuoh, T. 1971. Women's Place in the World, Not in the Home: Interviews. *Atlas* 20:39.

148   Lacey, Linda. 1981. Urban Migration in Developing Countries: A Case Study of Three Cities in Nigeria. Ph.D. Dissertation. Cornell University. Ithaca.

149   Lambo, T. Adeoye. 1969. The Child and Mother-Child Relationship in Major Cultures of Africa. *Assignment Children* 10:61-74.

150   ----. 1969. Socio-economic Change and its Impact on the Family, with Special Emphasis on the Role of Women. *Ibadan* 26:30-35.

151   Lamphere, Louise. Strategies, Cooperation and Conflict Among Women in Domestic Groups. In *Woman, Culture and Society*, ed. Michelle Rosaldo and Louise Lamphere, pp. 97-112. Stanford: Stanford University Press.

152   Leis, Nancy Boric. 1971. Virilocality, Polygamy and Women's Associations in West Africa. Paper presented at the 70th annual Meeting of the American Anthropological Association. New York.

153   Little, Kenneth. 1959. Some Urban Patterns of Marriage and Domesticity in West Africa. *The Sociological Review* 7(1):65-82.

154   ---- 1959. Urbanism in West Africa. *The Sociological Review* 7(1):5-13.

155   ----. 1960. The West African Town: Its Social Basis. *Diogenes* 29:16-31.

156   ----. 1973. *African Women in Towns*. London: Cambridge University Press.

157   ----. 1977. Women's Strategies in Modern Marriage in Anglophone West Africa: An Ideo-
        logical and Sociological Appraisal. *Journal of Comparative Family Studies*
        8(3):341-356.

158   Lloyd, Barbara B. 1966. Education and Family Life in the Development of Class
        Identification Among the Yoruba. In *New Elites of Tropical Africa*, ed. P.C. Lloyd,
        pp. 163-183. London: Oxford University Press.

159   ----. 1970. Yoruba Mothers' Reports of Child-Rearing. In *Socialisation: The Approach From
        Social Anthropology*, ed. Philip Mayer, pp. 75-107. London: Tavistock Publica-
        tions.

160   Lloyd, Peter C. 1959. Family Property Among the Yoruba. *Journal of African Law* 3:105.

161   ----. 1959. Some Notes on the Yoruba Rules of Succession and on Family Property. *Journal
        of African Law* 3(1):6-18.

162   ----. 1962. *Yoruba Land Law*. London: Oxford University Press.

163   ----. 1966. Agnatic and Cognatic Descent Among the Yoruba. *Man* 1(4):484-500.

164   ----. 1966. *The New Elites of Tropical Africa*. London: Oxford University Press for the
        International African Institute.

165   Lock, Max. 1974. Women in Maiduguri: Some Aspects of Their Lives. In *Maiduguri: Sur-
        veys and Planning Reports*. pp. 7.6.1-7.6.34 UK: Warminster Press for Max Lock
        Group Ltd.

166   Longhurst, Richard. 1982. Resource Allocation and the Sexual Division of Labor: A Case
        Study of a Moslem Hausa Village in Northern Nigeria. In *Women and Develop-
        ment*, ed. L. Beneria, pp. 95-117. New York: Praeger.

167   Lucas, David. 1973. Nigerian Women and Family Resources. Paper presented at the Family
        Research Seminar of the Institute of African Studies, University of Ghana. Accra.

168   Mabogunje, A. L. 1958. The Yoruba Home. *Odu* 5:28-35.

169   ----. 1977. The Urban Situation in Nigeria. In *Patterns of Urbanization: Comparative Coun-
        try Studies*, ed. S. Goldstein and D.F. Sly, pp. 569-641. Dolhain: Ordina Editions.

170   MacCormack, Carol P., ed. 1982. *Ethnography of Fertility and Birth*. London: Academic Press.

171   Mack, Delores E. 1978. Husbands and Wives in Lagos: The Effects of Socioeconomic Status on the Patterns of Family Living. *Journal of Marriage and the Family* 40(4):807-816.

172   Maclean, Catherine M. Una. 1966. Yoruba Mothers: A Study of Changing Methods of Childbearing in Rural and Urban Nigeria. *Journal of Tropical Medicine and Hygiene* 69(11):253-263.

173   Mair, Lucy. 1969. *African Marrriage and Social Change*. London: Oxford University Press.

174   Malcolm, L. W. G. 1925. Some Notes on the Seclusion of Girls Among the Efik of Old Calabar. *Man* 25:113-114.

175   Maqsud, Muhammad. 1974. The Impact of Cultural Values on the Development of Moral Judgements of Hausa Muslim Children in Kano. *Kano Studies* 1:45-53.

176   Marris, Peter. 1960. Slum Clearance and Family Life in Lagos. *Human Organizations* 19:123-128.

177   ----. 1961. *Family and Social Change in an African City: A Study of Rehousing in Lagos*. London: Routledge and Kegan Paul.

178   Marshall, Gloria Albertha. 1964. Women, Trade, and the Yoruba Family. Ph.D. Dissertation. Columbia University. New York.

179   Meek, Charles Kingsley. 1955. Ibo Law. In *Readings in Anthropology*, ed. E. Adamson Hoebel, pp. 234-249. New York: McGraw-Hill.

180   Miner, Horace. 1972. The Zaria Hausa in a Rural Ecosystem. Paper presented at the African Studies Association Meeting. Philadelphia.

181   Mohammed, A. 1975. Prostitution as a Social Problem in the North-Western State: Sabon Garin Sokoto Case Study. B.Sc. Essay. Ahmadu Bello University. Zaria.

182   ----. 1980. Home Outside the Home (A Sociological Concept of Prostitution Among the Hausa). Seminar paper. Department of Sociology. Bayero University. Kano.

183   Moore, J. Aduke. 1960. The Sphere and Influence of Women in Africa. *Journal of Human Relations* 8(3-4):709-717.

184   Morgan, R. W., and Immerwahr, George E. Family Structure in Lagos, Nigeria. Department of Community Health, University of Lagos College of Medicine and the Department of International Health, Johns Hopkins School of Hygiene and Public Health.

185   Morton-Williams, Peter. 1978. Family Structures in an Egbado Yoruba Community. In *Marriage, Fertility and Parenthood in West Africa.*, ed. C. Oppong, G. Adaba, M. Bekombo-Priso and J. Mogey, pp. 69-102. Canberra: Australian National University, Dept. of Demography. Changing African Family Project Monograph Series, No. 4, Vol.1.

186   Muhammad, Yahaya. 1967. The Legal Status of Women in the Northern States of Nigeria. *Journal of Islamic Legal Studies* 1(2):1-38.

187   Muller, Jean-Claude. 1969. Preferential Marriage Among the Rukuba of Benue-Plateau State, Nigeria. *American Anthropologist* 71:1057-1061.

188   ----. 1970. Rukuba Kinship and Marriage. Ph.D. Dissertation. University of Rochester. Rochester.

189   ----. 1972. Ritual Marriage, Symbolic Fatherhood and Initiation Among the Rukuba, Benue-Plateau State, Nigeria. *Man* 7(2):283-295.

190   ----. 1973. On Preferential/Prescriptive Marriage and the Function of Kinship Systems: The Rukuba Case. *American Anthropologist* 75:1563-1576.

191   ----. 1980. On the Relevance of Having Two Husbands: Contribution to the Study of Polygynous/Polyandrous Marital Forms of the Jos Plateau. *Journal of Comparative Family Studies* 11:359-369.

192   Nafziger, E. W. 1969. The Effect of Nigerian Extended Family on Entrepreneurial Activity. *Economic Development and Cultural Change* 18:25-33.

193   National Seminar on Women. 1979. Laws and Customs Affecting Women. Resolutions issued by a National Seminar on Women. CenSCER. Benin.

194   Netting, Robert. 1964. Beer as a Locus of Value Among the West African Kofyar. *American Anthropologist* 66:375-385.

195   ----. 1969. Marital Relations in the Jos Plateau of Nigeria, Women's Weapons: The Politics of Domesticity Among the Kofyar. *American Anthropologist* 71(6):1037-1076.

196   Newman, Jeanne S. 1984. *Women of the World: Sub-Saharan Africa*. Washington, D.C.: WID-USAID and U.S. Department of Commerce, Bureau of the Census.

197   Nigeria. Federal Government. 1971. *Survey of Working Women with Family Responsibilities.* Federal Ministry of Labour.

198   Ntiri, Daphne Williams. 1983. *The African Woman in a Transitional Society.* Troy, MI.: Bedford Publishers, Inc.

199   Nwabara, Comfort Chisaraokwu. 1977. Factors Affecting Formal Education Decisions In Extended Kin Families of the Ibo of Nigeria. Ph.D. Dissertation. Michigan State University. East Lansing.

200   Nwabueze, B. O. 1968. Family Law in Nigeria. In *Le droit de la Famille en Afrique noire et a Madagascar,* ed. Keba M'Baye, pp. 117-157. Paris: Maisonneuve et Larose.

201   Nwogugu, E. I. 1964. Legitimacy in Nigerian Law. *Journal of Nigerian Law* 8(2):91-105.

202   ----. 1974. *Family Law in Nigeria.* Ibadan: Heinemann.

203   Nzekwu, O. 1959. Iria Ceremony. *Nigeria* 63,34.

204   Nzimiro, I. 1962. Family and Kinship in Iboland. Ph.D. Dissertation. University of Cologne. Cologne.

205   Obi, S. N. C. 1962. Women's Property and Succession in Modern Ibo Law, Eastern Nigeria. *Journal of African Law* 6(1):6-18.

206   ----. 1963. *Ibo Law of Property.* London: Butterworth.

207   Obi, S. N. Chinwuba. 1966. *Modern Family Law in Southern Nigeria.* London: Sweet and Maxwell.

208   Oduntan, S. O. 1976. The Status of Women in Family Planning. Paper presented at the Conference on Nigerian Women and Development in Relation to Changing Family Structure, April 26-30. Department of Preventive and Social Medicine. University of Ibadan. Ibadan.

209   Offonry, H. Kanu. 1951. The Strength of the Ibo Clan Feeling. *West Africa* 1787:467.

210   Ogunbiyi, I. A. 1969. The Position of Muslim Women as Stated by Uthman B. Fudi. *Odu* 2:43-60.

211   Ogunsheye, F. A. 1960. The Women of Nigeria. *Presence Africaine* 4(32):33-49.

212   Oguntoye, O. A. 1968. Occupational Survey of Old Bussa. Nigerian Institute of Social and Economic Research. Ibadan.

213 Ohadike, P. O. 1968. A Demographic Note on Marriage, Family, and Family Growth in Lagos, Nigeria. In *The Population of Tropical Africa*, ed. J.C. Caldwell and C. Okonjo, pp. 379-392. London: Longmans.

214 ----. 1968. Urban Social Structure, Marital Patterns, Variations and Attitudes in a Major West African City (Lagos, Nigeria). University of East Africa Social Sciences Council Conference Papers. Makerere Institute of Social Research. Vol.2, pp. 416-428. Makerere University. Kampala.

215 Okadigho, Miriam. 1977. Discriminative Provisions in the Draft Constitution: Two Points of Dissent. Paper presented at the Nigerian Political Science Symposium.

216 Okali, C. 1979. The Changing Economic Position in Rural Communities in West Africa. *Africana Marburgensia* 12(1/2):59-93.

217 Okediji, O. O., and Okediji, Francis Olu. 1966. Marital Stability and Social Structure in an African City. *Nigerian Journal of Economic and Social Studies* 8(1):151-163.

218 Okere, L. C. 1983. *The Anthropology of Food in Rural Igboland, Nigeria*. New York: University Press of America.

219 Okojie, C. G. 1960. *Ishan Native Laws and Customs*. Yaba: John Okwesa & Co. and the Nigeria National Press.

220 Okonjo, C. 1971. Nigeria, Marriage, Kinship, and Fertility. In *The Demographic Transition in Tropical Africa*, pp. 267-273. Paris: Organisation for Economic Cooperation and Development, Development Center.

221 Okonjo, Isabel Kamene. 1975. The Role of Women in Development of Culture in Nigeria. In *Women Cross-Culturally: Change and Challenge*, ed. R. Rohrlich-Leavitt, pp. 31-40. The Hague: Mouton.

222 ----. 1976. The Dual-Sex Political System in Operation: Igbo Women and Community Politics in Midwestern Nigeria. In *Women in Africa: Studies in Social and Economic Change*, ed. N.J. Hafkin and Edna Bay, pp. 45-58. Stanford: Stanford University Press.

223 ----. 1976. The Role of Women in Social Change Among the Igbo of Southeastern Nigeria Living West of the River Niger. Ph.D. Dissertation. Boston University. Boston.

224 Okonjo, Unokanma. 1970. The Impact of Urbanization on the Ibo Family Structure. Ph.D. Dissertation. Gottingen University.

225 Okore, A. O. 1977. The Value of Children Among Ibo Households in Nigeria: A Study of Arochukwu Division and Urban Umuahia in Imo State. Ph.D. Dissertation. Australian National University. Canberra.

226   Okoro, N. A. 1966. *The Customary Laws of Succession in Eastern Nigeria and the Statutory and Judicial Rules Concerning Their Application*. London: Sweet and Maxwell.

227   Olusanya, P. O. 1978. Women's Changing Intra-Familial Role and Its Impact on Population Attitudes and Reproductive Behavior in a Nigerian Metropolis. Paper presented at the International Seminar on Integration of Theory and Policy in Population Studies. Legon.

228   Onwuejeogwu, Michael. 1969. The Cult of the Bori Spirits among the Hausa. In *Man in Africa*, ed. Mary Douglas and Phyllis M. Kaberry, pp. 279-305. London: Tavistock Publications.

229   Oppong, C. 1979. Family Structure and Women's Reproductive and Productive Roles: Some Conceptual and Methodological Issues. Population and Labour Policies Programme Working Paper No. 79. World Employment Programme Research. ILO. Geneva.

230   ----. 1982. Maternal Role Rewards, Opportunity Costs and Fertility. World Employment Programme. Population and Labour Policies Programme Working Paper No. 120. ILO. Geneva.

231   ----. 1983. *Female and Male in West Africa*. London: George Allen and Unwin.

232   Oppong, C.; Adaba, G.; Bekombo-Priso, M.; and Mogey, J., eds. 1978. *Marriage, Fertility and Parenthood in West Africa*. Canberra: Australian National University, Dept. of Demography, Changing African Family Monograph Series, No.4.

233   Orubuloye, I. O. 1977. Family Obligations and Fertility in Nigeria: The Case of the Yoruba of Western Nigeria. In *The Economic and Social Supports for High Fertility: Proceedings of the Conference held on Family and Fertility Change, November 16-18, 1976.*, pp. 203-217. Canberra: Australian National University, Department of Demography, Changing African Family Project Companion Series, No. 2.

234   Otite, Onigu. 1971. Process of Family Formation Among The Urhobo of Midwestern Nigeria. *International Journal of Sociology of the Family* 1(2):125-136.

235   Ottenberg, Phoebe. 1958. Marriage Relationships in the Double Descent System of the Afikpo Ibo of South-eastern Nigeria. Ph.D. Dissertation. Northwestern University. Evanston.

236   Ottenberg, Simon. 1957. The System of Authority of the Afikpo Ibo of Southeastern Nigeria. Ph.D. Dissertation. Northwestern University. Evanston.

237   ----. 1965. Inheritance and Succession in Afikpo. In *Studies in the Laws of Succession in Nigeria: Essays*, ed. J.D. Derrett, pp. 33-90. London: Oxford University Press.

238   ----. 1968. *Double Descent in an African Society: The Afikpo Village-Group*. Seattle: University of Washington Press.

239   Oyediran, M. A., and Bamisaiye, A. 1983. A Study of the Childcare Arrangements and the Health-Status of Preschool-Children of Employed Women in Lagos. *Public Health* 97(5):267-274.

240   Peil, Margaret. 1975. Female Roles in West African Towns. In *Changing Social Structure in Ghana*, ed. J. Goody, pp. 73-90. London: International African Institute.

241   ----. 1983. Urban Contacts: A Comparison of Women and Men. In *Female and Male in West Africa*, ed. C. Oppong, pp. 275-282. London: George Allen and Unwin.

242   Peshkin, Alan. 1972. *Kanuri Schoolchildren: Education and Social Mobilization in Nigeria*. New York: Holt, Rinehart, amd Winston.

243   Philips, Arthur. 1953. *Survey of African Marriage and Family Life*. London: Oxford University Press.

244   ----. 1955. Conflict Between Statutory and Customary Law: Marriage in Nigeria. *Modern Law Review* 18:73-76.

245   Pittin, Renee. 1979. Marriage and Alternative Strategies: Career Patterns of Hausa Women in Katsina City. Ph.D. Dissertation. The School of Oriental and African Studies, University of London. London.

246   ----. 1979. Hausa Women and Islamic Law: Is Reform Necessary?. Paper presented at the 22nd Annual Meeting of the African Studies Association. Los Angeles.

247   ----. 1983. Houses of Women: A Focus on Alternative Life-Styles in Katsina City. In *Female and Male in West Africa*, ed. C. Oppong, pp. 291-302. London: George Allen and Unwin.

248   Plotnicov, Leonard. 1970. Rural-Urban Communications in Contemporary Nigeria: The Persistence of Traditional Social Institutions. *Journal of Asian and African Studies* 5:66-82.

249   Radcliffe-Brown, A. R., and D. Forde. 1950. *African Systems of Kinship and Marriage*. London: Oxford University Press.

250   Ransome-Kuti, F. 1961. The Status of Women in Nigeria. *Journal of Human Relations* 10(1):67-72.

251   Raphael, Dana. 1975. *Being Female: Reproduction, Power, and Change*. The Hague: Mouton.

252 Remy, Dorothy. 1973. Adaptive Strategies of Men and Women in Zaria, Nigeria: Industrial Workers and Their Wives. Ph.D. Dissertation. University of Michigan. Ann Arbor.

253 Rendel, Margherita. 1981. *Women, Power, and Political Systems*. London: Croomhelm.

254 Riches, David. 1979. On the Presentation of the Tiv Segmentary Lineage System, or, Speculations on Tiv Social Organisation. *Queen's University Papers in Social Anthropology* 4:69-90.

255 Roberts, S. *Law and the Family in Africa*. The Hague: Mouton.

256 Sacks, Karen. 1979. *Sisters and Wives: The Past and Future of Sexual Inequality*. Westport, CT.: Greenwood Press.

257 Sagay, I. 1974. Widow Inheritance Versus Monagomous Marriage: The Oba's Dilemma. *Journal of African Law* 18:168-172.

258 Salacuse, J. W. 1964. Birth, Death, and the Marriage Act: Some Problems in Conflict of Laws. *Nigerian Law Journal* 1:59.

259 ----. 1965. *Selective Survey of Family Law in Northern Nigeria*. Zaria: Institute of Administration.

260 Salamone, Frank A. 1971. Some Aspects of Social Stratification Among the Hausa. *International Journal of Group Tensions* 1(4):335-349.

261 Sangree, Walter H. 1969. Going Home to Mother: Traditional Marriage Among the Irigwe of Benue-Plateau State, Nigeria. *American Anthropologist* 71(6):1049-1057.

262 ----. 1974. Prescriptive Polygamy and Complementary Filiation Among the Irigwe of Nigeria. *Man* 9:44-52.

263 Saunders, Margaret Overholt. 1980. Women's Role in a Muslim Hausa Town. In *A World of Women: Anthropological Studies of Women in Societies of the World*, ed. E. Bourguignon, pp. 57-86. New York: Praeger.

264 Schildkrout, Enid. 1978. Age and Gender in Hausa Society. In *Sex and Age as Principles of Social Differentiation*, ed. J.S. LaFontaire, pp. 109-137. New York: Academic Press.

265 ----. 1978. Thoughts on Child Labor, Education and Marriage in Kano City. Paper presented at the African Studies Association Meeting. Baltimore.

266   ----. 1979. Women's Work and Children's Work: Variations Among Moslems in Kano. In *Social Anthropology of Work*, ed. S. Wallman, pp. 69-85. London: Academic Press.

267   ----. 1980. Children's Work Reconsidered. *International Social Science Journal* 32:479-489.

268   ----. 1981. The Employment of Children in Kano, Nigeria. In *Participation or Exploitation? The Economic Roles of Children in Low-Income Countries*, ed. G. Rogers and G. Standing, pp. 81-112. Geneva: ILO.

269   ----. 1983. Dependence and Autonomy: The Economic Activities of Secluded Hausa Women in Kano. In *Female and Male in West Africa*, ed. C. Oppong, pp. 107-126. London: George Allen and Unwin.

270   Schwab, W. B. 1955. Kinship and Lineage Among the Yoruba. *Africa* 25(4):352-374.

271   ----. 1962. Continuity and Change in the Yoruba Lineage System. *Annals of the New York Academy of Sciences* 96:590-605.

272   Simmons, Donald C. 1960. Sexual Life, Marriage and Childhood Among the Efik. *Africa* 30(1):153-165.

273   Smedley, Audrey. 1974. Women of Udu: Survival in a Harsh Land. In *Many Sisters: Women in Cross-Cultural Perspective*, ed. C.J. Mathiasson, pp. 205-228. London: Collier Macmillan.

274   Smith, M. G. 1955. *The Economy of Hausa Communities of Zaria, Colonial Research Studies No. 16*. London: H.M. Stationery Office.

275   ----. 1962. Exchange and Marketing Among the Hausa. In *Markets in Africa*, ed. P. Bohannan and G. Dalton, pp. 299-334. Evanston: Northwesten University Press.

276   Smith, Mary F. 1954. *Baba of Karo*. London: Faber and Faber.

277   Sokoto, Mohammed Abubakar. 1975. Prostitution as a Social Problem in the North Western State: Sabon Gari, Sokoto Case Study. B.Sc. Essay. Dept. of Sociology. Ahmadu Bello University. Zaria.

278   Southall, Aidan W. 1961. The Position of Women and the Stability of Marriage. In *Social Change in Modern Africa*, ed. A.W. Southall. London: Oxford University Press.

279   Starns, William W., Jr. 1974. *Land Tenure Among the Rural Hausa*. Madison: Land Tenure Center, University of Wisconsin.

280 Stenning, Derrick J. 1966. Household Viability Among the Pastoral Fulani. In *The Development Cycle in Domestic Groups*, ed. Jack Goody, pp. 92-119. Cambridge: Cambridge University Press.

281 Sudarkasa, Niara. 1976. Where Women Work - Study of Yoruba Women in the Market Place and in the Home. *Africa* 46(3):295.

282 Sutter, John William. 1982. Peasants, Merchant Capital and Rural Differentiation: A Nigerian Hausa Case Study. Ph.D. Dissertation. Cornell University. Ithaca.

283 Temple, Olive. 1914. Women in Northern Nigeria. *Blackwood's Magazine* 196:257-267.

284 Tiffany, Sharon. 1982. *Women, Work and Motherhood: The Anthropological Perspective on Working Women*. New York: Prentice-Hall Spectrum Books.

285 Trager, Lillian. 1977. Role of Women Traders in Urban and Regional Economy of Ilesha, Nigeria. *Urban Anthropology* 6:183.

286 Trevor, Jean. 1975. Family Change in Sokoto: A Traditional Moslem Fulani/Hausa City. In *Population Growth and Socioeconomic Change in West Africa*, ed. John C. Caldwell, pp. 236-253. New York/London: Columbia University Press.

287 Uba-Mgbemena, Asonye. 1982. The Role of 'Ifo' in the Training of the Igbo Child. *Nigeria Magazine* 143:53-58.

288 Uchendu, Victor C. 1965. Concubine Among the Ngwa Igbo of Southern Nigeria. *Africa* 35(21):187-197.

289 Ukaegbu, Alfred O. 1975. Marriage and Fertility in East Central Nigeria: A Case Study of Ngwa Igbo Women. Ph.D. Dissertation. University of London. London.

290 ----. 1976. The Role of Traditional Marriage Habits in Population Growth: The Case of Rural Eastern Nigeria. *Africa* 46:390-398.

291 UNECA. 1979. Law and the Status of Women in Nigeria. ATRCW and Ford. ECA/ATRCW/RE801/79. New York.

292 Usoro, Eno J. 1961. The Place of Women in Nigerian Society. *African Women* 4(2):27-30.

293 Uyanga, Joseph. 1980. Rural-Urban Differences in Child Care and Breastfeeding Behavior in Southeastern Nigeria. *Social Science and Medicine* 14D:23-29.

294 ----. 1980. The Value of Children and Childbearing in Rural Southeastern Nigeria. *Rural Africana* 7:37-54.

295   Van Allen, J. 1972. "Sitting on a Man": Colonialism and the Lost Political Institutions of Igbo Women. *Canadian Journal of African Studies* 6(2):165-181.

296   ----. 1976. Aba Riots' or Igbo 'Women's War'? Ideology, Stratification, and the Invisibility of Women. In *Women in Africa: Studies in Social and Economic Change*, ed. N.J. Hafkin and E. Bay, pp. 59-86. Stanford: Stanford University Press.

297   Vanden Driesen, I. H. 1972. Some Observations on the Family Unit, Religion, and the Practice of Polygyny in the Ife Division of Western Nigeria. *Africa* 42(1):44-56.

298   Ward, Edward. 1938. *The Yoruba Husband-Wife Code*. Washington, D.C.: Catholic University of America.

299   Ware, Helen. 1975. The Relevance of Changes in Women's Roles to Fertility Behavior: The African Experience. Paper presented at the Population Association of America Meeting. Seattle, WA.

300   ----. 1979. Polygyny: Women's Views in a Transitional Society, Nigeria 1975. *Journal of Marriage and the Family* 41:185-195.

301   ----. 1981. *Women, Education and Modernization of the Family in West Africa*. Canberra: Australian National University, Dept. of Demography. Changing African Family Project Series Monograph No.7.

302   ----. 1983. Female and Male Life-Cycles. In *Female and Male in West Africa*, ed. C. Oppong, pp. 6-31. London: George Allen and Unwin.

303   Westfall, G. D. 1974. Nigerian Women: A Bibliographical Essay. *Africana Journal* 5:99-138.

304   World Health Organization. 1983. *Women and Breastfeeding*. Geneva: World Health Organization.

305   Yahaya, I. Y. 1973. Kishi: A Feeling Among the Hausa Co-wives. *Kano Studies* 1:83-98.

306   Yahaya, Muhammed. 1967. The Legal Status of Muslim Women in the Northern States of Nigeria. *Journal of the Centre for Islamic Legal Studies* 1(2):1-38.

307   Yeld, Rachael E. 1961. Educational Problems Among Women and Girls in Sokoto Province of Northern Nigeria. *Sociologus* 11:160-173.

308   Young, Kate; Wolkowitz, Carol; and McCullagh, Roslyn. 1981. *Of Marriage and the Market: Women's Subordination in International Perspective*. London: CSE Books.

Chapter Four
Marriage and Divorce

1   Abba, Isa A. 1980. Kulle (Purdah) Among the Muslims in the Northern States of Nigeria: Some Clarifications. *Kano Studies* 2:45-50.

2   Abdullahi, Umaru. 1974. The Influence of Customs to Marriage Under Islamic Law in the Far Northern States of Nigeria. Paper presented at the Workshop on African Indigenous Laws. University of Nigeria. Nsukka.

3   Aborampah, Osei Mensah. 1981. Plural Marriage, Post-partum Abstinence and Fertility among the Yoruba of Western Nigeria. Ph.D. Dissertation. University of Wisconsin. Madison.

4   Achike, Okay. 1967. Statutory and Customary Marriage: A Comparison. *Nigerian Law Journal* 2(1):49-61.

5   ----. 1974. Problems of Creation and Dissolution of Customary Marriages and Legitimation of Children under Customary Law in Nigeria. Paper presented at the seminar New Directions in African Family Law. Leiden.

6   ----. 1977. Problems of Creation and Dissolution of Customary Marriages in Nigeria. In *Law and the Family in Africa*, ed. Simon Roberts, pp. 145-158. The Hague: Mouton.

7   Adegbola, O., and Page, H. 1982. Nuptiality and Fertility in Metropolitan Lagos: Components and Compensating Mechanisms. In *Nuptiality and Fertility: Proceedings of a Seminar Held in Bruges, Belgium January 8-11, 1979*, ed. L.T. Ruzicka, pp. 337-362. Liege: Ordina Editions.

8   Ademola, Ade. 1982. Changes in the Patterns of Marriage and Divorce in a Yoruba Town. *Rural Africana* 14:1-24.

9   Adesanya, S. A. 1968. Marriage According to the Local Islamic Rites of Southern Nigeria. *Journal of Marriage and the Family* 2:26-44.

10   ----. 1973. *Laws of Matrimonial Causes*. Ibadan: University Press.

11   ----. 1974. Aspects of the Status of Women Under Nigerian Marriage Laws. *Odu* 10:3-29.

12   ----. 1976. Divorce in Ghana and Nigeria: A Comparative Study in Legislative Reform. *Review of Ghana Law* 8:91-115.

13   Adewolo, E. D. 1982. Islamic Marriage System and the Extent of Its Adoption by the Yoruba Muslims of Nigeria. *Orita* 14:16-33.

14   Adewoye, O. 1973. Law and Social Change in Nigeria. *Journal of the Historical Society of Nigeria* 7(1):149-158.

15   Agbede, I. O. 1968. Recognition of Double Marriage in Nigerian Law. *International Comparative Law Quarterly* 17:17-35.

16   Aguda, A. 1966. *The Marriage Laws of Nigeria*. Ibadan: Mustard Printers.

17   Aig-Ojehomon-Ketting, R. 1975. Modern Marriage in Benin City: A Power Struggle Between Men and Women. *Kroniek von Afrika* 4:60-71.

18   Akande, J. O. 1978. Law, Status of Women and Family Welfare: Matrimonial Causes Decree 1970. Paper read at the International Planned Parenthood Federation Regional Conference. Nairobi.

19   ----. 1979. Law and the Status of Women in Nigeria. Economic Commision for Africa. (ECA/ATRCW/RE801/79). Addis Ababa: ATRCW.

20   Akande, S. 1971. *Marriage and Homemaking in Nigerian Society*. Ibadan: Daystar Press.

21   Aluko, Timothy. 1950. Polygamy and the Surplus of Women. *The West African Review* 21(270):259-260.

22   Amechi, E. E. A. 1979. The Legal Status of Nigerian Women. Ph.D. Dissertation. Institute of Oriental and African Studies. University of London. London.

23   Anderson, J. N. D. 1967. *Family Law in Asia and Africa*. New York: Praeger.

24   ----. 1970. *Islamic Law in Africa*. London: Frank Cass.

25   ----. 1976. *Law Reform in the Muslim World*. London: The Athlone Press. University of London Legal Series XI.

26   Andreski, Iris. *Old Wives' Tales: Life Histories From Iboland*. London: Routledge and Kegan Paul.

27   Aniagolu, A. N., Date unknown. Aspects of Customary Marriage and Divorce and Their Influence Upon Family Life. Paper presented at the Workshop on African Indigenous Laws. University of Nigeria. Nsukka.

28   Ardener, E. 1962. *Divorce and Fertility: An African Study*. London: Oxford University Press.

29   Arikpo, Okoi. 1955. The Future of Bride Price. *West Africa* 2018:1017.

30   Ariwoola, Olagoke. 1965. *The African Wife*. London: The Author (35 Linthorpe Rd., No. 16).

31   Arousi, M. E. 1977. Judicial Dissolution of Marriage. *Journal of Islamic and Comparative Law* 7:13-20.

32   Babotunde, S. O. 1973. Changes in Yoruba Marriage and Family. B.Sc. Essay. University of Ibadan. Ibadan.

33   Balogun, I. A. B. 1972. Islam, Polygamy and Family Planning in Nigeria. *Birthright* 7(1):35-42.

34   Barkow, Jerome H. 1971. The Institution of Courtesanship in the Northern States of Nigeria. *Africa* 10:58-73.

35   ----. 1972. Hausa Women and Islam. *Canadian Journal of African Studies* 6:317-328.

36   ----. 1973. Muslims and Maguzawa in the North Central State of Nigeria. *Canadian Journal of African Studies* 2(1):59-76.

37   Barnes, Sandra T. 1974. Forms of Marriage in Urban Nigeria. Paper presented at the American Anthropological Association Meeting. Mexico City.

38   Bascom, William. 1942. The Principle of Seniority in the Social Structure of the Yoruba. *American Anthropologist* 44:37-46.

39   Beier, H. 1955. The Position of Yoruba Women. *Presence Africaine* 1(2):39-46.

40   Bird, Mary. 1958. Social Change in Kinship and Marriage Among the Yoruba in Nigeria. Ph.D. Dissertation. University of Edinburgh. Edinburgh.

41   ----. 1963. Urbanization, Family and Marriage in Western Nigeria. In *Proceedings of the Inaugural Seminar, Centre of African Studies*, pp. 59-74. Edinburgh: University of Edinburgh.

42   Caldwell, John C. 1976. Marriage, the Family and Fertility in Sub-Saharan Africa With Special Reference to Research Programmes in Ghana and Nigeria. In *Family and Marriage in Some African and Asiatic Countries*, ed. S.A. Huzayyin and G.T. Acsadi, pp. 359-371. Cairo: Cairo Demographic Centre.

43   Callaway, Barbara J. 1984. Ambiguous Consequences of the Socialisation and Seclusion of Hausa Women. *The Journal of Modern African Studies* 22(3):429-450.

44   Chalifoux, Jean-Jacques. 1980. Secondary Marriage and Levels of Seniority Among the Abisi(Piti), Nigeria. *Journal of Comparative Family Studies* 11(3):325-334.

58

45   Childs, Stanley H. 1946. Christian Marriage in Nigeria. *Africa* 16(1):238-246.

46   Chojnacka, Helena. 1980. Polygamy and the Rate of Population Growth. *Population Studies* 34:91-107.

47   Clignet, R. 1970. *Many Wives, Many Powers: Authority and Power in Polygynous Families.* Evanston, IL.: Northwestern University Press.

48   Cohen, Ronald. 1961. Marriage and Instability Among the Kanuri of Northern Nigeria. *American Anthropologist* 63:1123-1241.

49   ----. 1967. Family Life in Bornu. *Anthropologica* 9(1):21-42.

50   ----. 1969. A Multimethod Approach to the Study of Marriage and Divorce: A Study Among the Kanuri of Bornu, Nigeria. *Journal of Business and Social Sciences* 2:53-69.

51   ----. 1970. Brittle Marriage as a Stable System. In *Divorce and After*, ed. P. Bohannan, pp. 182-212. New York: Doubleday.

52   ----. 1971. *Dominance and Defiance: A Study of Marital Instability in an Islamic African Society.* Washington, D.C.: American Anthropological Association, Anthropological Studies No.6.

53   Coker, G. B. A. 1966. *Family Property Among the Yoruba.* London: Sweet and Maxwell.

54   Coleman, R. W. A. 1949. Changing Customs in Nigeria. *West African Review* 20(263):897-899.

55   Coles, Catherine M. 1982. Urban Muslim Women and Social Change in Northern Nigeria. Working Papers on Women in International Development, No.19. Michigan State University. East Lansing.

56   ----. 1983. Muslim Women in Town: Social Change Among the Hausa of Northern Nigeria. Ph.D. Dissertation. University of Wisconsin. Madison.

57   Cotton, J. C. 1905. The Calabar Marriage Law and Custom. *Journal of the African Society* 4(16):427-432.

58   Damachi, U. G. 1972. *Nigerian Modernization.* New York: The Third Press.

59   Delano, I. O. 1958. The Yoruba Family as the Basis of Yoruba Culture. *Odu* 2:2.

60   Denga, Daniel T. 1982. Childlessness and Marital Adjustment in Northern Nigeria. *Journal of Marriage and the Family* 44:799-802.

61   Doi, A. Rahman I., and Parratt, J. I. 1968. Polygamy in Yoruba Society: A Religious or Sociological Issue. *African Quarterly* 8(1):52-58.

62   Donnerreichle, C. 1979. Role of Women in Africa - Marriage, Birth and Disease in the Lives of the Hausa Women in Nigeria. *Argument* 21:766-768.

63   Dorjahn, Vernon. 1954. The Demographic Aspects of African Polygamy. Ph.D. Dissertation. Northwestern University. Evanston.

64   ----. 1959. The Factor of Polygamy in African Demography. In *Continuity and Change in African Cultures*, ed. M. Herskovitz and W. Bascom, pp. 87-112. Chicago: University of Chicago Press.

65   Driesen, V. I. H. 1972. Some Observations on the Family Unit, Religion and the Practice of Polygamy in the Ife Division of Western Nigeria. *Africa* 42(1):44-56.

66   Dry, D. P. L. 1956. Some Aspects of Hausa Family Structure. In *Proceedings of the Third International West African Conference, held at Ibadan, Nigeria. December 12-21, 1949*, pp. 158-163. Lagos: Nigerian Museum.

67   Duru, Augustine I. 1964. Christian and Nigerian Marriages: A Comparative Study. Ph.D. Dissertation. Pontificia Universitas Urbaniana. Rome.

68   Eekelaar, J. M., and Katz, S. N. 1980. *Marriage and Cohabitation in Contemporary Societies*. Toronto: Butterworth.

69   Egboh, E. O. 1972. Polygamy in Iboland with Special Reference to Polygamy Practice Among Christian Ibos. *Civilisations* 22:431-444.

70   ----. 1973. The Place of Women in the Ibo Society of South-Eastern Nigeria From the Earliest Times to the Present. *Civilisations* 23/24:305-316.

71   Eghareuba, J. 1946. *Benin Laws and Customs*. Benin: Service Press Ltd.

72   Ehiagbe, I. 1970. Marital Instability: A Look on Traditional Africa. B.Sc. Thesis. Dept. of Sociology, University of Lagos. Lagos.

73   Ekanem, Ita I. 1974. Influence of Polygyny on Fertility in Eastern Nigeria. In *Sub-fertility and Infertility in Africa: Report of an International Workshop, Ibadan, Nigeria, 1973*, ed. B.K. Adadevoh, pp. 56-64. Ibadan: Caxton Press.

74   Ekechi, F. K. 1976. African Polygamy and Western Christian Ethnocentrism. *Journal of African Studies* 3(3):329-349.

75   Ekundare, Olufemi Richard. 1974. The Impact of Economic Development on Customary Marriages in Nigeria. Paper presented at the seminar New Directions in African Family Law. Leiden.

76   ----. 1969. *Marriage and Divorce Under Yoruba Customary Law*. Ile Ife: University of Ife Press.

77   Elias, Taslim Olawale. 1957. Hausa Marriage. *Nigeria Magazine* 53:135-149.

78   ----. 1962. *Nigerian Land Law and Custom*. London: Routledge and Kegan Paul.

79   El-Imairi, M. T. 1977. Marriage in Islam: Its Basic Rules and Regulations. *Al-Ilm* 2.

80   Ellison, R. E. 1936. Marriage and Child-birth Among the Kanuri. *Africa* 9(4):524-535.

81   Ema, Udo A. J. 1940. Fattening Girls in Oron, Calabar Province. *Nigeria* 21:386-389.

82   Esenwa, F. E. 1948. Marriage Customs in Asaba Division. *Nigerian Field* 13(2):71-81.

83   Ezeani, A. O. N. 1965. Legal Effect of Religious Marriages. *Nigerian Law Journal* 1:1-227.

84   Ezimora, Chike. 1972. Taking a Wife in Iboland. *Daily Times* 14.

85   Fadipe, N. A.; Okediji, Francis; and Oladejo, O. 1970. *The Sociology of the Yoruba*. Ibadan: University Press.

86   Forde, Daryll. 1940. Yako Marriage. *Man* 40(66):57-58.

87   ----. 1941. *Marriage and the Family Among the Yako of Southeastern Nigeria*. London: Lund Humphries.

88   ----. 1950. Double Descent Among the Yako. In *African Systems of Kinship and Marriage*, ed. A.R. Radcliffe-Brown and Daryll Forde, pp. 285-332. London: Oxford University Press.

89   Frantz, Charles. 1978. Ecology and Social Organization Among Nigerian Fulbe. In *The Nomadic Alternative: Modes and Models of Interaction in the African-Asian Deserts and Steppes*, ed. Wolfgang Weissleder, pp. 97-118. The Hague: Mouton.

90 Ghani, W. 1976. Customary Marriage and Change in Marwa Society. Research paper. Ahmadu Bello University. Zaria.

91 Grossbard, Amyra S. 1976. An Economic Analysis of Polygyny: The Case of Maiduguri. *Current Anthropology* 17(4):701-707.

92 ----. 1980. The Economics of Polygamy. In *Research in Population Economics, Vol.2*, ed. Julian L. Simon and Julie DaVanzo, pp. 321-350. Greenwich, CT.: JAI Press, Inc.

93 Gugler, Josef, and Flanagan, William. 1978. *Urbanization and Social Change in West Africa*. Cambridge, England: Cambridge University Press.

94 Harrington, Judith A. 1978. Some Micro-Socioeconomics of Female Status in Nigeria. Paper presented at the Conference on Women in Poverty: What Do We Know?. International Centre for Research on Women. Washington, D.C.

95 ----. 1983. Nutritional Stress and Economic Responsibility: A Study of Nigerian Women. In *Women and Poverty in the Third World*, ed. M. Buvinic, pp. 130-156. Baltimore: Johns Hopkins University Press.

96 Hay, Margaret Jean, and Stichter, Sharon. 1984. *African Women South of the Sahara*. London, New York: Longman.

97 Hickey, Joseph. 1978. Shifting Marital Alliances Among the Bokkos Fulanis. *Ethnology* 17(1):25-37.

98 Hoch-Smith, J. 1978. Radical Yoruba Female Sexuality. In *Women in Ritual and Symbolic Roles*, ed. J. Hoch-Smith and A. Spring, pp. 245-267. New York: Plenum Press.

99 Igbafe, P. A. 1970. Tradition and Change in the Benin Marriage System. *Nigerian Journal of Economic and Social Studies* 12(1):73-102.

100 Ijalaye, D. A. 1967. Capacity to Marry Under Nigerian Customary Law. *Nigerian Bar Journal* 8:1-20.

101 Ijaodola, J. O. 1969. The Proper Place of Islamic Law in Nigeria. *Nigerian Law Journal* 3:129-140.

102 ----. 1970. Proper Place of Islamic Law in Nigeria. *Nigerian Law Journal* 4:1-129.

103 ----. 1971. Aspects of the Matrimonial Causes Decree 1970. *Nigerian Law Journal* 5:144-158.

104 Ijomah, B. I. C. The Prostitutes of Nsukka. In *The Social Structure of Contemporary Society*, ed. A. Akiwowo. New York: Macmillan Press.

105   Ilegbune, C. U. 1970. A Critique of the Nigerian Law of Divorce Under the Matrimonial Causes Decree 1970. *Journal of African Law* 14:178-197.

106   Imam, Ayesha. 1985. Ideology, the Mass Media and Women: A Study from Radio Kaduna, Nigeria. Presented at the Seminar on Nigerian Women and Development, June 20-21 1985. Institute of African Studies, University of Ibadan. Ibadan.

107   Imam, Ibrahim. 1969. Kanuri Marriage. *Nigeria Magazine* 102:512-515.

108   Imoagene, S. O. 1970. The Marriage System of the Weppa-Wano (Midwestern Nigeria). *African Studies* 29:207-218.

109   Iro, M. I. 1976. The Pattern of Elite Divorce in Lagos: 1961-1973. *Journal of Marriage and the Family* 38:177-182.

110   ----. 1978. *Social Correlates of Divorce Among Lagos Elites Who Married in Nigeria.* Canberra: Australian National University, Dept. of Demography. Changing African Family Project Monograph Series, No. 4, Vol.2.

111   Isichei, P. A. C. 1973. Sex in Traditional Asaba. *Cahiers d'Etudes Africanes* 13(52):682-699.

112   Izzet, A. 1961. Family Life Among the Yoruba in Lagos, Nigeria. In *Social Change in Modern Africa*, ed. A. Southall, pp. 305-315. London: Oxford University Press.

113   Jeffreys, M. D. W. 1950. Age Groups Among the Ika and Kindred People. *African Studies* 9(4):157-166.

114   ----. 1969. Some Notes on the Igbo Female. *Afrika und Ubersee* 53(1):37-44.

115   Jones, G. I. 1961. Ecology and Social Structure Among the North-Eastern Ibo. *Africa* 31(2):117-134.

116   Karanja-Diejomaoh, W. M. 1978. Disposition of Incomes by Husbands and Wives: An Exploratory Study of Families in Lagos. In *Marriage, Fertility and Parenthood in West Africa*, ed. C. Oppong, G. Adaba, M. Bekombo-Priso and J. Mogey, pp. 407-432. Canberra: Australian National University, Dept. of Demography. Changing African Family Project Monograph Series, No. 4, Vol.2.

117   ----. 1983. Conjugal Decision-Making: Some Data From Lagos. In *Female and Male in West Africa*, ed. C. Oppong, pp. 236-241. London: George Allen and Unwin.

118   Kasunmu, Alfred B. 1963. Marriage and Divorce Among the Yoruba. Masters Thesis. University of London. London.

119   ----. 1964. Integration of the Law of Husband and Wife in Western Nigeria. Paper presented at the Fourth Conference on the Integration of Customary and Modern Legal Systems in Africa. University of Ife. Ile-Ife.

120   ----. 1964. Principle of Acknowledgement or Recognition of Paternity Under Customary Law in Nigeria. *International Comparative Law Quarterly* 13:1093-1104.

121   ----. 1977. Economic Consequences of Divorce: A Case Study of Some Judicial Decisions in Lagos. In *Law and the Family in Africa*, ed. S. Roberts, pp. 129-143. The Hague: Mouton.

122   Kasunmu, Alfred B., and Salacuse, Jeswald B. 1966. *Nigerian Family Law*. London: Butterworth African Law Series (No.12).

123   Khalil, K. H. 1976. Some Notes on Marriage and Family Relations in Senegal and Nigeria. Paper presented at the Seminar on Marriage and Family in Some Arab and African Countries. Cairo Demographic Center. Cairo.

124   Kirk-Green, A. H. M. 1957. A Lala Initiation Ceremony. *Man* 57(5):9-11.

125   Kisekka, Mere Nakateregga. 1975. Sex and Marital Differences in Sexism Among Zaria Residents. Presented at the Nigerian Psychological Society Conference. Ahmadu Bello University. Zaria.

126   ----. 1976. Polygyny and the Status of African Women. Paper presented at the National Conference on Nigerian Women and Development in Relation to Changing Family Structure. University of Ibadan. Ibadan.

127   ----. 1980. Marital and Familial Patterns in Zaria, Nigeria. *Africana Marburgensia* 13:43-50.

128   ----. 1981. The Role of Women in Socioeconomic Development: Indicators as Instruments of Social Analysis--The Case of Nigeria and Uganda. In *Women and Development*, pp. 33-47. Paris: UNESCO.

129   Koripamo, P. A. 1973. Marital Instability Among the Kolokumo Ijos. Research essay. Ahmadu Bello University. Zaria.

130   Kwaghbo, Gwar. 1968. Iee: A Local Tiv Festival. *Nigerian Field* 33(2):74-75.

131   Leis, Nancy Boric. 1964. Economic Independence and Ijaw Women: A Comparative Study of Two Communities in the Niger Delta. Ph.D. Dissertation. Northwestern University. Evanston.

132   ----. 1971. Virilocality, Polygamy and Women's Associations in West Africa. Paper presented at the 70th annual Meeting of the American Anthropological Association. New York.

133   Little, Kenneth. 1959. Some Urban Patterns of Marriage and Domesticity in West Africa. *The Sociological Review* 7(1):65-82.

134   ----. 1959. Urbanism in West Africa. *The Sociological Review* 7(1):5-13.

135   ----. 1960. The West African Town: Its Social Basis. *Diogenes* 29:16-31.

136   ----. 1977. Women's Strategies in Modern Marriage in Anglophone West Africa: An Ideological and Sociological Appraisal. *Journal of Comparative Family Studies* 8(3):341-356.

137   Little, Kenneth, and Price, Anne. 1967. Some Trends in Modern Marriage Among West Africans. *Africa* 37(4):407-424.

138   Lloyd, P. C. 1955. The Yoruba Lineage. *Africa* 25.

139   Lloyd, Peter C. 1959. Family Property Among the Yoruba. *Journal of African Law* 3:105.

140   ----. 1959. Some Notes on the Yoruba Rules of Succession and on Family Property. *Journal of African Law* 3(1):6-18.

141   ----. 1966. Agnatic and Cognatic Descent Among the Yoruba. *Man* 1(4):484-500.

142   ----. 1968. Divorce Among the Yoruba. *American Anthropologist* 70:67-81.

143   Lock, Max. 1974. Women in Maiduguri: Some Aspects of Their Lives. In *Maiduguri: Surveys and Planning Reports*. pp. 7.6.1-7.6.34 UK: Warminster Press for Max Lock Group Ltd.

144   Lucas, David. 1974. A Demographic Study of a South-Eastern Ibibio Village. Research Paper No.2. Lagos.

145   ----. 1974. Occupation, Marriage and Fertility Among Nigerian Women in Lagos. Human Resources Research Unit. Research Bulletin No.3/001. University of Lagos. Lagos.

146   ----. 1974. Some Aspects of Marriage, Fertility and Migration Among Women in Lagos. University of Lagos Research Bulletin. Lagos.

147   Mabogunje, A. L. 1958. The Yoruba Home. *Odu* 5:28-35.

148   ----. 1977. The Urban Situation in Nigeria. In *Patterns of Urbanization: Comparative Country Studies*, ed. S. Goldstein and D.F. Sly, pp. 569-641. Dolhain: Ordina Editions.

149   Mack, Delores E. 1978. Husbands and Wives in Lagos: The Effects of Socioeconomic Status on the Patterns of Family Living. *Journal of Marriage and the Family* 40(4):807-816.

150   Maiduguri, Theresa. 1972. I Was Bundled Into Marriage. *Daily Times* 16-17.

151   Mair, Lucy. 1969. *African Marriage and Social Change*. London: Oxford University Press.

152   Marasinghe, M. L. 1968. Monogamy, Polygamy, and Bigamy. *Journal of Islamic and Comparative Law* 2:54-78.

153   Marris, Peter. 1961. *Family and Social Change in an African City: A Study of Rehousing in Lagos*. London: Routledge and Kegan Paul.

154   Marshall, Gloria Albertha. 1964. Women, Trade, and the Yoruba Family. Ph.D. Dissertation. Columbia University. New York.

155   Mayo, Marjorie. 1969. Two Steps Forward, One Step Back: An Account of Some of the Difficulties That Can Plague Work Among Women. *Community Development Journal* 4(2):93-98.

156   Mba, Cyriacus. 1964. Matrimonial Consent in Igbo Marriages. Ph.D. Dissertation. Pontificia Universitas Gregoriana. Rome.

157   Meek, Charles Kingsley. 1936. Marriage by Exchange in Nigeria, a Disappearing Institution. *Africa* 9(1):64-74.

158   ----. 1955. Ibo Law. In *Readings in Anthropology*, ed. E. Adamson Hoebel, pp. 234-249. New York: McGraw-Hill.

159   Mohammed, A. 1975. Prostitution as a Social Problem in the North-Western State: Sabon Garin Sokoto Case Study. B.Sc. Essay. Ahmadu Bello University. Zaria.

160   ----. 1980. Home Outside the Home (A Sociological Concept of Prostitution Among the Hausa). Seminar paper. Department of Sociology. Bayero University. Kano.

161   Mott, Frank L. 1974. *The Dynamics of Demographic Change in a Nigerian Village*. Lagos: University of Lagos, Human Resources Research Unit, Monograph No.2.

162   Muhammad, Yahaya. 1967. The Legal Status of Women in the Northern States of Nigeria. *Journal of Islamic Legal Studies* 1(2):1-38.

163   Muller, Jean-Claude. 1969. Preferential Marriage Among the Rukuba of Benue-Plateau State, Nigeria. *American Anthropologist* 71:1057-1061.

164   ----. 1970. Rukuba Kinship and Marriage. Ph.D. Dissertation. University of Rochester. Rochester.

165   ----. 1972. Ritual Marriage, Symbolic Fatherhood and Initiation Among the Rukuba, Benue-Plateau State, Nigeria. *Man* 7(2):283-295.

166   ----. 1973. On Preferential/Prescriptive Marriage and the Function of Kinship Systems: The Rukuba Case. *American Anthropologist* 75:1563-1576.

167   ----. 1978. On Bridewealth and Marriage Among the Rukuba, Plateau State, Nigeria. *Africa* 48(2):161-175.

168   ----. 1980. On the Relevance of Having Two Husbands: Contribution to the Study of Polygynous/Polyandrous Marital Forms of the Jos Plateau. *Journal of Comparative Family Studies* 11:359-369.

169   Muller, Jean-Claude, and Sangree, W. H. 1973. Irigwe and Rukuba Marriage: A Comparison. *Canadian Journal of African Studies* 7:27-57.

170   Musa, Ayuba Zakirai. 1981. Assessment of Societal Perceptions and Attitudes Toward Marriage and Educated Hausa Women in the Northern States of Nigeria. Ph.D. Dissertation. Ohio University.

171   National Seminar on Women. 1979. Laws and Customs Affecting Women. Resolutions issued by a National Seminar on Women. CenSCER. Benin.

172   Netting, Robert. 1969. Marital Relations in the Jos Plateau of Nigeria, Women's Weapons: The Politics of Domesticity Among the Kofyar. *American Anthropologist* 71(6):1037-1076.

173   Newman, Jeanne S. 1984. *Women of the World: Sub-Saharan Africa*. Washington, D.C.: WID-USAID and U.S. Department of Commerce, Bureau of the Census.

174   Nigeria. Eastern Region. 1955. *Report of the Eastern Region's Committee on Bride Price*. Enugu: Government Printer.

175   Ntiri, Daphne Williams. 1983. *The African Woman in a Transitional Society*. Troy, MI.: Bedford Publishers, Inc.

176   Nwabueze, B. O. 1968. Family Law in Nigeria. In *Le droit de la Famille en Afrique noire et a Madagascar*, ed. Keba M'Baye, pp. 117-157. Paris: Maisonneuve et Larose.

177   Nwogugu, E. I. 1964. Legitimacy in Nigerian Law. *Journal of Nigerian Law* 8(2):91-105.

178   ----. 1971. A Critical Analysis of the Grounds for Divorce Under the Matrimonial Causes Decree 1970. *Nigerian Law Journal* 5:76-91.

179   ----. 1974. *Family Law in Nigeria*. Ibadan: Heinemann.

180   ----. 1974. Problems of Dissolution of Customary Law Marriages in Nigeria. Paper presented at the seminar. New Directions in African Family Law. Leiden.

181   ----. 1980. Formal Marriage Law and Its Underlying Assumptions in Nigeria. In *Marriage and Cohabitation in Contemporary Societies*, ed. J.M. Eekelaar and S.N. Katz, pp. 116-123. Toronto: Butterworth.

182   Obi, Celestine A. 1970. Christianity and Igbo Marriage. Ph.D. Dissertation. Pontificia Universitas Urbaniana. Rome.

183   Obi, S. N. C. 1962. The Effect of Ordinance Marriage on the Rights and Status of the Spouses. *Journal of African Law* 6(1):49-52.

184   ----. 1962. Women's Property and Succession in Modern Ibo Law, Eastern Nigeria. *Journal of African Law* 6(1):6-18.

185   ----. 1963. *Ibo Law of Property*. London: Butterworth.

186   Obi, S. N. Chinwuba. 1966. *Modern Family Law in Southern Nigeria*. London: Sweet and Maxwell.

187   Odulana, J. 1978. Family Welfare Laws in Ten African Countries: Report of the Africa Regional Law Panel Field Trips,1977/78, Vol.1. International Planned Parenthood Federation, Africa Region. Nairobi.

188   Offonry, H. Kanu. 1951. The Strength of the Ibo Clan Feeling. *West Africa* 1787:467.

189   Ogunbiyi, I. A. 1969. The Position of Muslim Women as Stated by Uthman B. Fudi. *Odu* 2:43-60.

190   Ogunrotimi, T. O. 1973. Traditional Marriage in Ode-Ekiti. B.Sc. Essay. University of Ibadan. Ibadan.

191   Ogunsheye, F. A. 1960. The Women of Nigeria. *Presence Africaine* 4(32):33-49.

192   Ohadike, P. O. 1968. A Demographic Note on Marriage, Family, and Family Growth in Lagos, Nigeria. In *The Population of Tropical Africa*, ed. J.C. Caldwell and C. Okonjo, pp. 379-392. London: Longmans.

193   ----. 1968. Urban Social Structure, Marital Patterns, Variations and Attitudes in a Major West African City (Lagos, Nigeria). University of East Africa Social Sciences Council Conference Papers. Makerere Institute of Social Research. Vol.2, pp. 416-428. Makerere University. Kampala.

194   Ojiako, John. 1966. Bride Price among the Ibos of Southeastern Nigeria: A Sociological and Theoretical Investigation. Ph.D. Dissertation. Theology University of Innsbruck. Innsbruck.

195   Okadigho, Miriam. 1977. Discriminative Provisions in the Draft Constitution: Two Points of Dissent. Paper presented at the Nigerian Political Science Symposium.

196   Okediji, Francis Olu. 1974. Population Dynamics Research in Nigeria: Achievements and New Horizons. In *Population Dynamics Research in Africa*, ed. F.O. Okediji, pp. 3-18. Washington,D.C.: Smithsonian Institute, Interdisciplinary Communications Program.

197   Okediji, Francis Olu; Caldwell, John C.; Caldwell, Pat; and Ware, Helen. 1976. The Changing African Family Project: A Report With Special Reference to the Nigeria Segment. *Studies in Family Planning* 7(5):126-136.

198   Okediji, Francis Olu; Caldwell, John; Caldwell, Pat; and Ware, Helen. 1978. *The Changing African Family Project: A Report With Special Reference to the Nigerian Segment*. Canberra: Australian National University, Dept. of Demography. Changing African Family Project Monograph Series, No.4, Vol.2.

199   Okediji, O. O., and Okediji, Francis Olu. 1966. Marital Stability and Social Structure in an African City. *Nigerian Journal of Economic and Social Studies* 8(1):151-163.

200   Okonjo, C. 1971. Nigeria, Marriage, Kinship, and Fertility. In *The Demographic Transition in Tropical Africa*, pp. 267-273. Paris: Organisation for Economic Cooperation and Development, Development Center.

201   Oloruntimehin, O. 1975. Some Factors Affecting the Stability of Marriage in Nigeria. Paper presented at the Conference of Social Research and National Development. University of Ibadan. Ibadan.

202   Olusanya, P. O. 1970. A Note on Some Factors Affecting the Stability of Marriage Among the Yoruba of Western Nigeria. *Journal of Marriage and the Family* 32:150-155.

203   ----. 1971. The Problem of Multiple Causation in Population Analysis with Particular Reference to the Polygamy-Fertility Hypothesis. *The Sociological Review* 19:165-178.

204 Olusanya, Philip O. 1981. Patterns of Nuptiality in Nigeria. *Research for Development: A Journal of the Nigerian Institute of Social and Economic Reseach* 2(2):152-184.

205 Onwuejeogwu, Michael. 1969. The Cult of the Bori Spirits among the Hausa. In *Man in Africa*, ed. Mary Douglas and Phyllis M. Kaberry, pp. 279-305. London: Tavistock Publications.

206 Opaluwa, A. A. 1976. The Impact of Modernisation on Marriage Customs Among the Igala. Research paper. Ahmadu Bello Univeristy. Zaria.

207 Oppong, C. 1979. Family Structure and Women's Reproductive and Productive Roles: Some Conceptual and Methodological Issues. Population and Labour Policies Programme Working Paper No. 79. World Employment Programme Research. ILO. Geneva.

208 Oppong, C.; Adaba, G.; Bekombo-Priso, M.; and Mogey, J., eds. 1978. *Marriage, Fertility and Parenthood in West Africa*. Canberra: Australian National University, Dept. of Demography, Changing African Family Monograph Series, No.4.

209 Otite, Onigu. 1971. Process of Family Formation Among The Urhobo of Midwestern Nigeria. *International Journal of Sociology of the Family* 1(2):125-136.

210 Ottenberg, Phoebe. 1958. Marriage Relationships in the Double Descent System of the Afikpo Ibo of South-eastern Nigeria. Ph.D. Dissertation. Northwestern University. Evanston.

211 Ottenberg, Simon. 1968. *Double Descent in an African Society: The Afikpo Village-Group*. Seattle: University of Washington Press.

212 Otterbein, Keith F. 1969. Higi Marriage System. *Bulletin of the Cultural Research Institute* 8(1-2):16-20.

213 Ottong, G. J. 1978. Factors Affecting Marriage and Fertility in Shika, Zaria. Paper presented at the International Seminar on Integration of Theory and Policy in Population Studies. Legon.

214 Peil, Margaret. 1975. Female Roles in West African Towns. In *Changing Social Structure in Ghana*, ed. J. Goody, pp. 73-90. London: International African Institute.

215 ----. 1983. Urban Contacts: A Comparison of Women and Men. In *Female and Male in West Africa*, ed. C. Oppong, pp. 275-282. London: George Allen and Unwin.

216 Philips, Arthur. 1953. *Survey of African Marriage and Family Life*. London: Oxford University Press.

217   ----. 1955. Conflict Between Statutory and Customary Law: Marriage in Nigeria. *Modern Law Review* 18:73-76.

218   ----. 1971. *Marriage Laws in Africa.* London: Oxford University Press.

219   Pittin, Renee. 1979. Marriage and Alternative Strategies: Career Patterns of Hausa Women in Katsina City. Ph.D. Dissertation. The School of Oriental and African Studies, University of London. London.

220   ----. 1979. Hausa Women and Islamic Law: Is Reform Necessary?. Paper presented at the 22nd Annual Meeting of the African Studies Association. Los Angeles.

221   ----. 1983. Houses of Women: A Focus on Alternative Life-Styles in Katsina City. In *Female and Male in West Africa,* ed. C. Oppong, pp. 291-302. London: George Allen and Unwin.

222   Radcliffe-Brown, A. R., and D. Forde. 1950. *African Systems of Kinship and Marriage.* London: Oxford University Press.

223   Ransome-Kuti, F. 1961. The Status of Women in Nigeria. *Journal of Human Relations* 10(1):67-72.

224   Rehfisch, F. 1966. Mambila Marriage, Prohibitions, Incest Regulations and the Role System. *Journal of Asian and African Studies* 1(4):298-309.

225   Remy, Dorothy. 1973. Adaptive Strategies of Men and Women in Zaria, Nigeria: Industrial Workers and Their Wives. Ph.D. Dissertation. University of Michigan. Ann Arbor.

226   Roberts, S. *Law and the Family in Africa.* The Hague: Mouton.

227   Sagay, I. 1974. Widow Inheritance Versus Monagomous Marriage: The Oba's Dilemma. *Journal of African Law* 18:168-172.

228   Salacuse, J. W. 1964. Birth, Death, and the Marriage Act: Some Problems in Conflict of Laws. *Nigerian Law Journal* 1:59.

229   ----. 1965. *Selective Survey of Family Law in Northern Nigeria.* Zaria: Institute of Administration.

230   Salamone, Frank A. 1971. Some Aspects of Social Stratification Among the Hausa. *International Journal of Group Tensions* 1(4):335-349.

231   ----. 1981. Levirate, Widows and Types of Marriage among the Dukana of Northern Nigeria. *Afrika und Ubersee* 64:129-136.

232   Salawu, S. A. I. 1977. Effects of Marriage Practices in Maternal Health Care in the Northern States. *Abumed* 1(5):35-38.

233   Sangree, Walter H. 1969. Going Home to Mother: Traditional Marriage Among the Irigwe of Benue-Plateau State, Nigeria. *American Anthropologist* 71(6):1049-1057.

234   ----. 1972. Monagamous Hangups and Complementary Filiation in Polygamous Society. Paper Presented at the 12th Annual Meeting of the Northeastern Anthropological Association. Buffalo.

235   ----. 1972. Secondary Marriage and Tribal Solidarity in Irigwe, Nigeria. *American Anthropologist* 74:1234-1243.

236   ----. 1974. The Dodo Cult, Witchcraft, and Secondary Marriage in Irigwe, Nigeria. *Ethnology* 13(3):261-278.

237   ----. 1974. Prescriptive Polygamy and Complementary Filiation Among the Irigwe of Nigeria. *Man* 9:44-52.

238   ----. 1980. The Persistence of Polyandry in Irigwe, Nigeria. *Journal of Comparative Family Studies* 11:335-343.

239   Saunders, Margaret Overholt. 1978. Marriage and Divorce in a Muslim Hausa Town (Mirria, Niger Republic). Ph.D. Dissertation. Indiana University. Bloomington.

240   ----. 1980. Women's Role in a Muslim Hausa Town. In *A World of Women: Anthropological Studies of Women in Societies of the World*, ed. E. Bourguignon, pp. 57-86. New York: Praeger.

241   Schildkrout, Enid. 1978. Thoughts on Child Labor, Education and Marriage in Kano City. Paper presented at the African Studies Association Meeting. Baltimore.

242   ----. 1983. Dependence and Autonomy: The Economic Activities of Secluded Hausa Women in Kano. In *Female and Male in West Africa*, ed. C. Oppong, pp. 107-126. London: George Allen and Unwin.

243   Sembajwe, Israel. 1979. Effect of Age at First Marriage, Number of Wives, and Type of Marital Union on Fertility. *Journal of Biosocial Science* 11:341-351.

244   Shani, M. I. n.d. The Impact of Custom in the Islamic Law of Divorce in the Northern States of Nigeria. Centre for Islamic Legal Studies. Ahmadu Bello University. Zaria.

245   Simmons, Donald C. 1960. Sexual Life, Marriage and Childhood Among the Efik. *Africa* 30(1):153-165.

246   Smedley, Audrey. 1974. Women of Udu: Survival in a Harsh Land. In *Many Sisters: Women in Cross-Cultural Perspective*, ed. C.J. Mathiasson, pp. 205-228. London: Collier Macmillan.

247   ----. 1980. The Implications of Birom Cicisbeism. *Journal of Comparative Family Studies* 11:345-357.

248   Smith, M. G. 1953. Secondary Marriage in Northern Nigeria. *Africa* 23(4):298-323.

249   ----. 1955. *The Economy of Hausa Communities of Zaria, Colonial Research Studies No. 16.* London: H.M. Stationery Office.

250   ----. 1969. Idda and Secondary Marriage Among the Northern Kadara. In *Ideas and Procedures of African Customary Law*, ed. M. Gluckman, pp. 210-222. New York: Oxford University Press for International African Institute.

251   ----. 1980. After Secondary Marriage, What?. *Ethnology* 19(3):265-277.

252   Smith, Mary F. 1954. *Baba of Karo*. London: Faber and Faber.

253   Sofoluwe, G. O. 1965. A Study of Divorce Cases in Igbo-Ora. *Nigerian Journal of Economics and Social Studies* 7(1):51-62.

254   Sokoto, Mohammed Abubakar. 1975. Prostitution as a Social Problem in the North Western State: Sabon Gari, Sokoto Case Study. B.Sc. Essay. Dept. of Sociology. Ahmadu Bello University. Zaria.

255   Southall, Aidan W. 1961. The Position of Women and the Stability of Marriage. In *Social Change in Modern Africa*, ed. A.W. Southall. London: Oxford University Press.

256   Sporndli, J. 1942. Marriage Customs Among the Ibos. *Anthropos* 37-40:113-121.

257   Stenning, Derrick J. 1966. Household Viability Among the Pastoral Fulani. In *The Development Cycle in Domestic Groups*, ed. Jack Goody, pp. 92-119. Cambridge: Cambridge University Press.

258   Temietan, S. O. 1938. Marriage Among the Jekri Tribes as Contrasted with that Amongst the Hausa Tribes. *Nigeria* 13:75-78.

259   Temple, Olive. 1914. Women in Northern Nigeria. *Blackwood's Magazine* 196:257-267.

260   Trevor, Jean. 1975. Family Change in Sokoto: A Traditional Moslem Fulani/Hausa City. In *Population Growth and Socioeconomic Change in West Africa*, ed. John C. Caldwell, pp. 236-253. New York/London: Columbia University Press.

261   Tschudis, Jolantha. 1970. The Social Life of the Afo, Hill Country of Nasarawa Nigeria. *African Notes* 6(1):87-89.

262   Uchendu, Victor C. 1965. Concubine Among the Ngwa Igbo of Southern Nigeria. *Africa* 35(21):187-197.

263   Ukaegbu, Alfred O. 1975. Marriage and Fertility in East Central Nigeria: A Case Study of Ngwa Igbo Women. Ph.D. Dissertation. University of London. London.

264   ----. 1976. The Role of Traditional Marriage Habits in Population Growth: The Case of Rural Eastern Nigeria. *Africa* 46:390-398.

265   ----. 1977. Fertility of Women in Polygynous Unions in Rural Eastern Nigeria. *Journal of Marriage and the Family* 39:397-404.

266   ----. 1977. Socio-cultural Determination of Fertility: A Case Study of Rural Eastern Nigeria. *Journal of Comparative Family Studies* 8:99-115.

267   Ukah, L. 1972. On Ibo Traditional Marriage. *Bulletin of the International Committee on Urgent Anthropological and Ethnological Research* 14:37-41.

268   UNECA. 1979. Law and the Status of Women in Nigeria. ATRCW and Ford. ECA/ATRCW/RE801/79. New York.

269   Vanden Driesen, I. H. 1972. Some Observations on the Family Unit, Religion, and the Practice of Polygyny in the Ife Division of Western Nigeria. *Africa* 42(1):44-56.

270   Ward, Edward. 1937. *Marriage Among the Yoruba*. Washington, D.C.: Catholic University of America.

271   ----. 1938. *The Yoruba Husband-Wife Code*. Washington, D.C.: Catholic University of America.

272   Ware, Helen. 1975. The Relevance of Changes in Women's Roles to Fertility Behavior: The African Experience. Paper presented at the Population Association of America Meeting. Seattle, WA.

273   ----. 1979. Polygyny: Women's Views in a Transitional Society, Nigeria 1975. *Journal of Marriage and the Family* 41:185-195.

274   ----. 1981. *Women, Education and Modernization of the Family in West Africa*. Canberra: Australian National University, Dept. of Demography. Changing African Family Project Series Monograph No.7.

275 ----. 1983. Female and Male Life-Cycles. In *Female and Male in West Africa*, ed. C. Oppong, pp. 6-31. London: George Allen and Unwin.

276 Weischhoff, Heinz A. 1941. Divorce Laws and the Practices in Modern Ibo Culture. *Journal of Negro History* 26:299-324.

277 Westfall, G. D. 1974. Nigerian Women: A Bibliographical Essay. *Africana Journal* 5:99-138.

278 Williamson, Kay. 1962. Changes in the Marriage System of the Okrika Ijo. *Africa* 32:53-60.

279 Yahaya, I. Y. 1973. Kishi: A Feeling Among the Hausa Co-wives. *Kano Studies* 1:83-98.

280 Yahaya, Muhammed. 1967. The Legal Status of Muslim Women in the Northern States of Nigeria. *Journal of the Centre for Islamic Legal Studies* 1(2):1-38.

281 Yaro, S. V. A. 1976. Marriage and Marriage Stability: A Comparative Study of Two Villages Near Kubanni Dam. Research paper. Ahmadu Bello University. Zaria.

282 Young, Kate; Wolkowitz, Carol; and McCullagh, Roslyn. 1981. *Of Marriage and the Market: Women's Subordination in International Perspective*. London: CSE Books.

283 Zabel, S. 1969. A Comparative Study of the Law of Marriage in the Sudan and Nigeria. *Utah Law Review* 1:22-53.

284 ----. 1969. A Legislative History of the Gold Coast and Nigerian Marriage Ordinances. *Journal of African Law* 13(2):64-79.

Chapter Five
Religion and Ritual

1   Abba, Isa A. 1980. Kulle (Purdah) Among the Muslims in the Northern States of Nigeria: Some Clarifications. *Kano Studies* 2:45-50.

2   Abdul, M. O. A. 1970. Yoruba Divination and Islam. *Orita: Ibadan Journal of Religious Studies* 4:17-25.

3   Abdullahi, Umaru. 1974. The Influence of Customs to Marriage Under Islamic Law in the Far Northern States of Nigeria. Paper presented at the Workshop on African Indigenous Laws. University of Nigeria. Nsukka.

4   Abimbola, Wande. 1977. The Ifa Divination System. *Nigeria Magazine* 122/123:35-76.

5   Achike, Okay. 1967. Statutory and Customary Marriage: A Comparison. *Nigerian Law Journal* 2(1):49-61.

6   Adesanya, S. A. 1968. Marriage According to the Local Islamic Rites of Southern Nigeria. *Journal of Marriage and the Family* 2:26-44.

7   ----. 1974. Aspects of the Status of Women Under Nigerian Marriage Laws. *Odu* 10:3-29.

8   Adewolo, E. D. 1982. Islamic Marriage System and the Extent of Its Adoption by the Yoruba Muslims of Nigeria. *Orita* 14:16-33.

9   Ajose, O. A. 1954. Old and New in Nigeria: Custom, Religion, and Disease. *Lancet* CCXXVI:1024-1025.

10   Anderson, J. N. D. 1970. *Islamic Law in Africa*. London: Frank Cass.

11   ----. 1976. *Law Reform in the Muslim World*. London: The Athlone Press. University of London Legal Series XI.

12   Andreski, Iris. *Old Wives' Tales: Life Histories From Iboland*. London: Routledge and Kegan Paul.

13   Aronson, D. R. 1978. *The City is Our Farm: Seven Migrant Ijebu Yoruba Families*. Boston, MA.: Schenkman.

14   Arousi, M. E. 1977. Judicial Dissolution of Marriage. *Journal of Islamic and Comparative Law* 7:13-20.

15   Awolalu, J. Omosade. 1981. Continuity and Discontinuity in African Religion: The Yoruba Experience. *Orita* 13:3-20.

16   Awolalu J. Omosade. 1979. *Yoruba Beliefs and Sacrificial Rites*. London: Longman.

17   Balogun, I. A. B. 1976. Teachings and Practices of Islam and the Status of Nigerian Muslim Women. Paper presented at the National Conference on Nigerian Women and Development in Relation to Changing Family Structure. University of Ibadan. Ibadan.

18   Barkow, Jerome H. 1970. Hausa and Maguzawa: Process of Group Differentiation in a Rural Area of North Central State, Nigeria. Ph.D. Dissertation. University of Chicago. Chicago.

19   ----. 1972. Hausa Women and Islam. *Canadian Journal of African Studies* 6:317-328.

20   ----. 1973. Muslims and Maguzawa in the North Central State of Nigeria. *Canadian Journal of African Studies* 2(1):59-76.

21   Bascom, William. 1944. The Sociological Role of the Yoruba Cult Group. *American Anthropologist* 46.

22   ----. 1969. *Ifa Divination: Communication between Gods and Man in West Africa*. Bloomington: Indiana University Press.

23   Beck, Lois, and Keddi, Nikki. 1978. *Women in the Muslim World*. Cambridge, MA.: Harvard University Press.

24   Beckett, P. A., and O'Connell, J. 1976. Education and the Situation of Women: Background and Attitudes of Christian and Muslim Female Students at a Nigerian University. *Cultures et Developpement* 8:242-265.

25   Besmer, F. E. 1977. Initiation Into the Bori Cult--A Case Study in Ningi Town. *Africa* 47:1-13.

26   Bohannan, Paul. 1975. Tiv Divination. In *Studies in Social Anthropology: Essays in Memory of E.E. Evans-Pritchard by His Former Oxford Colleagues*, ed. J.M.H. Beattie et al., pp. 149-166. Oxford: Oxford University Press.

27   Callaway, Barbara J. 1984. Ambiguous Consequences of the Socialisation and Seclusion of Hausa Women. *The Journal of Modern African Studies* 22(3):429-450.

28   Childs, Stanley H. 1946. Christian Marriage in Nigeria. *Africa* 16(1):238-246.

29   Clarke, J. D. 1944. Three Yoruba Fertility Ceremonies. *Journal of the Royal Anthropological Institute* LXXIV(1-2):91-96.

30   Damachi, U. G. 1972. *Nigerian Modernization.* New York: The Third Press.

31   Doi, A. Rahman I. 1972. Islamic Education in Nigeria. *Islamic Culture* 46(1):1-16.

32   ----. 1978. Islam in Nigeria: Changes Since Independence. In *Christianity in Independent Africa,* ed. Edward Fashole-Luke, pp. 334-353. London: R. Collings.

33   Downes, R. M. 1971. *Tiv Religion.* Ibadan: University Press.

34   Drewal, Henry J., and Drewal, Margaret T. 1983. *Gelede: Art and Female Power Among the Yoruba.* Bloomington: Indiana University Press.

35   Dry, D. P. L. 1952. The Place of Islam in Hausa Society. Ph.D. Dissertation. Oxford University. Oxford.

36   Duru, Augustine I. 1964. Christian and Nigerian Marriages: A Comparative Study. Ph.D. Dissertation. Pontificia Universitas Urbaniana. Rome.

37   Duru, Mary Steimel. 1980. Socialization Among the Igbo: An Intergenerational Study of Cultural Patterns, Familial Roles and Child Rearing Practices. Ph.D. Dissertation. University of Maryland. College Park.

38   Egboh, E. O. 1972. Polygamy in Iboland with Special Reference to Polygamy Practice Among Christian Ibos. *Civilisations* 22:431-444.

39   Ekechi, F. K. 1976. African Polygamy and Western Christian Ethnocentrism. *Journal of African Studies* 3(3):329-349.

40   El-Imairi, M. T. 1977. Marriage in Islam: Its Basic Rules and Regulations. *Al-Ilm* 2.

41   Ema, Udo A. J. 1940. Fattening Girls in Oron, Calabar Province. *Nigeria* 21:386-389.

42   Fadipe, N. A.; Okediji, Francis; and Oladejo, O. 1970. *The Sociology of the Yoruba.* Ibadan: University Press.

43   Galadanci, Alhaji S. A. 1971. Education of Women in Islam with Reference to Nigeria. *Nigerian Journal of Islam* 1(2):5-10.

44   Ginat, Joseph. 1980. *Women in Muslim Rural Society.* New Brunswick, N.J.: Transaction Books.

45 Hay, Margaret Jean, and Stichter, Sharon. 1984. *African Women South of the Sahara*. London, New York: Longman.

46 Henderson, Helen Kreider. 1969. Ritual Roles of Women in Onitsha Ibo Society. Ph.D. Dissertation. University of California. Berkeley.

47 Hiskett, M. 1975. Islamic Education in the Traditional and State Systems in Northern Nigeria. In *Conflict and Harmony in Education in Tropical Africa*, ed. G.N. Brown and M. Hiskett, pp. 134-151. London: Allen and Unwin.

48 Hoch-Smith, J. 1978. Radical Yoruba Female Sexuality. In *Women in Ritual and Symbolic Roles*, ed. J. Hoch-Smith and A. Spring, pp. 245-267. New York: Plenum Press.

49 Ijaodola, J. O. 1969. The Proper Place of Islamic Law in Nigeria. *Nigerian Law Journal* 3:129-140.

50 ----. 1970. Proper Place of Islamic Law in Nigeria. *Nigerian Law Journal* 4:1-129.

51 Ilogu, E. 1974. *Christianity and Ibo Culture*. Leiden: Brill.

52 ----. 1975. The Problem of Christian Ethics Among the Igbo of Nigeria. *Ikenga* 3:38-52.

53 Jeffreys, M. D. W. 1965. The Nyama Society of the Ibibio Women. *African Studies* 15(1):15-28.

54 Kanam, Yahaya. 1968. The Effect of Custom on Certain Apsects of Maliki Law in the Northern States of Nigeria. *Journal of Islamic and Comparative Law* 2:79-87.

55 Kirk, Dudley. 1965. Factors Affecting Moslem Natality. United Nations World Population Conference, Vol.2. New York.

56 Kirk-Green, A. H. M. 1957. A Lala Initiation Ceremony. *Man* 57(5):9-11.

57 Kisekka, Mere Nakateregga. 1980. Marital and Familial Patterns in Zaria, Nigeria. *Africana Marburgensia* 13:43-50.

58 Kumo, S. 1977. The Applications of Islamic Law in Northern Nigeria: Problems and Prospects. *Journal of Islamic and Comparative Law* 7:21-30.

59 Maqsud, Muhammad. 1974. The Impact of Cultural Values on the Development of Moral Judgements of Hausa Muslim Children in Kano. *Kano Studies* 1:45-53.

60   Mitchell, Robert Cameron. 1970. Religious Protest and Social Change: The Origins of the Aladura Movement in Western Nigeria. In *Protest and Power in Black Africa*, ed. I. Rotberg and A.A. Mazrui, pp. 458-496. New York: Oxford University Press.

61   Muhammad, Yahaya. 1967. The Legal Status of Women in the Northern States of Nigeria. *Journal of Islamic Legal Studies* 1(2):1-38.

62   Muller, Jean-Claude. 1978. Ritual Legitimacy and Demography Among the Rukuba. *Canadian Journal of African Studies* 12(1):61-81.

63   Nadel, S. F. 1937. Gunnu, A Fertility Cult of the Nupe in Northern Nigeria. *Royal Anthropological Institute* 67:91-130.

64   Nzekwu, O. 1959. Iria Ceremony. *Nigeria* 63,34.

65   Obi, Celestine A. 1970. Christianity and Igbo Marriage. Ph.D. Dissertation. Pontificia Universitas Urbaniana. Rome.

66   Offonry, H. Kanu. 1951. The Strength of the Ibo Clan Feeling. *West Africa* 1787:467.

67   Ogunbiyi, I. A. 1969. The Position of Muslim Women as Stated by Uthman B. Fudi. *Odu* 2:43-60.

68   Ojo, G. J. Afolabi. 1966. *Yoruba Culture*. Ibadan: The Caxton Press (West Africa) Ltd.

69   Okadigho, Miriam. 1977. Discriminative Provisions in the Draft Constitution: Two Points of Dissent. Paper presented at the Nigerian Political Science Symposium.

70   Omoyajowa, J. Akin. 1970. The Cherubim and Seraphim Movement: A Study of Interaction. *Orita: Ibadan Journal of Religious Studies* 4:124-139.

71   Onwuejeogwu, Michael. 1969. The Cult of the Bori Spirits among the Hausa. In *Man in Africa*, ed. Mary Douglas and Phyllis M. Kaberry, pp. 279-305. London: Tavistock Publications.

72   Oppong, C. 1983. *Female and Male in West Africa*. London: George Allen and Unwin.

73   Osunulu, Clara. 1976. Religion and the Status of Nigerian Women. Paper presented at the National Conference of Nigerian Women and Development in Relation to Changing Family Structure. University of Ibadan. Ibadan.

74   Oyelade, E. O. 1982. Trends in Hausa/Fulani Islam Since Independence: Aspects of Islamic Modernisation in Nigeria. *Orita* 4:3-15.

75   Peel, J. D. Y. 1967. Religious Change in Yorubaland. *Africa* 37(3):292-306.

76   Philips, Arthur. 1955. Conflict Between Statutory and Customary Law: Marriage in Nigeria. *Modern Law Review* 18:73-76.

77   Pittin, Renee. 1979. Hausa Women and Islamic Law: Is Reform Necessary?. Paper presented at the 22nd Annual Meeting of the African Studies Association. Los Angeles.

78   Sangree, Walter H. 1969. Going Home to Mother: Traditional Marriage Among the Irigwe of Benue-Plateau State, Nigeria. *American Anthropologist* 71(6):1049-1057.

79   ----. 1974. The Dodo Cult, Witchcraft, and Secondary Marriage in Irigwe, Nigeria. *Ethnology* 13(3):261-278.

80   Schacht, J. 1957. Islam in Northern Nigeria. *Studia Islamica* 8:123-146.

81   Sembajwe, Israel. 1980. Religious Fertility Differentials Among the Yoruba of Western Nigeria. *Journal of Biosocial Science* 12:153-164.

82   Shani, M. I. n.d. The Impact of Custom in the Islamic Law of Divorce in the Northern States of Nigeria. Centre for Islamic Legal Studies. Ahmadu Bello University. Zaria.

83   Simpson, George E. 1980. *Yoruba Religion and Medicine in Ibadan*. Ibadan: Ibadan University Press.

84   Smith, Mary F. 1954. *Baba of Karo*. London: Faber and Faber.

85   Talbot, P. A. 1927. *Some Nigerian Fertility Cults*. London: Humphrey Milford.

86   Tasie, G. O. M. 1977. *Kalabau Traditional Religion*. Berlin: Dietrich Reimer.

87   Trevor, Jean. 1974. Moslem School Girls: Did Our School Help or Hinder Them?. *New Era* 55:156-160.

88   ----. 1975. Western Education and Muslim Fulani-Hausa Women in Sokoto, Northern Nigeria. In *Conflict and Harmony in Education in Tropical Africa*, ed. G.N. Brown and M. Hiskett. London: Allen and Unwin.

89   Trimingham, J. S. 1959. *Islam in West Africa*. Oxford: Clarendon Press.

90   Tukur, Bashiru. 1963. Koranic Schools in Northern Nigeria. *West African Journal of Education* 7(3):149-152.

91   Uyanga, Joseph. 1979. The Charactersistics of Patients of Spiritual Healing Homes and Traditional Doctors in Southeastern Nigeria. *Social Science and Medicine* 13A:323-334.

92   ----. 1979. The Medical Role of Spiritual Healing Churches in Southern Nigeria. *Nigerian Behavioral Sciences Journal* 2:48-52.

93   Vanden Driesen, I. H. 1972. Some Observations on the Family Unit, Religion, and the Practice of Polygyny in the Ife Division of Western Nigeria. *Africa* 42(1):44-56.

94   Westfall, G. D. 1974. Nigerian Women: A Bibliographical Essay. *Africana Journal* 5:99-138.

95   Yahaya, Muhammed. 1967. The Legal Status of Muslim Women in the Northern States of Nigeria. *Journal of the Centre for Islamic Legal Studies* 1(2):1-38.

96   Yeld, Rachael E. 1960. Islam and Social Stratification in Northern Nigeria. *British Journal of Sociology* 11:112-128.

Chapter Six
Associations and Networks

1 Adepoju, Aderanti. 1974. Migration and Socio-Economic Links Between Urban Migrants and their Home Communities in Nigeria. *Africa* 44:383-396.

2 ----. 1974. Rural-Urban Socio-Economic Links: The Example of Migrants in South-West Nigeria. In *Modern Migrations in Western Africa*, ed. Samir Amin, pp. 127-137. London: Oxford University Press.

3 ----. 1975. Some Aspects of Migration and Family Relationships in South-West Nigeria. In *Changing Family Studies*, ed. C. Oppong, pp. 148-156. Legon: University of Ghana, Institute of African Studies.

4 Adeyokunnu, Tomilayo. 1970. The Markets for Foodstuffs in Western Nigeria. *Odu* 3:71-86.

5 Ardener, Shirley. 1953. The Social and Economic Significance of the Contributions Club Among a Section of the Southern Ibo. In *Proceedings of the Second Conference of the West African Institute of Social and Economic Research, 1953*, pp. 128-142. Ibadan: University College.

6 Aronson, D. R. 1978. *The City is Our Farm: Seven Migrant Ijebu Yoruba Families*. Boston, MA.: Schenkman.

7 Awoliyi, E. A. 1967. Role of Women and Women's Organizations in the Solution of Problems of Environmental Hygiene in Nigeria. *Journal of the Society of Health* 2(2):7-8.

8 Balogun, S. 1974. Pressure Groups and Interest Articulation: A Study of the Egba Women's Union, 1947-1951. B.Sc. Essay. University of Ibadan. Ibadan.

9 Barnes, Sandra T. 1975. Social Involvement of Migrants in Lagos, Nigeria. Paper presented at the Internal Migration Conference. University of Ife. Ile-Ife.

10 ----. 1975. Voluntary Associations in a Metropolis: The Case Study of Lagos, Nigeria. *African Studies Review* 18(2):75-87.

11 Barnes, Sandra T., and Margaret Peil. 1977. Voluntary Association Membership in Five West African Cities. *Urban Anthropology* 6(1):83-106.

12 Bascom, William. 1952. The Esusu: A Credit Institution of the Yoruba. *Journal of the Royal Anthropological Institute* 82:63-69.

13 Buvinic, Mayra et al. 1979. Credit for Rural Women: Some Facts and Lessons. International Center for Research on Women. Washington, D.C.

14   Cole, C. 1973. The Socio-Economic Inter-Relationship Between Rural and Urban Centres: A Case Study of Ikorodu and Lagos. Research essay. Ahmadu Bello University. Zaria.

15   Coleman, James. 1952. The Role of Tribal Associations in Nigeria. West African Institute of Social and Economic Research, Annual Conference, pp. 61-66. Ibadan.

16   Collins, J. D. 1977. Political and Economic Change in Rural Hausaland: A Study of Peanut Markets and Cooperatives in the Magaria Region of Niger. Ph.D. Dissertation. Johns Hopkins University. Baltimore, MD.

17   Fadipe, N. A.; Okediji, Francis; and Oladejo, O. 1970. *The Sociology of the Yoruba*. Ibadan: University Press.

18   Fallers, L. A. 1967. *Immigrants and Associations*. The Hague: Mouton.

19   Fischer, C. S.; Jackson, R. M.; Stueve, C. A.; Gerson, K.; Jones, L.; and Baldassare, M. 1977. *Networks and Places: Social Relations in the Urban Setting*. New York: Free Press.

20   Grant, B., and Anthonio, Q. B. O. 1973. Women's Cooperatives in the Western State of Nigeria. *Bulletin of Rural Economics and Sociology* 8:7-35.

21   Gugler, Josef. 1971. Life in a Dual Town System: Eastern Nigerians in Town, 1961. *Cahiers d'Etudes Africaines* 11(3):400-421.

22   Hay, Margaret Jean, and Stichter, Sharon. 1984. *African Women South of the Sahara*. London, New York: Longman.

23   Hill, Polly. 1969. Hidden Trade in Hausaland. *Man* 4(3):392-409.

24   Keirn, S. M. 1970. Voluntary Associations Among Urban African Women. In *Culture Change in Contemporary Africa. Communications From the African Studies Center*, ed. B.M. Du Toit. Gainsville, FL: University of Florida.

25   Ladipo, P. A. 1981. Developing Women's Cooperatives: An Experiment in Rural Nigeria. *Journal of Development Studies* 17(3):123-136.

26   Lamphere, Louise. Strategies, Cooperation and Conflict Among Women in Domestic Groups. In *Woman, Culture and Society*, ed. Michelle Rosaldo and Louise Lamphere, pp. 97-112. Stanford: Stanford University Press.

27   Leis, Nancy Boric. 1971. Virilocality, Polygamy and Women's Associations in West Africa. Paper presented at the 70th annual Meeting of the American Anthropological Association. New York.

28   ----. 1974. Women in Groups: Ijaw Women's Associations. In *Women, Culture, and Society*, ed. Michelle Rosaldo and Louise Lamphere, pp. 223-242. Stanford: Stanford University Press.

29   Little, Kenneth. 1957. The Role of Voluntary Associations in West African Urbanization. *American Anthropologist* 59:579-596.

30   ----. 1960. The West African Town: Its Social Basis. *Diogenes* 29:16-31.

31   ----. 1970. *West African Urbanization: A Study of Voluntary Associations in Social Change.* Cambridge: Cambridge University Press.

32   ----. 1972. Voluntary Associations and Social Mobility Among West African Women. *Canadian Journal of African Studies* 6(2):275-288.

33   Lloyd, P. C. 1953. Craft Organisation in Yoruba Towns. *Africa* 23.

34   Mabogunje, A. L. 1961. The Market Woman. *Ibadan* 11:14-17.

35   Mohamed, M. Z. 1973. Changes in Patterns of Association: A Focus on Non-Kinship Relations in Katsina Town. Research essay. Ahmadu Bello University. Zaria.

36   Morrill, W. T. 1963. Immigrants and Associations: The Ibo in Twentieth Century Calabar. *Comparative Studies in Society and History* 5(4):424-448.

37   Odoma, S. S. 1973. Oja: A Sociological Analysis of the Indigenous Cooperative Credit Association of the Igala-Speaking Peoples. Research essay. Ahmadu Bello University. Zaria.

38   Ogunsheye, F. A. 1960. The Women of Nigeria. *Presence Africaine* 4(32):33-49.

39   Okediji, O. O. 1975. On Voluntary Associations as Adaptive Mechanisms in West African Urbanization: Another Perspective. *African Urban Notes* B(2):51-73.

40   Okojie, C. G. 1960. *Ishan Native Laws and Customs.* Yaba: John Okwesa & Co. and the Nigeria National Press.

41   Okonjo, Isabel Kamene. 1979. Rural Women's Credit Systems: A Nigerian Example. *Studies in Family Planning* 10(11/12):326-331.

42   Okorie, F. A., and Miller, L. T. 1976. Esusu Clubs and Their Performance in Mobilizing Rural Savings and Extended Credit, Ohaozara Sub-Division, East Central State, Nigeria. Technical Report, Dept. of Agricultural Economics. University of Ibadan. Ibadan.

43   Olmsted, Nora. 1980. More Money Needed For Women. *West Africa* 3293:1650-1651.

44   Olusanya, Philip O. 1972. Urban-Rural Contacts and the Diffusion of Antinatal Attitudes Among a West African Peasant Group: The Case of Western Rural Nigeria. In *Symposium of Implications of Population Trends for Policy Measures in West Africa*, ed. N.O. Addo, pp. 147-156. Legon: University of Ghana, Dept. of Sociology.

45   Oppong, C. 1983. *Female and Male in West Africa*. London: George Allen and Unwin.

46   Ottenberg, Simon. 1968. The Development of Credit Associations on the Changing Economy of the Afikpo Igbo. *Africa* 38(3):237-252.

47   Peil, Margaret. 1983. Urban Contacts: A Comparison of Women and Men. In *Female and Male in West Africa*, ed. C. Oppong, pp. 275-282. London: George Allen and Unwin.

48   Plotnicov, Leonard. 1970. The Modern African Elite of Jos, Nigeria. In *Social Stratification in Africa*, ed. Arthur Tuden and Leonard Plotnicov, pp. 269-302. New York: The Free Press.

49   ----. 1970. Rural-Urban Communications in Contemporary Nigeria: The Persistence of Traditional Social Institutions. *Journal of Asian and African Studies* 5:66-82.

50   Remy, Dorothy. 1973. Adaptive Strategies of Men and Women in Zaria, Nigeria: Industrial Workers and Their Wives. Ph.D. Dissertation. University of Michigan. Ann Arbor.

51   ----. 1974. Social Networks and Patron-Client Relations: Ibadan Market Women. Dept. of Urban Studies. Federal City College. Washington, D.C.

52   Russell, Muriel J. 1974. Women's Participation in Cooperatives. Paper presented to the Workshop on Participation of Women in Handicrafts and Small Industries. Kitwe, Zambia.

53   Soyemi, A. I. 1972. *Directory of Voluntary Organizations in Western Nigeria*. Ibadan: Nigerian Institute of Social and Economic Research.

54   Trager, Lillian. 1981. Customers and Creditors: Variations in Economic Personalism in a Nigerian Marketing System. *Ethnology* 20:133-146.

55   Uchendu, Patrick Kenechukwu. 1981. The Changing Cultural Role of Igbo Women in Nigeria 1914-1975. Ph.D. Dissertation. New York University. New York.

56   Uzoma, Adoaha C. 1971. The Changing Postion of Married Women of One Ibo Community in Township and Village: A Socioeconomic Analysis. *Der Ostblock and die Entwicklungslander* 44:113-150.

57   Yeld, Rachael E. 1960. A Study of the Social Position of Women in Kebbi (Northern Nigeria). Masters Thesis. London University. London.

58   Yusuf, Ahmed B. 1974. A Reconsideration of Urban Conceptions: Hausa Urbanization and the Hausa Rural-Urban Continuum. *Urban Anthropology* 3:200-221.

Chapter Seven
Education

1   Adamu, H. 1971. *The North and Nigerian Unity: Some Reflections on the Political, Social and Educational Problems of Northern Nigeria.* Zaria: Gaskiya Corporation.

2   Adeniyi, A. 1972. *A Philosophy for Nigerian Education.* Ibadan: Heinemann.

3   Adesanya, S. A. 1974. Aspects of the Status of Women Under Nigerian Marriage Laws. *Odu* 10:3-29.

4   Adesina, Segun. 1977. *Planning and Educational Development in Nigeria.* Lagos: Educational Industries Nigeria Ltd.

5   Adewuyi, A. O. 1973. The Need for Home Economics in Nigerian Development. Master's Thesis. Texas Women's University. Denton, TX.

6   African Women. 1955. Problems of Girls' Education in Nigeria, Northern Region. *African Women* 1(3):68-70.

7   Agusiobo, O. N. 1973. Implications of Vocational Educational Programmes for the Nigerian School System. *West African Journal of Education* 17:51-70.

8   Ahwan, Abasiya Magaji. 1981. An Analysis of Goals in Post-Primary Institutions in Nigeria with Special Reference to Kaduna-State. Ph.D. Dissertation. North Texas State University. Denton.

9   Ajaegbu, H. I. 1976. The Increasing Elite Group in Nigeria's Population: Their Demographic-Economic Role and Their Implications for Development Planning. *Jimlar Mutane* 1(1):113-123.

10   Amon-Nikoi, Gloria. 1978. Women and Work in Africa. In *Human Resources and African Development,* ed. U.G. Damachi and U.P. Diejomaoh, pp. 188-219. New York: Praeger.

11   Anaza, J. A. 1975. The Labour Market Implications of UPE. Paper presented to the Conference on Economic Development and Employment Generation in Nigeria. NISER. University of Ibadan. Ibadan.

12   Anwukah, Anthony Gozie. 1978. A History of the Development of Nigerian Education 1960-1976. Ph.D. Dissertation. University of Washington. Seattle.

13   Anyanwu, C. N. 1981. *Principles and Practice of Adult Education and Community Development.* Ibadan: Abiprint Publishing Co.

14 Armer, Michael J. 1967. Psychological Impact of Education in Northern Nigeria. Paper delivered at the 10th annual meeting of the African Studies Association. New York.

15 Arowolo, Oladele O. 1981. Fertility and Mortality Trends: Implications for Education, Health and Housing Expenditures in Nigeria. In *Population and Economic Development in Nigeria in the 1980's*, ed. H. Chojnacka, P.O. Olusanya and F. Ojo, pp. 77-89. New York: United Nations Dept. of Technical Co-operation for Development.

16 Audu, I. S. 1975. Higher Education for Development: Case Study, Ahmadu Bello University. New York International Council for Educational Development. New York.

17 Awe, Bolanle. 1964. University Education for Women in Nigeria. *Ibadan* 18:57-61.

18 Aweda, David A. 1978. Educated Elite and Their Attitude Toward Family Planning and Fertility. *Odu* 17:64-84.

19 Awosika, Keziah. 1976. Nigerian Women in the Labour Force: Implications for National Economic Planning. Paper presented at the National Conference on Women and Development in Relation to Changing Family Structure. University of Ibadan. Ibadan.

20 ----. 1981. Women's Education and Participation in the Labour Force: The Case of Nigeria. In *Women, Power and Political Systems*, ed. M. Rendel, pp. 81-93. London: Croomhelm.

21 Beckett, P. A., and O'Connell, J. 1976. Education and the Situation of Women: Background and Attitudes of Christian and Muslim Female Students at a Nigerian University. *Cultures et Developpement* 8:242-265.

22 Boulding, E. 1976. *Handbook of International Data on Women*. New York: Wiley.

23 Bray, T. M. 1977. Universal Primary Education in Kano State: The First Year. *Savanna* 6(1):3-14.

24 ----. 1978. Universal Primary Education in Kano State: The Second Year. *Savanna* 7(2):176-178.

25 ----. 1981. *Universal Primary Education in Nigeria: A Study of Kano State*. London: Routledge.

26 Brown, G. N., and Hiskett, M. 1975. *Conflict and Harmony in Education in Tropical Africa*. London: George Allen and Unwin.

27   Brown, Lalage J. 1976. Adult Education, The Community and the Nigerian University. In *Education and Community in Africa*, ed. Kenneth King, pp. 247-270. Edinburgh: Centre of African Studies, University of Edinburgh.

28   Burness, H. M. 1955. The Position of Women in Gwandu and Yauri. *Overseas Education* 26(4):143-152.

29   ----. 1957. Women in Katsina Province, Northern Nigeria. *Overseas Education* 29(3):116-122.

30   ----. 1959. The War Against Ignorance. *African Women* 3(3):49-53.

31   Caldwell, John C. 1979. Education as a Factor in Mortality Decline: An Examination of Nigerian Data. *Population Studies* 33:395-413.

32   Callaway, Archibald. 1964. Nigeria's Indigenous Education: The Apprentice System. *Odu* 1(1).

33   Callaway, Barbara J. 1984. Ambiguous Consequences of the Socialisation and Seclusion of Hausa Women. *The Journal of Modern African Studies* 22(3):429-450.

34   Callaway, Barbara J., and Kleeman, Katherine E. 1985. Women in Nigeria--Three Women of Kano: Modern Women and Traditional Life. *Africa Report* 30(2):26-29.

35   Congleton, F. I. 1958. Some Problems of Girls' Education in Northern Nigeria. *Overseas Education* 30(2):73-79.

36   Damachi, U. G. 1972. *Nigerian Modernization*. New York: The Third Press.

37   Dambatta, A. H. 1976. Parental Objection to Primary School Education in Dambatta District of Kano State. B.A. Essay. Bayero Univeristy. Kano.

38   Doi, A. Rahman I. 1972. Islamic Education in Nigeria. *Islamic Culture* 46(1):1-16.

39   Dow, Thomas E., Jr. 1977. Breastfeeding and Abstinence Among the Yoruba. *Studies in Family Planning* 8(8):209-214.

40   Due, Jean M. 1982. Constraints to Women and Development in Africa. *Journal of Modern African Studies* 20(1):155-166.

41   Ebigbola, J. A. 1981. Population and Education in the Third National Development Plan and Recommendations for the Next Plan Period: A Case Study of the UPE Scheme in Nigeria. In *Population and Economic Development in Nigeria in the 1980's*, ed. Helena Chojnacka, P.O. Olusanya and F. Ojo, pp. 117-127. New York: United Nations Dept. of Technical Cooperation for Development.

42   Egboh, E. O. 1973. The Place of Women in the Ibo Society of South-Eastern Nigeria From the Earliest Times to the Present. *Civilisations* 23/24:305-316.

43   Fafunwa, A. B. 1974. *History of Education in Nigeria*. London: Allen and Unwin.

44   Fajana, A. 1966. Some Aspects of Yoruba Traditional Education. *Odu: University of Ife Journal of African Studies* 3(1):16-28.

45   Fapohunda, Eleanor R. 1978. Women at Work in Nigeria: Factors Affecting Modern Sector Employment. In *Human Resources and African Development*, ed. U.G. Damachi and V.P. Diejomaoh, pp. 220-241. New York/London: Praeger.

46   Fapohunda, O. J. 1976. Population Increases and Educational Policies in Nigeria. *Jimlar Mutane* 1(2):253-271.

47   Fatunde, S. S. 1972. Adult Education for Social Development: Women's Programme in the Western State of Nigeria. Federal Ministry of Education. Lagos.

48   Foster, Joan. 1960. Women's Teacher Training in Northern Nigeria. *Overseas Education* 31(4):147-155.

49   Galadanci, Alhaji S. A. 1971. Education of Women in Islam with Reference to Nigeria. *Nigerian Journal of Islam* 1(2):5-10.

50   Green, R. H., and Singer, Hans. 1984. Sub-Saharan Africa in Depression: The Impact on the Welfare of Children. *World Development* 12(3):283-295.

51   Gugler, Josef, and Flanagan, William. 1978. *Urbanization and Social Change in West Africa*. Cambridge, England: Cambridge University Press.

52   Gwatkin, Davidson R. 1972. Policies Affecting Population in West Africa. *Studies in Family Planning* 3(9):214-221.

53   Harrington, Judith A. 1978. Education, Female Status, and Fertility in Nigeria. Population Association of America Annual Meeting, April 13-15, 1978. Collected papers, Vol.3., pp. 274-324. Atlanta, Georgia.

54   Haub, C. 1983. Nigeria. *Intercom* 11:11-12.

55   Hiskett, M. 1975. Islamic Education in the Traditional and State Systems in Northern Nigeria. In *Conflict and Harmony in Education in Tropical Africa*, ed. G.N. Brown and M. Hiskett, pp. 134-151. London: Allen and Unwin.

56   Imoagene, Oshomha. 1976. *Social Mobility in Emergent Society: A Study of the New Elite in Western Nigeria.* Canberra: Australian National University, Department of Demography. Changing African Family Project Monograph Series, No. 4, Vol.2.

57   International Family Planning Perspectives. 1980. More Education Leads to Higher Fertility for Rural Nigerian Women. *International Family Planning Perspectives* 6(4):149-151.

58   Iro, M. I. 1976. The Pattern of Elite Divorce in Lagos: 1961-1973. *Journal of Marriage and the Family* 38:177-182.

59   ----. 1978. *Social Correlates of Divorce Among Lagos Elites Who Married in Nigeria.* Canberra: Australian National University, Dept. of Demography. Changing African Family Project Monograph Series, No. 4, Vol.2.

60   Jibowu, Deborah. 1969. Education of Women: Nigeria. Paper presented to the Nigerian National Curriculum Conference, pp. 130-136. Lagos.

61   Kaita, Malama Hassu Iro. 1969. Women's Education in Nigeria. Paper presented to the Nigerian National Curriculum Conference, pp. 141-147. Lagos.

62   ----. 1973. Women's Education in the Northern States of Nigeria 1950-1972. Diploma of Education Thesis. University of Nottingham.

63   Lawal, Ano. 1976. The History and Involvement of Literate Women in the Adult Education Programmes in Ilorin Division of Kwara State. Research essay. Dept. of Education. Ahmadu Bello University. Zaria.

64   Leith-Ross, Sylvia. 1956. The Rise of the New Elite Amongst Women of Nigeria. *International Social Science Bulletin* 8(3):481-488.

65   ----. 1965. The Rise of a New Elite Amongst the Women of Nigeria. In *Africa: Social Problems of Change and Conflict,* ed. P. Van den Berghe, pp. 221-229. San Fransico: Chandler.

66   Lemu, A. 1976. *Women's Education in Nigeria.* Kano: I.I.S.F.

67   Leo, Mother Mary. 1959. Preparing a Nigerian Girl for Life. *Overseas Education* 31(3):109-111.

68   Liman, Alhaji M. 1974. Home Economics in the Third National Development Plan, 1975-1980. Paper presented at the National Seminar on Home Economics Development Planning held at the International Institute of Tropical Agriculture, Ibadan, 8-14, December 1974. Federal Department of Agriculture. Lagos.

69   Little, Kenneth, and Price, Anne. 1967. Some Trends in Modern Marriage Among West Africans. *Africa* 37(4):407-424.

70   Lloyd, Barbara B. 1966. Education and Family Life in the Development of Class Identification Among the Yoruba. In *New Elites of Tropical Africa*, ed. P.C. Lloyd, pp. 163-183. London: Oxford University Press.

71   Lloyd, Peter C. 1966. *The New Elites of Tropical Africa*. London: Oxford University Press for the International African Institute.

72   Lucas, David. 1974. Demographic Class Project 1971-1972: Occupation and Family Size of Lagos Wives. *Lagos Notes and Records* 5:68-69.

73   ----. 1974. Female Employment in Lagos. *Manpower and Unemployment Research in Africa: A Newsletter* 7:37-41.

74   ----. 1976. Participation of Women in the Nigerian Labour Force Since the 1950's with Particular Reference to Lagos. Ph.D. Dissertation. Dept. of Economics. University of London. London.

75   Mabogunje, A. L. 1977. The Urban Situation in Nigeria. In *Patterns of Urbanization: Comparative Country Studies*, ed. S. Goldstein and D.F. Sly, pp. 569-641. Dolhain: Ordina Editions.

76   McDowell, D. W. 1971. Education and Occupational and Residential Mobility in an Urban Nigerian Community. Ph.D. Dissertation. Columbia University. New York.

77   McQueen, A. J. 1965. Aspirations and Problems of Nigerian School Leavers. *Bulletin of Inter-African Labour Institute* 12:35-42.

78   Magdalen, Sister M. C. 1928. Education of Girls in Southern Nigeria. *International Review of Missions* 17:505-514.

79   Majasan, J. A. 1976. Traditional System of Education in Nigeria. *Nigeria Magazine* 119:23-29.

80   Makinwa, Pauline K. 1979. The Theory of the Demographic Transition and the Fertility of Urban and Educated Women in Nigeria. Paper presented at the Annual Conference of the Nigeria Anthropological and Sociological Association. University of Nigeria. Nsukka.

81   Mangvwat, Joyce Amina. 1981. Home Economics In Northern Nigeria: An Historical Study (1842-1980). Ph.D. Dissertation. University of Wisconsin. Madison.

82   Martin, Carol. 1981. Women Job Seekers in Bauchi State, Nigeria: Policy Options for Employment Training. Ed.D. Dissertation. University of Massachusetts. Amherst.

83   ----. 1983. Skill-Building or Unskilled Labour For Female Youth: A Bauchi Case. In *Female and Male in West Africa*, ed. C. Oppong, pp. 223-235. London: George Allen and Unwin.

84   Melie, Edith Ememgene. 1980. Returning Nigerian and American College Women: A Cross-Cultural Analysis of their Motivational Orientations. Ph.D. Dissertation. University of Wisconsin. Madison.

85   Moore, J. Aduke. 1960. The Sphere and Influence of Women in Africa. *Journal of Human Relations* 8(3-4):709-717.

86   Muckenhirn, Erma F. 1966. Secondary Education and Girls in Western Nigeria. Comparative Education Dissertation Series 9. University of Michigan. Ann Arbor.

87   Musa, Ayuba Zakirai. 1981. Assessment of Societal Perceptions and Attitudes Toward Marriage and Educated Hausa Women in the Northern States of Nigeria. Ph.D. Dissertation. Ohio University.

88   National Seminar on Women. 1979. Laws and Customs Affecting Women. Resolutions issued by a National Seminar on Women. CenSCER. Benin.

89   Nevadomsky, J. 1981. Motivations of Married-Women to Higher-Education in Nigeria. *International Journal of Sociology of the Family* 11:73-85.

90   Nigeria. Federal Department of Agriculture. 1974. Report of the National Seminar on Home Economics Development Planning. Institute of Tropical Agriculture, 8-14 December, 1974. Ibadan.

91   Nigerian Association of University Women. 1963. *Survey of Women's Education in Western Nigeria.* Ibadan.

92   Nwabara, Comfort Chisaraokwu. 1977. Factors Affecting Formal Education Decisions In Extended Kin Families of the Ibo of Nigeria. Ph.D. Dissertation. Michigan State University. East Lansing.

93   Odita, Florence Chinyere. 1972. Differences in Pay, Promotion, Job Title and Other Related Factors Between Employed Male and Female College Graduates as Indicators of Sex Discrimination. Ph.D. Dissertation. Ohio State University.

94   Odokara, Elijah O. 1967. A Theoretical Basis for Analysis of Adult Education in Developing Countries: A Review of Adult Education Programs in Rural Communities of Eastern Nigeria. Ph.D. Dissertation. Michigan State University. East Lansing.

95   Ogunsheye, F. A. 1960. The Women of Nigeria. *Presence Africaine* 4(32):33-49.

96   Ogunsola, A. F. 1974. *Legislation and Education in Northern Nigeria*. Ibadan: Oxford University Press.

97   Okediji, Francis Olu; Caldwell, John C.; Caldwell, Pat; and Ware, Helen. 1976. The Changing African Family Project: A Report With Special Reference to the Nigeria Segment. *Studies in Family Planning* 7(5):126-136.

98   Okonjo, Isabel Kamene. 1976. The Role of Women in Social Change Among the Igbo of Southeastern Nigeria Living West of the River Niger. Ph.D. Dissertation. Boston University. Boston.

99   Olayinka, M. S. 1973. Job Aspirations of the Youth and the Educational Provisions in Lagos. *West African Journal of Education* 17:41-49.

100   Olusanya, P. O. 1967. The Education Factor in Human Fertility: A Case Study of the Residents of a Suburban Area in Ibadan, Western Nigeria. *Nigerian Journal of Economic and Social Studies* 9(3):351-374.

101   ----. 1970. A Note on Some Factors Affecting the Stability of Marriage Among the Yoruba of Western Nigeria. *Journal of Marriage and the Family* 32:150-155.

102   ----. 1971. Status Differentials in Fertility Attitudes of Married Women in Two Communities in Western Nigeria. *Economic Development and Cultural Change* 19:641-651.

103   Omojola, S. 1976. Some Factors Influencing Low Motivation for Education Among Secondary Students in Kano City. P.D.G.E. Thesis. Institute of Education. Ahmadu Bello University. Zaria.

104   Omololu, A. 1969. Education of Women: Nigeria. Paper presented to the Nigerian National Curriculum Conference, pp. 136-141. Lagos.

105   Onah, J. Onuora, and Iwuji, E. C. 1976. Urban Poverty in Nigeria. *South African Journal of Economics* 44(2):185-193.

106   Oppong, C. 1983. *Female and Male in West Africa*. London: George Allen and Unwin.

107   Ottenberg, Phoebe, and Ottenberg, Simon. 1964. Ibo Education and Social Change. In *Education and Politics in Nigeria*, ed. H.N. Weiler, pp. 25-63. Freiburg: Rombach.

108   Oyelade, E. O. 1982. Trends in Hausa/Fulani Islam Since Independence: Aspects of Islamic Modernisation in Nigeria. *Orita* 4:3-15.

109 Peel, J. D. Y. 1978. Olaju: A Yoruba Concept of Development. *Journal of Development Studies* 14(2):139.

110 Peshkin, Alan. 1981. Social Change in Northern Nigeria: The Acceptance of Western Education. In *Social Change and Economic Development in Nigeria*, ed. U.G. Damachi and H.D. Siebel, pp. 149-171. New York: Praeger Press.

111 Plotnicov, Leonard. 1970. The Modern African Elite of Jos, Nigeria. In *Social Stratification in Africa*, ed. Arthur Tuden and Leonard Plotnicov, pp. 269-302. New York: The Free Press.

112 Poole, Howard E. 1971. A Study of Sex Role and Learning in a Changing Society. *West African Journal of Education* 15:167-171.

113 Prior, Kenneth. 1955. Rural Training at Asaba. *Nigeria* 47:184-212.

114 Ritsert, Katrina. 1960. Adult Education Experiment in Northern Nigeria. *African Women* 3(4):82-85.

115 Santow, Gigi. 1978. A Microsimulation of Yoruba Fertility. *Mathematical Biosciences* 42:93-117.

116 Schildkrout, Enid. 1978. Thoughts on Child Labor, Education and Marriage in Kano City. Paper presented at the African Studies Association Meeting. Baltimore.

117 ----. 1979. The Impact of Western Education on Women and Children in Northern Nigeria. Paper presented at the Conference on Women and Work in Africa, Urbana, Illinois, April 29-May 1. Champagne-Urbana.

118 Seers, Dudley. 1981. What Needs Are Really Basic in Nigeria: Some Thoughts Prompted by an ILO Mission. *International Labour Review* 120(6):741-750.

119 Smythe, Hugh H., and Smythe, M. M. 1960. *The New Nigerian Elite*. Stanford: Stanford University Press.

120 Spence, Annette. 1954. Adult Education for Women (Calabar Province). *Community Development Bulletin* 6(1):10-12.

121 Taiwo, C. O. 1980. *The Nigerian Education System: Past, Present and Future*. London: Allen and Unwin.

122 Tibenderana, P. K. 1979. The Beginning of Girls' Education in Native Administration Schools in Northern Nigeria, 1930-1945. *Savanna* 3:2.

123   Trevor, Jean. 1974. Moslem School Girls: Did Our School Help or Hinder Them?. *New Era* 55:156-160.

124   ----. 1975. Western Education and Muslim Fulani-Hausa Women in Sokoto, Northern Nigeria. In *Conflict and Harmony in Education in Tropical Africa*, ed. G.N. Brown and M. Hiskett. London: Allen and Unwin.

125   Tukur, Bashiru. 1963. Koranic Schools in Northern Nigeria. *West African Journal of Education* 7(3):149-152.

126   Uka, N. 1974. The Nigerian Youth and Vocational Education. *West African Journal of Education* 18:39-43.

127   UNECA. 1973. Nigeria Country Report on Vocational Training Opportunites for Girls and Women. Women's Programme Unit. Addis Abada.

128   ----. 1973. Nigerian Country Report. Economic Commission for Africa. Addis Ababa.

129   UNICEF. 1969. Assessment of Programmes for the Preparation and Training of Women and Girls for Family and Community Responsibilities in Western State of Nigeria. Lagos.

130   Ware, Helen. 1981. *Women, Education and Modernization of the Family in West Africa*. Canberra: Australian National University, Dept. of Demography. Changing African Family Project Series Monograph No.7.

131   ----. 1983. Female and Male Life-Cycles. In *Female and Male in West Africa*, ed. C. Oppong, pp. 6-31. London: George Allen and Unwin.

132   West African Review. 1934. Female Education in Southern Nigeria. *West African Review* 5(86):5-6.

133   Wheeler, A. C. R. The Organization of Educational Planning in Nigeria. In *Educational Development in Africa, Vol. 1*, pp. 243-306. UNESCO.

134   Williams, Grace Alele. 1976. Education and Status of Nigerian Women. Paper presented at the National Conference on Nigerian Women and Development in Relation to the Changing Family Structure. University of Ibadan. Ibadan.

135   Women's Study Group, Benin City, Midwestern State, Nigeria. 1969. Memorandum on Women's Education: Nigeria. Paper presented to the Nigerian National Curriculum Conference, pp. 265-272. Lagos.

136   Yeld, Rachael E. 1961. Educational Problems Among Women and Girls in Sokoto Province of Northern Nigeria. *Sociologus* 11:160-173.

137   Zaria, Mallam Aliju. 1937. Education of Women and Girls in the Northern Provinces. *Nigeria* 10:51-52.

138   Zollner, Joy. 1970. Roles of Women in National Development in African Countries. *International Labour Review* 101:399-401.

139   ----. 1971. African Conference on the Role of Women in National Development. *International Labour Review* 104:555-557.

Chapter Eight
Health and Nutrition

1   Abudu, O., and Akinkugbe, A. 1982. Clinical Causes and Classification of Perinatal Mortality in Lagos. *International Journal of Gynaecology and Obstetrics* 20:443-447.

2   Adadevoh, B. K. 1971. Effect of Small and Large Number of Children on the Welfare and Health of Individual Families. A Micro-Case Study: Nigeria. Paper presented at the African Population Cenference. Accra.

3   Adadevoh, B. K., and Gardiner, Robert K. A. 1974. *Sub-Fertility and Infertility in Africa: Report of an International Workshop on Correlates of Sub-Fertility and Fertility in Africa, University of Ibadan, November 26-30, 1973.* Ibadan: Caxton Press.

4   Adegbola, O. 1977. New Estimates of Fertility and Child Mortality in Africa South of the Sahara. *Population Studies* 31(3):467-486.

5   Ademuwagun, Z. A. 1974. The Meeting Point of Orthodox Health Personnel and Traditional Healers/Midwives in Nigeria; The Patterns of Utilization of Health Services in Ibarapa Division. *Rural Africana* 26:55-77.

6   Adeokun, L. A. 1978. Fixed Point Approach to Health Care Delivery in Nigeria. *Nigerian Medical Journal* 8(5):480-483.

7   Adeokun, Lawrence A. 1978. Population Composition and Family Welfare in S.W. Nigeria. Paper presented at the National Workshop on the Introduction of Population Concepts into the Curricula of Agricultural Training Institutions. University of Ife. Ile-Ife.

8   Adeokun, Lawrence A., and Odebiyi, A. I. 1977. Physical Planning and Cultural Factors Deterring Optimum Utilization of Modern Health Facilities in Nigeria. *Journal of Medical and Pharmaceutical Marketing* 5(5):266-275.

9   Ajaegbu, H. I., and Mann, C. E. 1975. Human Population and the Disease Factor in the Development of Nigeria. In *The Population Factor in African Studies*, ed. R.P. Moss et al, pp. 123-138. London: University of London Press.

10   Ajose, O. A. 1954. Old and New in Nigeria: Custom, Religion, and Disease. *Lancet* CCXXVI:1024-1025.

11   ----. 1957. Preventive Medicine and Superstition in Nigeria. *Africa* 27(3):268-274.

12   Akhihiero, K. O. 1966. Collection of Vital and Health Statistics in Nigeria. Statistics Division, Ministry of Finance and Economic Development. Benin.

13   Akingba, J. B. 1977. Abortion, Maternity and Other Health Problems in Nigeria. *Nigerian Medical Journal* 7(4):465-471.

14   Akinla, Oladele, and Adadevoh, K. A. 1969. Abortion: A Medical-Social Problem. *Journal of the Nigerian Medical Association* 6(3):16-22.

15   Akinla, Oladele. 1967. Social Obstetrics. Paper presented at the IPPF Seminar held on The Role of Family Planning in African Development. University College. Nairobi.

16   Akinsanya, A. 1977. Traditional Medical Practice and Therapeutics in Nigeria. *Conch* 8(1/2):231-241.

17   Animashaun, A. 1977. Abandoned Children in Lagos. *Nigerian Medical Journal* 7(4):408-411.

18   Arowolo, Oladele O. 1981. Fertility and Mortality Trends: Implications for Education, Health and Housing Expenditures in Nigeria. In *Population and Economic Development in Nigeria in the 1980's*, ed. H. Chojnacka, P.O. Olusanya and F. Ojo, pp. 77-89. New York: United Nations Dept. of Technical Co-operation for Development.

19   Awoliyi, E. A. 1967. Role of Women and Women's Organizations in the Solution of Problems of Environmental Hygiene in Nigeria. *Journal of the Society of Health* 2(2):7-8.

20   Ayangade, Samuel Okun. 1981. Maternal Mortality in a Semi-urban Nigerian Community. *Journal of the National Medical Association* 73:137-140.

21   Ayeni, Olusola. 1974. Demographic Characteristics of Nigeria: An Analysis of Population Data. Ph.D. Dissertation. University of London. London.

22   Ayeni, Olusola, and Oduntan, S. Olu. 1978. The Effect of Sex, Birthweight, Birth Order and Maternal Age on Infant Mortality in a Nigerian Community. *Annals of Human Biology* 5:353-358.

23   ----. 1980. Infant Mortality Rates and Trends in a Nigerian Rural Population. *Journal of Tropical Pediatrics* 26:7-10.

24   Ayonrinde, Akolawole. 1976. Marriage, Family Planning and Mental Health Status of Nigerian Women. Paper presented to the National Conference on Nigerian Women and Development in Relation to Changing Family Structure. University of Ibadan. Ibadan.

25   Barber, C. R. 1966. An Enquiry into Possible Social Factors Making for Acceptances of Institutional Delivery in a Predominantly Rural Area in Western Nigeria. *The Journal of Tropical Medicine and Hygiene* 69(3):63-65.

26   Bascom, William. 1942. The Principle of Seniority in the Social Structure of the Yoruba. *American Anthropologist* 44.

27   Batley, S. K. 1959. The Privately Owned Maternity Home in Nigeria. *African Women* 3(2):38-41.

28   Besmer, F. E. 1977. Initiation Into the Bori Cult--A Case Study in Ningi Town. *Africa* 47:1-13.

29   Brass, W.; Coale, A.; Demeny, P.; Heisel, D.; Lorimer, F.; Romaniuk, A.; and Van de Walle, E. 1968. *The Demography of Tropical Africa*. Princeton: Princeton University Press.

30   Caffrey, K. T. 1979. Maternal Mortality--A Continuing Challenge in Tropical Practice: A Report From Kaduna, Northern Nigeria. *East African Medical Journal* 56(6):274-277.

31   Caldwell, John C. 1979. Education as a Factor in Mortality Decline: An Examination of Nigerian Data. *Population Studies* 33:395-413.

32   Caldwell, John C., and McDonald, P. 1981. Influence of Maternal Education on Infant and Child Mortality: Levels and Causes. In *International Population Conference: Solicited Papers (Vol.2)*, pp. 79-96. Liege: International Union for the Scientific Study of Population, Ordina Editions.

33   Caldwell, John C., and Okonjo, Chukuka. 1968. *The Population of Tropical Africa*. New York: Columbia University Press.

34   Cantrelle, P.; Ferry, B.; and Mondot, J. 1978. Relationships Between Fertility and Mortality in Tropical Africa. In *The Effects of Infant and Child Mortality on Fertility*, ed. S.H. Preston, pp. 181-205. New York: Academic Press.

35   Coale, A. J. 1968. Estimates of Fertility and Mortality in Tropical Africa. In *The Population of Tropical Africa*, ed. J.C. Caldwell and C. Okonjo, pp. 179-186. London: Longmans.

36   Coale, A. J., and Lorimer, F. 1968. Summary of Estimates of Fertility and Mortality. In *The Demography of Tropical Africa*, ed. W. Brass, A. Coale, P. Demeny, D. Heisel, F. Lorimer, A. Romaniuk and E. Van de Walle, pp. 151-182. Princeton: Princeton University Press.

37   Courtney, L. D. 1973. Infant Weight, Prematurity Rate, Sex-ratio and Mortality Rate in a Tropical Center. *Journal of the Irish Medical Association* 66(19):540-541.

38   Darrah, Allan C. 1975. Birth, Medicine of Death: Some Implications of Metaphorizing Alimentation as Reproduction. Sociology Department. Ahmadu Bello University. Zaria.

39   De Benko, Eugene. 1972. Rural Health in Africa: A Selected Bibliography. *Rural Africana* 17:118-131.

40   Donnerreichle, C. 1979. Role of Women in Africa - Marriage, Birth and Disease in the Lives of the Hausa Women in Nigeria. *Argument* 21:766-768.

41   Dopamu, P. A. 1982. Obstetrics and Gynecology Among the Yoruba. *Orita* 14:34-42.

42   Doyle, P.; Morley, David; Woodland, Margaret; and Cole, Jane. 1978. Birth Intervals, Survival and Growth in a Nigerian Village. *Journal of Biosocial Science* 10:81-94.

43   Dyson, Tim P. 1977. An Analysis of Village Fertility, Mortality and Growth. In *The Feasibility of Fertility Planning: Micro Perspectives*, ed. T.S. Epstein and D. Jackson, pp. 21-41. Elmsford, N.Y.: Pergamon Press.

44   Ebigbo, P. O., and Chukudebelu, W. O. 1980. Child Spacing and Child Mortality Among Nigerian Igbos. *International Journal of Gynecology and Obstetrics* 18(5):372-374.

45   Eicher, C. K. 1967. Food, Nutrition, Population, and Income Interrelationships in West Africa. Paper delivered at the 10th annual meeting of the African Studies Association. New York.

46   Ekanem, Ita I. et al. 1975. The Role of Traditional Birth Attendants (TBAs) in the South Eastern State of Nigeria. Institute of Population and Manpower Series Publication No.3. Faculty of Social Sciences, University of Ife. Ile-Ife.

47   Ekpo, Eme Udofia. 1983. Economic and Non-economic Barriers to the Utilization of Orthodox Obstetric Services in Cross-River State, Nigeria. Ph.D. Dissertation. Saint Louis University. Saint Louis.

48   Etkin, Nina. 1979. Indigenous Medicine Among the Hausa of Northern Nigeria. *Medical Anthropology* 3(4):401-429.

49   Farooq, Ghazi M., and Adeokun, Lawrence A. 1976. The Impact of Rural Family Planning Program in Ishan, Nigeria, 1969-72. *Studies in Family Planning* 7:158-169.

50   Fikry, M. 1977. *Traditional Maternal and Child Health Care and Related Problems in the Sahel: A Bibliographic Study*. Ann Arbor, MI.: United States Agency for International Development.

51   Gaisie, S. K. 1980. Some Aspects of Socio-Economic Determinants of Mortality in Tropical Africa. *Population Bulletin of the United Nations*, No.13, pp. 16-25. New York.

52   Gardner, R. F. R., and Elizabeth, S. 1958. Infant Mortality in Northern Nigeria With Special Reference to the Birom Tribe. *Journal of Gynaecology and Obstetrics of the British Empire* 65(5):749-758.

53   Gesler, Wilbert M. 1979. Illness and Health Practitioner Use in Calabar, Nigeria. *Social Science and Medicine* 13D:23-30.

54   Grayson, J. 1981. Third World Policies and Realities. *Lancet* 3217(1):445-446.

55   Green, R. H., and Singer, Hans. 1984. Sub-Saharan Africa in Depression: The Impact on the Welfare of Children. *World Development* 12(3):283-295.

56   Gwatkin, Davidson R. 1972. Policies Affecting Population in West Africa. *Studies in Family Planning* 3(9):214-221.

57   Hanck, H. M. 1963. Child Mortality in Awo Omamma, Eastern Nigeria. *Journal of Obstetrics and Gynaecology of the British Commonwealth* 70:1076-1080.

58   Harrington, Judith A. 1983. Nutritional Stress and Economic Responsibility: A Study of Nigerian Women. In *Women and Poverty in the Third World*, ed. M. Buvinic, pp. 130-156. Baltimore: Johns Hopkins University Press.

59   Harrison, K. A. 1977. Maternal Mortality in Zaria. Paper read at the 1st International Congress of the Society of Gynaecology and Obstetrics of Nigeria. University of Ibadan. Ibadan.

60   ----. 1978. Childbearing in Zaria. Public Lecture Series. Ahmadu Bello University. Zaria.

61   ----. 1979. Approaches to Reducing Maternal and Perinatal Mortality in Africa. In *Maternity Services in the Developing World: What the Community Needs*, ed. R.H. Philpott, pp. 52-69. London: Royal College of Obstetricians and Gynaecologists.

62   ----. 1979. Nigeria. *Lancet* 157(4):1229-1232.

63   Hartfield, V. J. 1980. Maternal Mortality in Nigeria Compared with Earlier International Experience. *International Journal of Gynaecology and Obstetrics* 18:70-75.

64   Hauck, H. M. 1963. Child Mortality in Awo Omamma, Eastern Nigeria. *Journal of Obstetrics and Gynaecology of the British Commonwealth* 70:1076-1080.

65   Hendrickse, R. G. 1967. *Major Causes of Death in Infancy and Early Childhood at University College Hospital, Ibadan.* Dakar: International Children's Centre.

66   Hughes, Charles C. 1976. Culture and Health Planning for the Yoruba of Western Nigeria. *Medical Anthropological Newsletter* 8(1):14-18.

67   Hunponu-Wusu, O. O. 1976. Current Mortality Patterns Among Nigerians in the Age-Group 15-44 Years. *Jimlar Mutane* 1(1):34-40.

68   Igun, A. A. *The Role of Obstetrics and Gynaecology in Population Movement in Nigeria*. Ile-Ife: University of Ife.

69   Igun, A. A., and Acsadi, G. T. 1972. *Demographic Statistics in Nigeria*. Ile-Ife: University of Ife.

70   Johnson, B. C. 1981. Traditional Practices Affecting the Health of Women and Children. In *Female Circumcision, Childhood Marriage, Nutritional Taboos, etc. Vol. 2. Second ed.*, pp. 7-20. Alexandria, Egypt: WHO Regional Office for the Eastern Mediterranean.

71   Johnson, T. O.; Akinla, O.; Kuku, S. B.; and Oyediran, M. A. 1974. Infertility in Lagos. In *Sub-fertility and Infertility in Africa: Report of an International Workshop, Ibadan, Nigeria, 1973*, ed. B.K. Adadevoh, pp. 94-95. Ibadan: Caxton Press.

72   Kisekka, Mere Nakateregga. 1981. The Role of Women in Socioeconomic Development: Indicators as Instruments of Social Analysis--The Case of Nigeria and Uganda. In *Women and Development*, pp. 33-47. Paris: UNESCO.

73   Ladipo, P. A., and Balogun, E. K. 1978. Sources of Medical Care in the Isoya Project Villages. *Odu* 17:99-109.

74   Lang, J. R. 1970. A Further Study on Foetal Loss and Child Mortality in the North of Nigeria. *Journal of Obstetrics and Gynaecology of the British Commonwealth* 77(5):427-434.

75   Laoye, Ade J. 1975. Traditional Midwifery in Nigeria. *Journal of the Society of Health* 10(1):1-12.

76   Leighton, Alexander H., and Lambo, T. Adeoye. 1963. *Psychiatric Disorder Among the Yoruba*. Ithaca, N.Y.: Cornell University Press.

77   Lucas, David, and McWilliam, John. 1976. *A Survey of Nigeria's Population Literature*. Lagos: University of Lagos.

78   MacCormack, Carol P., Ed. 1982. *Ethnography of Fertility and Birth*. London: Academic Press.

79   McCulloch, W. E. 1930. *An Enquiry into the Dietaries of the Hausas and Town Fulani of Northern Nigeria*. Lagos.

80   MacGregor, Malcolm. 1958. Pediatrics in Western Nigeria. *Archives of Disease in Childhood* 33(170):277-291.

81   MacKenzie, P. 1979. The Delivery of Basic Health Care By the Calabar Rural Maternal-Child Health/Family Planning Program. International Working Papers No.6. Population Council. New York.

82   Maclean, Catherine M. Una. 1978. Choices of Treatment Among the Yoruba. In *Culture and Curing*, eds. Peter Morley and Roy Wallis, pp. 152-168. Pittsburgh: University of Pittsburgh Press.

83   ----. 1965. Traditional Medicine and its Practitioners in Ibadan, Nigeria. *Journal of Tropical Medicine and Hygiene* 68(10):237-244.

84   ----. 1966. Hospitals and Healers, an Attitude Survey in Ibadan. *Human Organization* 25(2):131-140.

85   ----. 1966. Yoruba Mothers: A Study of Changing Methods of Childbearing in Rural and Urban Nigeria. *Journal of Tropical Medicine and Hygiene* 69(11):253-263.

86   ----. 1969. In Defense of their Children. *New Society* 14:52-54.

87   ----. 1969. Traditional Healers and Their Female Clients: An Aspect of Nigerian Sickness Behavior. *Journal of Health and Social Behavior* 10:172-186.

88   ----. 1971. *Magical Medicine: A Nigerian Case-Study*. London: Allen Lane/Penguin Press.

89   ----. 1976. Some Aspects of Sickness Behavior Among the Yoruba. In *Social Anthropology and Medicine*, ed. J.B. Loudon, pp. 285-317. New York: Academic Press.

90   ----. 1980. African Medical Expertise, Its Transmission and Receipt. In *Experts in Africa: Proceedings of a Colloquium at the University of Aberdeen, March 1980*, ed. J.C. Stone, pp. 114-129. Aberdeen: Aberdeen University, African Studies Group.

91   ----. 1982. Folk Medicine and Fertility: Aspects of Yoruba Medical Practice Affecting Women. In *Ethnography of Fertility and Birth*, ed. Carol P. MacCormack, pp. 161-179. New York: Academic Press.

92   Makanjuola, R. O. A. 1982. Psychotic Disorders After Birth in Nigerian Women. *Tropical and Geographical Medicine* 34:67-72.

93   Margetts, E. L. 1965. Traditional Yoruba Healers in Nigeria. *Man* 65(102):115-118.

94   Matthews, D. S. 1956. A Preliminary Note on the Ethnological and Medical Significance of Breast-Feeding Among the Yoruba. In *Proceedings of the 3rd International West African Conference, Ibadan, 1949*, pp. 269-279. Lagos: Nigerian Museum.

95   Megafu, Uchenna. 1975. Causes of Maternal Deaths at the University of Nigeria Teaching Hospital. *The West African Medical Journal* 23(2):87-91.

96   Morgan, R. W. 1973. Migration as a Factor in the Acceptance of Medical Care. *Social Science and Medicine* 7(11):865-873.

97   ----. 1982. Distribution of Modern Contraceptive Use in a Medium Income Rural Population in Nigeria, in the Absence of an Adequate Health Care Delivery System: A Preliminary Determination of Relationships Between Modern Contraceptive Use and Levels of Nutrition, Child Mortality, and Fertility. Final report prepared for U.S. AID, Grant AID-DSPE-G-00008, Research Program by Boston University and the University of Ife, February 1979-1981.

98   Morgan, R. W., and Kannisto, V. 1973. A Population Dynamics Survey in Lagos, Nigeria. *Social Science and Medicine* 7(1):1-30.

99   Morley, David C. 1963. A Medical Service for Children Under Five Years of Age in West Africa. *Transactions of the Royal Society of Tropical Medicine and Hygiene* 57(2):78-80.

100   Mott, Frank L. 1974. *The Dynamics of Demographic Change in a Nigerian Village*. Lagos: University of Lagos, Human Resources Research Unit, Monograph No.2.

101   ----. 1974. Some Data Relating to Infertility in Nigeria. In *Sub-fertility and Infertility in Africa: Report of an International Workshop, Ibadan, Nigeria, 1973*, ed. B.K. Adadevoh, pp. 30-33. Ibadan: Caxton Press.

102   ----. 1975. The Relationships Between Demographic Phenomena and Maternal and Child Health. Presented at the African Health Training Institiutions Project Seminar/Workshop on Family Health.

103   ----. 1976. Some Aspects of Health Care In Rural Nigeria. *Studies in Family Planning* 7(4):109-114.

104   Mott, Frank L., and Fapohunda, O. J. 1975. *The Population of Nigeria*. Lagos: University of Lagos. Human Resources Research Unit Monograph No.3.

105   Murphy, Jane M. 1965. Cultural Change and Mental Health Among Yoruba Women of Nigeria. Paper presented at the African Studies Association Meeting. Philadelphia.

106   National Seminar on Women. 1979. Laws and Customs Affecting Women. Resolutions issued by a National Seminar on Women. CenSCER. Benin.

107   Newman, Jeanne S. 1984. *Women of the World: Sub-Saharan Africa*. Washington, D.C.: WID-USAID and U.S. Department of Commerce, Bureau of the Census.

108   Nicol, B. M. 1959. Fertility and Food in Northern Nigeria. *West African Medical Journal* 8(1):18-27.

109   Nigeria. Federal Government. 1975. Lagos Island Maternity Hospital--1975. Medical Statistics Division. Lagos.

110   Nigeria. Federal Office of Statistics. 1983. The Health of Nigerians: Results From a Pilot Survey in Four States in September 1982. Interim Report. Lagos.

111   Nnadi, Eucharia Enderline. 1982. Health Care Seeking Behavior in Nigeria--An Intertribal Perspective. Ph.D. Dissertation. University of Minnesota. Minneapolis.

112   Nylander, P. P. S. 1968. The Significance of Secondary Amenorrhea in Nigeria. *West African Medical Journal* 17(6):208-209.

113   ----. 1970. Maternal Age and Parity Distribution in Rural and Urban Communities in Western Nigeria. *African Journal of Medical Sciences* 3(1):285-289.

114   ----. 1971. Perinatal Mortality in Ibadan. *African Journal of Medical Sciences* 2:173-178.

115   Obi, J. O. 1979. Morbidity and Mortality of Children Under Five Years Old in a Nigerian Hospital. *Journal of the National Medical Association* 71(3):245-247.

116   Odulana, J. 1978. Family Welfare Laws in Ten African Countries: Report of the Africa Regional Law Panel Field Trips,1977/78, Vol.1. International Planned Parenthood Federation, Africa Region. Nairobi.

117   Oduntan, S. O., and Odunlami, V. B. 1975. Maternal Mortality in Western Nigeria. *Tropical and Geographical Medicine* 27:313-316.

118   Ogbeide, Osafu. 1980. Infant Mortality in Benin City. *Journal of Tropical Pediatrics* 26:199-202.

119   Ogunlesi, T. O. 1971. Population Control and National Health Policy. Paper presented at the Seminar on Population Problems and Policy in Nigeria. University of Ife. Ile-Ife.

120   Ogunlesi, T. O., and Adekunle, L. 1974. Igbo-Ora Infant Perinatal Morbidity and Mortality Survey: A Case Study of Record Linkage in a Rural Community. Paper presented at the Inaugural Conference of the Population Association of Africa. Ibadan.

121   Ogunode, F. A. 1981. Guidelines for the Fourth Development Plan and Population Policy for the 1980's. In *Population and Economic Development in Nigeria in the 1980's*, ed. Helena Chojnacka, P.O. Olusanya and F. Ojo, pp. 193-208. New York: United Nations Dept. of Technical Co-operation for Development.

122   Ohiaeri, A. E. 1963. *Research in the Traditional Medicine*. Nsukka: The Author.

123   Ojimba, Margaret Ijeuru. 1976. An Argument for the Integration of the Traditional Health System and the Modern Health Care Delivery System in Orlu Province Eastern Nigeria. Ph.D. Dissertation. Howard University. Washington, D.C.

124   Ojo, G. J. Afolabi. 1966. *Yoruba Culture*. Ibadan: The Caxton Press (West Africa) Ltd.

125   Ojo, O. A. 1968. Male Factor in Infertile Marriages in Nigeria. *West African Medical Journal* 17(1):210-211.

126   ----. 1974. A Ten Year Review of Maternal Mortality Rates in the University College Hospital, Ibadan, Nigeria. *West African Medical Journal* 22(2):33-36.

127   Ojo, O. A.; Ladipo, O. A.; and Adelowo, M. A. 1981. Maternity Care and Monitoring in Ibadan, Nigeria. *African Journal of Medicine and Medical Sciences* 10:49-56.

128   Okediji, Beatrice Olu, and Okediji, Peter Ade. 1978. The Interaction of Culture and Health: A Nigerian Case. *Psychopathologie Africaine* 14:99-109.

129   Okediji, Francis Olu. 1974. Population Dynamics Research in Nigeria: Achievements and New Horizons. In *Population Dynamics Research in Africa*, ed. F.O. Okediji, pp. 3-18. Washington,D.C.: Smithsonian Institute, Interdisciplinary Communications Program.

130   ----. 1975. Socioeconomic Status and Attitudes to Public Health Problems in the Western State: A Case Study of Ibadan. In *Population Growth and Socioeconomic Change in West Africa*, ed. John C. Caldwell, pp. 275-297. New York/London: Columbia University Press.

131   Okediji, Francis Olu; Caldwell, John C.; Caldwell, Pat; and Ware, Helen. 1976. The Changing African Family Project: A Report With Special Reference to the Nigeria Segment. *Studies in Family Planning* 7(5):126-136.

132   Olusanya, P. O. 1974. Reduced Fertility and Associated Factors in the Western State of Nigeria. In *Sub-fertility and Infertility in Africa: Report of an International Workshop, Ibadan, Nigeria, 1973*, ed. B.K. Adadevoh, pp. 43-53. Ibadan: Caxton Press.

133   Omu, A. E., and Akingba, J. B. 1983. The Contribution of Multiple Pregnancies to Perinatal Mortality in Benin City. *Journal of Obstetrics and Gynaecology* 3:227-232.

134   Onabamiro, S. D. 1953. *Food and Health*. London.

135   Onadeko, M. O. 1978. Public Health and the Nigerian Population Pressure. *Nigerian Medical Journal* 8(3):220-224.

136   Onokerhoraye, A. G. 1978. Spatial Aspects of the Health Care Problems in Nigeria: A Case Study of Kwara State. *Quarterly Journal of Administration* 12:241-255.

137   Orubuloye, I. O. 1981. The Significance of Breast-Feeding on Fertility and Mortality in Africa. In *Population Dynamics: Fertility and Mortality in Africa*, pp. 499-512. Addis Ababa: United Nations Economic Commission for Africa (UNECA).

138   Orubuloye, I. O., and Caldwell, J. C. 1975. The Impact of Public Health Services on Mortality: A Study of Mortality Differentials in a Rural Area of Nigeria. *Population Studies* 29:259-272.

139   Osborne, Oliver H. 1972. Social Structure and Health Care Systems: A Yoruba Example. *Rural Africana* 19:80-86.

140   Osuhor, P. C. 1979. Stillbirths in a Savannah District of Northern Nigeria: The Socio-Economic and Socio-Cultural Factors. *Nigerian Medical Journal* 9:481-485.

141   Oyakhire, G. K. 1980. Environmental Factors Influencing Maternal Mortality in Zaria, Nigeria. *Royal Society of Health Journal* 100:72-74.

142   Oyediran, M. A. 1981. Maternal and Child Health and Family Planning in Nigeria. *Public Health* 95:344-346.

143   Oyediran, M. A., and Bamisaiye, A. 1983. A Study of the Childcare Arrangements and the Health-Status of Preschool-Children of Employed Women in Lagos. *Public Health* 97(5):267-274.

144   Oyemade, A. 1975. Motherless Babies in Care in Nigeria. *Environmental Africa* 1(4):84-93.

145   Page, H. J. 1972. Fertility and Child Mortality South of the Sahara. In *Population Growth and Economic Development in Africa*, ed. S.H. Ominde and C.N. Ejiogu, pp. 51-66. London: Heinemann.

146   Ransome-Kuti, O. 1983. The Effect of Parity, Birth Intervals and Maternal Age on the Health of the Child. In *Primary Maternal and Neonatal Health: A Global Concern*, ed. F. Del Mundo, E. Ines-Cuyegkeng and D.M. Aviado, pp. 53-61. New York: Plenum.

147   Rehan, N. 1982. Still Births in a Hausa Community. *Journal of the Pakistan Medical Association* 32(7):156-162.

148   Romaniuk, A. 1968. Infertility in Tropical Africa. In *The Population of Tropical Africa*, ed. John C. Caldwell and C. Okonjo, pp. 214-224. New York: Columbia University Press.

149   Salawu, S. A. I. 1977. Effects of Marriage Practices in Maternal Health Care in the Northern States. *Abumed* 1(5):35-38.

150   Sangree, Walter H. 1974. The Dodo Cult, Witchcraft, and Secondary Marriage in Irigwe, Nigeria. *Ethnology* 13(3):261-278.

151   Seers, Dudley. 1981. What Needs Are Really Basic in Nigeria: Some Thoughts Prompted by an ILO Mission. *International Labour Review* 120(6):741-750.

152   Sembajwe, Israel. 1981. *Fertility and Infant Mortality Amongst the Yoruba in Western Nigeria*. Canberra: Australian National University, Department of Demography. Changing African Family Project Monograph Series No.6.

153   Simpson, George E. 1980. *Yoruba Religion and Medicine in Ibadan*. Ibadan: Ibadan University Press.

154   Sogbanmu, M. O. 1979. Perinatal Mortality and Maternal Mortality in General Hospital, Ondo, Nigeria: Use of High-Risk Pregnancy Predictive Scoring Index. *Nigerian Medical Journal* 9:475-479.

155   Sosanya, R. O. 1972. Midwifery Services in Nigeria. *Nigerian Nurse* 4:18-21.

156   Sullivan, J. H., and Chester, J. C. 1976. *U.S. Development Aid Programs in West Africa. 1.Population Planning Activities. 2.The Senegal River Basin Project 3.Reimbursable Development in Nigeria*. Washington, D.C.: U.S. Government Printing Office.

157   Tolani, Asuni. 1979. The Dilemma of Traditional Healing With Special Reference to Nigeria. *Social Sciences and Medicine* 13B:33-39.

158   Trevitt, Lorna. 1973. Attitudes and Customs in Childbirth Amongst the Hausa Women in Zaria City. *Savanna* 2(2):223-226.

159   Turtill, B. M. 1965. Midwifery and Midwife Training in Nigeria. *Nursing Times* 61(49):1664-1665.

160   Uche, Chukwudum. 1980. The Contexts of Mortality in Nigeria. Paper presented at the International Union for Scientific Study of Population Seminar on Biological and Social Aspects of Mortality and the Length of Life, May 13-16, Fuiuggi Terme, Italy.

161   UN. 1954. Foetal, Infant, and Early Childhood Mortality. United Nations, Vol. I. New York.

162   UNECA. 1963. Fertility, Mortality, International Migration and Population Growth in Africa. Conference held in Cairo, October-November 1962. E/CN.14/ASPP/L.2, E/CN.9/CONF.3/L.2. New York.

163   University of Ibadan. 1971. The Traditional Background to Medical Practice in Nigeria. Institute of African Studies. Ibadan.

164   Uyanga, Joseph. 1979. The Charactersistics of Patients of Spiritual Healing Homes and Traditional Doctors in Southeastern Nigeria. *Social Science and Medicine* 13A:323-334.

165   ----. 1979. The Medical Role of Spiritual Healing Churches in Southern Nigeria. *Nigerian Behavioral Sciences Journal* 2:48-52.

166   ----. 1980. Rural-Urban Differences in Child Care and Breastfeeding Behavior in Southeastern Nigeria. *Social Science and Medicine* 14D:23-29.

167   ----. 1981. Correlates of Population Pressure in Rural Households: A Nigerian Case Study. *Journal of Comparative Family Studies* 12:219-232.

168   ----. 1982. Child Mortality and Contraception Usage: A Study of Rural Acceptors in Nigeria. *Rural Africana* 14:61-68.

169   Waboso, Marcus F. 1965. Pregnancy. Official Report of Nigerian Midwives' Seminar. Federal Ministry of Health. Lagos.

170   ----. 1973. The Causes of Maternal Mortality in the Eastern States of Nigeria. *Nigerian Medical Journal* 3(2):99-104.

171   Ware, Helen. 1983. Female and Male Life-Cycles. In *Female and Male in West Africa*, ed. C. Oppong, pp. 6-31. London: George Allen and Unwin.

172   Weiss, Eugene, and Udo, A. A. 1981. The Calabar Rural Maternal and Child Health/Family Planning Project. *Studies in Family Planning* 12:47-57.

173   Wolff, N. H. 1979. Concepts of Causation and Treatment in the Yoruba Medical System: The Special Case of Barrenness. In *African Therapeutic Systems*, ed. Z.A. Ademuwagun, J.A. Ayoade, I.E. Harrison and D.M. Warren, pp. 125-131. Waltham, MA.: Crossroads Press.

174   World Health Organization. 1983. *Women and Breastfeeding*. Geneva: World Health Organization.

175   Zamani, J. E. 1976. A Study of the Factors Underlying Concern or Indifference to Medical Care Among the Hausa in Zaria. Research paper. Ahmadu Bello University. Zaria.

Chapter Nine
Fertility

1   Abbott, Joan. 1974. The Employment of Women and the Reduction of Fertility: Implications for Development. *World Development* 2:23-26.

2   Aborampah, Osei Mensah. 1981. Plural Marriage, Post-partum Abstinence and Fertility among the Yoruba of Western Nigeria. Ph.D. Dissertation. University of Wisconsin. Madison.

3   Acsadi, George T., and Johnson-Acsadi, Gwendolyn. 1983. Demand for Children and Spacing in Sub-Sahara Africa. Background paper for the report on Population Strategies for Sub-Saharan Africa. Washington, D.C.: The World Bank.

4   Acsadi, Gyorgy T. 1971. Some Problems of Yoruba Fertility and Its Regulation. Paper presented at the Faculty of Social Sciences Staff Seminar. University of Ife. Ile-Ife.

5   ----. 1972. Fertility Among the Yoruba. Presented to the Seminar on Family Planning in West Africa, pp. 7-12. University of Ibadan. Ibadan.

6   ----. 1972. Nigerian Vital Registration and Demographic Surveys. In *Demographic Statistics in Nigeria*, ed. A.A. Igun and G. Acsadi, pp. 198-213. Ile-Ife: University of Ife, Institute of Population and Manpower Studies.

7   ----. 1974. Fertility Change and Stability in Sub-Saharan Africa: Toward a Working Hypothesis of Demographic Transition. Paper presented at the Meetings of the Population Association of America. New York.

8   Acsadi, Gyorgy T.; Igun, Adenola A.; and Johnson, Gwendolyn Z. 1972. Surveys of Fertility, Family, and Family Planning in Nigeria. Institute of Population and Manpower Studies (IPMS), Publication No.2. University of Ife. Ile-Ife.

9   Adadevoh, B. K., and Gardiner, Robert K. A. 1974. *Sub-Fertility and Infertility in Africa: Report of an International Workshop on Correlates of Sub-Fertility and Fertility in Africa, University of Ibadan, November 26-30, 1973.* Ibadan: Caxton Press.

10 Adegbola, O. 1977. New Estimates of Fertility and Child Mortality in Africa South of the Sahara. *Population Studies* 31(3):467-486.

11 Adegbola, O., and Page, H. 1982. Nuptiality and Fertility in Metropolitan Lagos: Components and Compensating Mechanisms. In *Nuptiality and Fertility: Proceedings of a Seminar Held in Bruges, Belgium January 8-11, 1979*, ed. L.T. Ruzicka, pp. 337-362. Liege: Ordina Editions.

12   Adegbola, O.; Page, H.; and Lesthaeghe, R. 1980. Breast-Feeding and Post-Partum Abstinence in Metropolitan Lagos. Human Resources Research Unit Bulletin, No.80/03. University of Lagos. Lagos.

13   Adeniyi, E. O. 1978. *Population Growth and Fertility Among the Nupe of Nigeria*. Canberra: Australian National University, Dept. of Demography, Changing African Family Project Monograph Series, No. 4, Vol. 2.

14   Adeokun, Lawrence A. 1979. 1971-1975 National Survey of Fertility and Family Planning: Phase 1 Southwest Nigeria. Department of Demography and Social Statistics, DSS Monograph No.1. Faculty of Social Sciences, University of Ife. Ile-Ife.

15   ----. 1981. Lactation Abstinence in Family Building Among the Ekitis of Southwest Nigeria. In *Population and Economic Development in Nigeria in the 1980's*, ed. H. Chojnacka, P.O. Olusanya and F. Ojo, pp. 41-57. New York: United Nations Department of Technical Co-operation for Development.

16   ----. 1982. Marital Sexual Relationships and Birth Spacing Among Two Yoruba Subgroups. *Africa* 52:1-14.

17   Adeokun, Lawrence A., and Farooq, Ghazi M. 1974. Patterns of Fertility, Anti-Natal Knowledge and Practice: Impact of a Rural Family Planning Program. Ishan Division, Nigeria, 1969-1972. Institute of Population and Manpower Studies Report No.3. University of Ife. Ile-Ife.

18   Adepoju, Aderanti. 1977. Rationality and Fertility in the Traditional Yoruba Society, Southwest Nigeria. In *The Persistence of High Fertility*, ed. John C. Caldwell, pp. 123-152. Canberra: Australian National University.

19   ----. 1978. *Migration and Fertility: A Case Study in South-West Nigeria*. Canberra: Australian National University, Dept. of Demography. Changing African Family Project Monograph Series, No. 4, Vol.2.

20   Afigbo, A. E., and Nwabara, S. N. 1976. Black Civilization and the "Population Crises": A Cultural Approach. *Civilisations* 26:15-35.

21   Akingba, J. B. 1971. *The Problem of Unwanted Pregnancies in Nigeria Today*. Lagos: Heinemann.

22   Aluko, S. A. 1971. Population Growth and the Level of Income in Nigeria. Paper presented at the Seminar of Population Problems and Policy in Nigeria. University of Ife. Ile-Ife.

23   Ardener, E. 1962. *Divorce and Fertility: An African Study*. London: Oxford University Press.

24   Arowolo, Oladele O. 1976. Determinants of Fertility Among Yorubas of Nigeria. In *International Program for Population Analysis. Recent Empirical Findings on Fertility: Korea, Nigeria, Tunisia, Venezuela, Philippines*, pp. 27-45. Washington, D.C.: Smithsonian Institute, Interdisciplinary Communications Program.

25   ----. 1976. *Fertility Transition in Nigeria*. Washington, D.C.: Interdisciplinary Communications Program of the Smithsonian Institute. I.C.P. Monograph No.7.

26   ----. 1977. Fertility of Urban Yoruba Working Women: A Case Study of Ibadan City. *Nigerian Journal of Economic and Social Sciences* 19:37-66.

27   ----. 1978. *Female Labour Force Participation and Fertility: The Case of Ibadan City in the Western State of Nigeria*. Canberra: Australian National University. Changing African Family Project Monograph Series, No. 4, Vol.2.

28   ----. 1981. Fertility and Mortality Trends: Implications for Education, Health and Housing Expenditures in Nigeria. In *Population and Economic Development in Nigeria in the 1980's*, ed. H. Chojnacka, P.O. Olusanya and F. Ojo, pp. 77-89. New York: United Nations Dept. of Technical Co-operation for Development.

29   Aweda, David A. 1978. Educated Elite and Their Attitude Toward Family Planning and Fertility. *Odu* 17:64-84.

30   Ayangade, Samuel Okun. 1978. Birth Interval Study in a Culturally Stable Urban Population. *International Journal of Gynaecology and Obstetrics* 15:497-500.

31   Ayeni, Olusola. 1974. Demographic Characteristics of Nigeria: An Analysis of Population Data. Ph.D. Dissertation. University of London. London.

32   ----. 1975. Sex Ratio of Live Births in South-western Nigeria. *Annals of Human Biology* 2:137-141.

33   Bamisaiye, A.; De Sweemer, C.; and Ransome-Kuti, O. 1978. Developing a Clinic Strategy Appropriate to Community Family Planning Needs and Practices: An Experience in Lagos, Nigeria. *Studies in Family Planning* 9(2-3):44-48.

34   Barbour, K. M., and Prothero, R. M. 1961. *Essays on African Population*. London: Routledge and Kegan Paul.

35   Baum, S.; Hay, C.; and Huguet, J. 1972. An Inventory of Fertility and Related Surveys Conducted or Planned Since 1968 (Part 1). International Demographic Statistics Center. International Statistical Programs Division. U.S. Bureau of the Census. Washington, D.C.

36   Bongaarts, John. 1979. The Fertility Impact of Traditional and Changing Childspacing Practices in Tropical Africa. Center for Population Studies, Working Paper Number 42. The Population Council. New York.

37   Bongaarts, John; Frank, Odile; and Lesthaeghe, Ron. 1984. The Proximate Determinants of Fertility in Sub-Saharan Africa. *Population and Development Review* 10(3):511-537.

38   Brass, W.; Coale, A.; Demeny, P.; Heisel, D.; Lorimer, F.; Romaniuk, A.; and Van de Walle, E. 1968. *The Demography of Tropical Africa*. Princeton: Princeton University Press.

39   Bulatao, Rodolfo A. 1979. *Further Evidence of the Transition in the Value of Children*. Honolulu, HA.: East-West Population Institute.

40   Caldwell, John C. 1968. The Control of Family Size in Tropical Africa. *Demography* 5(2):598-619.

41   ----. 1968. *Population Growth and Family Change in Africa*. Canberra: Australian National University Press.

42   ----. 1976. Demographic and Contraceptive Innovators: A Study of Transitional African Society. *Journal of Biosocial Science* 8(4):347-365.

43   ----. 1976. Fertility and the Household Economy in Nigeria. *Journal of Comparative Family Studies* 7(2):193-253.

44   ----. 1976. Marriage, the Family and Fertility in Sub-Saharan Africa With Special Reference to Research Programmes in Ghana and Nigeria. In *Family and Marriage in Some African and Asiatic Countries*, ed. S.A. Huzayyin and G.T. Acsadi, pp. 359-371. Cairo: Cairo Demographic Centre.

45   ----. 1976. *The Socio-economic Explanation of High Fertility: Papers on the Yoruba Society of Nigeria*. Australian National University. Canberra: Department of Demography. Changing African Family Project Series, No.1.

46   ----. 1977. The Economic Rationality of High Fertility: An Investigation Illustrated with Nigerian Survey Data. *Population Studies* 31(1):5-27.

47   ----. 1977. The Study of Fertility and Fertility Change in Tropical Africa. Occasional Papers, No.7. World Fertility Survey. London.

48   ----. 1979. Variations in the Incidence of Sexual Abstinence and the Duration of Postnatal Abstinence Among the Yoruba of Nigeria. In *Natural Fertility: Patterns and Determinants of Natural Fertility*, ed. H. Leridon and J. Menken, pp. 397-407. Liege: Ordina Editions.

49   ----. 1982. *Theory of Fertility Decline*. London Academic Press.

50   Caldwell, John C., and Caldwell, Pat. 1977. The Role of Marital Sexual Abstinence in Determining Fertility: A Study of the Yorubas in Nigeria. *Population Studies* 31:193-217.

51   ----. 1978. The Achieved Small Family: Early Fertility Transition in an African City. *Studies in Family Planning* 9:2-18.

52   ----. 1981. Cause and Sequence in the Reduction of Postnatal Abstinence in Ibadan City, Nigeria. In *Child-spacing in Tropical Africa: Traditions and Change*, ed. H.J. Page and R. Lesthaeghe, pp. 181-199. New York: Academic Press.

53   Caldwell, John C.; Netting, Robert; Norman, D. W.; Hill, Polly; Weil, Peter; and Johnson, Robert. 1969. Population and Rural Development Research in West Africa. *Rural Africana* 8:5-60.

54   Caldwell, John C., and Okonjo, Chukuka. 1968. *The Population of Tropical Africa*. New York: Columbia University Press.

55   Caldwell, Pat, and Caldwell, John C. 1981. The Function of Child-spacing in Traditional Societies and the Direction of Change. In *Child-spacing in Tropical Africa: Traditions and Change*, ed. H.J. Page and R. Lesthaeghe, pp. 73-91. New York: Academic Press.

56   Cantrelle, P.; Ferry, B.; and Mondot, J. 1978. Relationships Between Fertility and Mortality in Tropical Africa. In *The Effects of Infant and Child Mortality on Fertility*, ed. S.H. Preston, pp. 181-205. New York: Academic Press.

57   Chadike, Patrick. 1969. The Possibility of Fertility Change in Modern Africa: A West African Case. *African Social Change* 602-614.

58   Changing African Family Project. 1974. *The Value of Children*. Canberra: Australian National University, Department of Demography. Changing African Family Project Series, No. 2.

59   Chojnacka, Helena. 1980. Polygamy and the Rate of Population Growth. *Population Studies* 34:91-107.

60   Chojnacka, Helena; Olusanya, P. O.; and Ojo, F., Eds. 1981. *Population and Economic Development in Nigeria in the 1980's. Proceedings of a National Workshop held at the University of Lagos, 12-14 September 1979*. New York: U.N. Department of Technical Co-operation for Development.

61   Clarke, J. D. 1944. Three Yoruba Fertility Ceremonies. *Journal of the Royal Anthropological Institute* LXXIV(1-2):91-96.

62   Clignet, R. 1970. *Many Wives, Many Powers: Authority and Power in Polygynous Families.* Evanston, IL.: Northwestern University Press.

63   Coale, A. J. 1968. Estimates of Fertility and Mortality in Tropical Africa. In *The Population of Tropical Africa*, ed. J.C. Caldwell and C. Okonjo, pp. 179-186. London: Longmans.

64   Coale, A. J., and Lorimer, F. 1968. Summary of Estimates of Fertility and Mortality. In *The Demography of Tropical Africa*, ed. W. Brass, A. Coale, P. Demeny, D. Heisel, F. Lorimer, A. Romaniuk and E. Van de Walle, pp. 151-182. Princeton: Princeton University Press.

65   Coles, Catherine M. 1983. Muslim Women in Town: Social Change Among the Hausa of Northern Nigeria. Ph.D. Dissertation. University of Wisconsin. Madison.

66   Denga, Daniel T. 1982. Childlessness and Marital Adjustment in Northern Nigeria. *Journal of Marriage and the Family* 44:799-802.

67   Dorjahn, Vernon. 1959. The Factor of Polygamy in African Demography. In *Continuity and Change in African Cultures*, ed. M. Herskovitz and W. Bascom, pp. 87-112. Chicago: University of Chicago Press.

68   Dow, Thomas E., Jr. 1977. Breastfeeding and Abstinence Among the Yoruba. *Studies in Family Planning* 8(8):209-214.

69   Doyle, P.; Morley, David; Woodland, Margaret; and Cole, Jane. 1978. Birth Intervals, Survival and Growth in a Nigerian Village. *Journal of Biosocial Science* 10:81-94.

70   Dyson, Tim P. 1977. An Analysis of Village Fertility, Mortality and Growth. In *The Feasibility of Fertility Planning: Micro Perspectives*, ed. T.S. Epstein and D. Jackson, pp. 21-41. Elmsford, N.Y.: Pergamon Press.

71   Ebigbo, P. O., and Chukudebelu, W. O. 1980. Child Spacing and Child Mortality Among Nigerian Igbos. *International Journal of Gynecology and Obstetrics* 18(5):372-374.

72   Ebigbo, P. O.; Ihezue, U. H.; and Chukudebelu, W. O. 1981. Attitudes of Expectant Nigerian Women Toward Pregnancy. *Advances in Planned Parenthood* 15(4):129-136.

73   Ekanem, Ita I. 1973. Fertility in Eastern Nigeria. Proceedings of the Workshop/Seminar on Population Dynamics Research in Africa. Lome, Togo.

74   ----. 1974. Correlates of Fertility in Eastern Nigeria. *Nigerian Journal of Economic and Social Studies* 16:115-127.

75   ----. 1978. *Ways of Controlling Family Size: A Case Study of Eastern Nigeria.* Canberra: Australian National University, Dept. of Demography. Changing African Family Project Monograph Series, No. 4, Vol.2.

76   ----. 1979. Ways of Controlling Family Size: A Case Study of the Eastern States of Nigeria. In *Population Education Source Book for Sub-Saharan Africa,* ed. R.K. Udo, pp. 280-289. Nairobi: Heinemann.

77   Ellison, R. E. 1936. Marriage and Child-birth Among the Kanuri. *Africa* 9(4):524-535.

78   Emereuwaonu, Ernest U. 1977. Marital Fertility, Desired Family Size, Communication Channels and Modern Reproductive Values in an African City. Ph.D. Dissertation. University of California. Los Angeles.

79   Epstein, T. S., and Jackson, D. 1977. *The Feasibility of Fertility Planning: Micro Perspectives.* Elmsford, N.Y.: Pergamon Press.

80   Fapohunda, O. J. 1974. Characteristics of the Unemployed in Lagos. *Human Resources Research Bulletin* 2(3).

81   ----. 1976. Population Increases and Educational Policies in Nigeria. *Jimlar Mutane* 1(2):253-271.

82   ----. 1980. Fertility Differentials Across Key Social Sectors in Nigeria. Paper presented at the I.U.S.S.P. Seminar. Colombo.

83   Farooq, Ghazi M. 1979. Household Fertility Decision-Making in Nigeria. World Employment Programme. Population and Employment Project, Working Paper No.75. ILO. Geneva.

84   Farooq, Ghazi M.; Ekanem, I. I.; and Ojelade, M. A. 1977. Family Size Preferences and Fertility in Southwestern Nigeria. World Employment Programme. Population and Employment Project, Working Paper Number 54. ILO. Geneva.

85   Fortes, Meyer. 1978. *Family, Marriage and Fertility in West Africa.* Canberra: Australian National University, Dept. of Demography. Changing African Family Project Monograph Series, No. 4, Vol.2.

86   Freedman, R. 1974. Examples of Community-Level Questionnaires From Sample Surveys About Fertility. World Fertility Survey Occasional Papers No.9. London.

87   Goody, Esther. 1978. *Some Theoretical and Empirical Aspects of Parenthood in West Africa.* Canberra: Australian National University, Dept. of Demography. Changing African Family Project Monograph Series, No.4, Vol.1.

88   Harrington, Judith A. 1978. Education, Female Status, and Fertility in Nigeria. Population Association of America Annual Meeting, April 13-15, 1978. Collected papers, Vol.3., pp. 274-324. Atlanta, Georgia.

89   Haub, C. 1983. Nigeria. *Intercom* 11:11-12.

90   Hibler, Michelle. 1980. On Women and Children. *Agenda* 10-11.

91   Hunponu-Wusu, O. O. et al. 1974. Demographic and Fertility Indicators Among Family Planning Acceptors in Kaduna, Northern Nigeria. *Savanna* 3:77-84.

92   Idele, S. I. 1977. *Fertility and Reproduction in the Bendel State of Nigeria.* Benin: University of Benin.

93   Igun, A. A., and Acsadi, G. T. 1972. *Demographic Statistics in Nigeria.* Ile-Ife: University of Ife.

94   Ilori, Felicia Adedoyin et al. 1979. Fertility Levels, Patterns and Differentials. In *1971-75 National Survey of Fertility, Family and Family Planning Phase 1: S.W. Nigeria,* ed. L.A. Adeokun. Ile-Ife: University of Ife.

95   Ilori, Felicia Adedoyin. 1976. *Factors Determining Rural-Urban Fertility Differentials in Western Oyo Province Nigeria: A Case Study of Ife, Ilesha and Selected Rural Areas.* Ile-Ife: University of Ife.

96   ----. 1976. Human Fertility as a Variable in Employment Development in Nigeria. Paper presented at the Conference on Employment Generation and Economic Development in Nigeria. Ibadan.

97   ----. 1978. The Effect of Female Labour Force Participation on Fertility Behavior and Family Welfare in South Western Nigeria. Paper presented at the National Workshop on the Introduction of Population Concepts into the Curricula of Agricultural Rural Development Training Institutions. University of Ife. Ile-Ife.

98   ----. 1978. Urbanization and Fertility: A Case Study of Western Nigeria. Paper presented at the International Seminar on the Integration of Theory and Policy in Population Studies, 2-5 January, 1978. University of Ghana. Legon.

99   ----. 1979. Background Characteristics of Total and Sample Population. In *1971-75 National Survey of Fertility, Family and Family Planning Phase 1: S.W. Nigeria,* ed. L.A. Adeokun. Ile-Ife: University of Ife.

100   ----. 1979. Recent Fertility Trends in Southwest Nigeria. Paper presented at the Annual Meeting of the Population Association of America, pp. 1-42. Philadelphia.

101   International Family Planning Perspectives. 1980. More Education Leads to Higher Fertility for Rural Nigerian Women. *International Family Planning Perspectives* 6(4):149-151.

102   Johnson, T. O.; Akinla, O.; Kuku, S. B.; and Oyediran, M. A. 1974. Infertility in Lagos. In *Sub-fertility and Infertility in Africa: Report of an International Workshop, Ibadan, Nigeria, 1973*, ed. B.K. Adadevoh, pp. 94-95. Ibadan: Caxton Press.

103   Kirk, Dudley. 1965. Factors Affecting Moslem Natality. United Nations World Population Conference, Vol.2. New York.

104   Kisekka, Mere Nakateregga. 1980. Marital and Familial Patterns in Zaria, Nigeria. *Africana Marburgensia* 13:43-50.

105   Kpedekpo, G. M. K. 1968. *The Eastern Regional Demography Survey. Technical Publication No.5.* Legon: University of Ghana, Institute of Statistics.

106   Lambo, T. Adeoye, and Bakare, C. G. M. 1971. The Psychological Dimensions of Fertility: An Intensive Study in Western State, Nigeria. *Rural Africana, Current Research in the Social Sciences* 14:82-88.

107   Lesthaeghe, R., and Bergen, H. 1975. Socioeconomic Distributions and Patterns of Natural Controlled Fertility: The Lagos Parity Study. Human Resources Research Unit. University of Lagos. Lagos.

108   Lesthaeghe, R., and Page, H. J. 1978. The Post Partum Non-Susceptible Period: Development and Applications of Model Schedules. Paper presented at the Annual Meetings of the Population Association of America Annual Conference. Atlanta. GA.

109   Lesthaeghe, R.; Page, H. J.; and Adegbola, O. 1981. Child-spacing and Fertility in Lagos. In *Child-spacing in Tropical Africa: Traditions and Change*, ed. H.J. Page and R. Lesthaeghe, pp. 147-179. New York: Academic Press.

110   Lucas, David. 1974. Demographic Class Project 1971-1972: Occupation and Family Size of Lagos Wives. *Lagos Notes and Records* 5:68-69.

111   ----. 1974. A Demographic Study of a South-Eastern Ibibio Village. Research Paper No.2. Lagos.

112   ----. 1974. Occupation, Marriage and Fertility Among Nigerian Women in Lagos. Human Resources Research Unit. Research Bulletin No.3/001. University of Lagos. Lagos.

113   ----. 1974. Some Aspects of Marriage, Fertility and Migration Among Women in Lagos. University of Lagos Research Bulletin. Lagos.

114 ----. 1976. Ethnic Fertility Differentials in Nigeria. Seminar paper presented in the Department of Demography. Australian National University. Canberra.

115 ----. 1977. Urban Rural Fertility in Southern Nigeria. In *The Economic and Social Supports for High Fertility: Proceedings of the Conference Held in Canberra, 16-18 November 1976*, ed. Lado T. Ruzicka, pp. 409-422. Canberra: Australian National University, Dept. of Demography.

116 ----. 1982. Some Remarks on the Paper by A. Okore, "Rural-Urban Fertility Differentials in Southern Nigeria: An Assessment of Some Available Evidence". *Population Studies* 36(3):475-476.

117 Lucas, David, and Fapohunda, O. J. 1973. Demographic Research in Lagos, Nigeria. In *Population Dynamics and Research in Africa*, ed. F.O. Okediji, pp. 71-86. Washington, D.C.: Interdisciplinary Communications Program, Smithsonian Institute.

118 Lucas, David, and McWilliam, John. 1976. *A Survey of Nigeria's Population Literature.* Lagos: University of Lagos.

119 Lucas, David; Sherlaimoff, Tania; Waddell-Wood, Peter; and Higman, Merle. 1985. *An Annotated Bibliography of the Nigerian Fertility and Family Planning Literature.* Canberra: Dept. of Demography, Australian National University.

120 Lucas, David, and Ukaegbu, A. 1977. Other Limits of Acceptable Family Size in Southern Nigeria. *Journal of Biosocial Science* 9:73-81.

121 Lucas, David, and Williams, G. 1973. Nigeria. In *Country Profiles.* New York: Population Council.

122 MacCormack, Carol P., Ed. 1982. *Ethnography of Fertility and Birth.* London: Academic Press.

123 Maclean, Catherine M. Una. 1982. Folk Medicine and Fertility: Aspects of Yoruba Medical Practice Affecting Women. In *Ethnography of Fertility and Birth*, ed. Carol P. MacCormack, pp. 161-179. New York: Academic Press.

124 Makinwa, Pauline K. Date unknown. Fertility in Urban Nigeria: The Case of Benin. In *Benin: Study of a Traditional African City*, ed. P.O. Sanda and P.K. Makinwa. Ibadan: Heinemann Educational.

125 ----. 1979. The Theory of the Demographic Transition and the Fertility of Urban and Educated Women in Nigeria. Paper presented at the Annual Conference of the Nigeria Anthropological and Sociological Association. University of Nigeria. Nsukka.

126 Makinwa-Adebusoye, P. K.; Nichols, D. J.; and Kelly, S. E. 1982. 1980 Lagos Contraception and Breast-feeding Study. Final Report. CenSCER. Univeristy of Benin. Benin.

127 Martin, W. J.; Morley, D.; and Woddland, M. 1964. Intervals Between Births in a Nigerian Village. *Journal of Tropical Pediatrics* 10(3):82-85.

128 Matthews, D. S. 1956. A Preliminary Note on the Ethnological and Medical Significance of Breast-Feeding Among the Yoruba. In *Proceedings of the 3rd International West African Conference, Ibadan, 1949*, pp. 269-279. Lagos: Nigerian Museum.

129 Meldrum, B., and Di Domenico, Catherine M. 1982. Women and Breastfeeding: Some Nigerian Examples. *Social Science and Medicine* 16:1247-1251.

130 Mellbring, G. 1971. *Report on Family Planning and Demography in Five West African Countries*. Paris: Organisation for Economic Co-operation and Development.

131 Mere, Ada, and Anikpo, Mark. The Impact of Wage-Employment of Women on Fertility in an Urban Town in Nigeria. Paper presented at CenSCER Conference, September 1980. CenSCER. University of Benin. Benin.

132 Morgan, R. W. 1969. A Population Dynamics Survey in Lagos, Nigeria. Preliminary Memorandum, Department of Community Health. College of Medicine. University of Lagos. Lagos.

133 ----. 1974. Traditional Contraceptive Techniques in Nigeria. In *Population in African Development. Vol.2.*, ed. P. Cantrelle, pp. 105-114. Liege, Belgium: International Union for the Scientific Study of Population.

134 ----. 1975. Fertility Levels and Fertility Change. In *Population Growth and Socioeconomic Change in West Africa*, ed. John C. Caldwell, pp. 187-235. New York: Columbia University Press [for] Population Council.

135 ----. 1976. Yoruba Modernization and Fertility in Lagos. In *Interdisciplinary Communications Programs, New Perspectives on the Demographic Transition*, pp. 1-51. Washington, D.C.: Smithsonian Institution. Occasional Monograph Series No. 4.

136 Morgan, R. W., and Kannisto, V. 1973. A Population Dynamics Survey in Lagos, Nigeria. *Social Science and Medicine* 7(1):1-30.

137 Mott, Frank L. 1974. *The Dynamics of Demographic Change in a Nigerian Village*. Lagos: University of Lagos, Human Resources Research Unit, Monograph No.2.

138 ----. 1974. Some Data Relating to Infertility in Nigeria. In *Sub-fertility and Infertility in Africa: Report of an International Workshop, Ibadan, Nigeria, 1973*, ed. B.K. Adadevoh, pp. 30-33. Ibadan: Caxton Press.

139   Mott, Frank L., and Fapohunda, O. J. 1975. *The Population of Nigeria*. Lagos: University of Lagos. Human Resources Research Unit Monograph No.3.

140   Nadel, S. F. 1937. Gunnu, A Fertility Cult of the Nupe in Northern Nigeria. *Royal Anthropological Institute* 67:91-130.

141   Newland, Kathleen. 1977. *Women and Population Growth: Choice Beyond Childbearing*. Washington, D.C.: Worldwatch Institute.

142   Newman, Jeanne S. 1984. *Women of the World: Sub-Saharan Africa*. Washington, D.C.: WID-USAID and U.S. Department of Commerce, Bureau of the Census.

143   Nicol, B. M. 1959. Fertility and Food in Northern Nigeria. *West African Medical Journal* 8(1):18-27.

144   Nigeria. Federal Government. 1968. Rural Demographic Sample Survey, 1965-1966, Lagos. Federal Office of Statistics. Lagos.

145   Nylander, P. P. S. 1968. The Significance of Secondary Amenorrhea in Nigeria. *West African Medical Journal* 17(6):208-209.

146   ----. 1970. Maternal Age and Parity Distribution in Rural and Urban Communities in Western Nigeria. *African Journal of Medical Sciences* 3(1):285-289.

147   Odulana, J. 1978. Family Welfare Laws in Ten African Countries: Report of the Africa Regional Law Panel Field Trips,1977/78, Vol.1. International Planned Parenthood Federation, Africa Region. Nairobi.

148   Ogum, G. E. 1980. Fertility Differentials in Nigeria. *Genus* 36:203-213.

149   Ogunnika, Olo. 1973. Fertility of Lagos Market Women. *Unilag Sociologist* 1(1):14-17.

150   Ohadike, P. O. 1967. Summary and Conclusion to a Social Demography Thesis on Modernisation, Fertility and Family Formation in an African City (Lagos, Nigeria). Canberra.

151   ----. 1968. A Demographic Note on Marriage, Family, and Family Growth in Lagos, Nigeria. In *The Population of Tropical Africa*, ed. J.C. Caldwell and C. Okonjo, pp. 379-392. London: Longmans.

152   ----. 1969. The Possibility of Fertility Change in Modern Africa: A West African Case. *African Social Research* 8:602-614.

124

153   Ojelade, Mukaila Adesina. 1982. The Socioeconomic Determinants of Fertility Behavior and Attitude in Southwest Nigeria, 1971-73. Ph.D. Dissertation. University of Pennsylvania. Philadelphia.

154   Ojo, O. A. 1968. Male Factor in Infertile Marriages in Nigeria. *West African Medical Journal* 17(1):210-211.

155   ----. 1970. The Problem of Fertility in Nigeria. In *The 6th World Congress on Fertility and Sterility, Tel Aviv, May 20-27, 1968 Proceedings*, pp. 128-132. Jerusalem, Israel: Israel Academy of Sciences and Humanities.

156   Ojo, Olufemi. 1971. Social and Economic Implications of Rapid Population Growth in Nigeria. Paper presented at the Seminar on Population Problems and Policy in Nigeria. University of Ife. Ile-Ife.

157   Okediji, Francis Olu. 1967. Some Social Psychological Aspects of Fertility Among Married Women in an African City. *Nigerian Journal of Economic and Social Studies* 9(1):67-68.

158   ----. 1968. *Differential Fertility in Ibadan City: Its Comparative Implications for Studying Population Change in Other African Societies*. Ibadan: University of Ibadan.

159   ----. 1968. Some Social-psychological Aspects of Fertility Among Married Women in an African City: Rejoinder. *Nigerian Journal of Economic and Social Studies* 10(1):125-133.

160   ----. 1969. Rural-Urban Fertility Differentials in Western Nigeria. *Population Studies* 23(3):363-378.

161   ----. 1969. Socio-Economic Status and Differential Fertility in an African City. *Journal of Developing Areas* 3:339-354.

162   ----. 1974. Population Dynamics Research in Nigeria: Achievements and New Horizons. In *Population Dynamics Research in Africa*, ed. F.O. Okediji, pp. 3-18. Washington,D.C.: Smithsonian Institute, Interdisciplinary Communications Program.

163   Okediji, Francis Olu; Caldwell, John C.; Caldwell, Pat; and Ware, Helen. 1976. The Changing African Family Project: A Report With Special Reference to the Nigeria Segment. *Studies in Family Planning* 7(5):126-136.

164   Okediji, Francis Olu; Caldwell, John; Caldwell, Pat; and Ware, Helen. 1978. *The Changing African Family Project: A Report With Special Reference to the Nigerian Segment*. Canberra: Australian National University, Dept. of Demography. Changing African Family Project Monograph Series, No.4, Vol.2.

165   Okonjo, C. 1971. Nigeria, Marriage, Kinship, and Fertility. In *The Demographic Transition in Tropical Africa*, pp. 267-273. Paris: Organisation for Economic Cooperation and Development, Development Center.

166   Okore, A. O. 1977. The Ibos of Arochukwu in Imo State, Nigeria. In *The Persistence of High Fertility*, ed. John C. Caldwell, pp. 313-330. Canberra: Australian National University.

167   ----. 1977. The Rationale for High Fertility in Rural Nigeria: The Case of the Ibos in Arochukwu in Iwo State. In *The Economic and Social Supports for High Fertility: Proceedings of the Conference on Family and Fertility Change, November 16-18, 1976*, pp. 253-274. Canberra: Australian National University. Changing African Family Project Companion Series No.2.

168   ----. 1977. The Rationality of Fertility Decisions in Iboland, Nigeria. Seminar paper presented in the Department of Demography, Australian National University. Canberra.

169   ----. 1977. The Value of Children Among Ibo Households in Nigeria: A Study of Arochukwu Division and Urban Umuahia in Imo State. Ph.D. Dissertation. Australian National University. Canberra.

170   ----. 1980. Rural-Urban Fertility Differentials in Southern Nigeria: An Assessment of Some Available Evidence. *Population Studies* 34:171-179.

171   ----. 1982. A Rejoinder to David Lucas' Urban Fertility Differentials. *Population Studies* 36(3):477-479.

172   Olusanya, P. O. 1967. The Education Factor in Human Fertility: A Case Study of the Residents of a Suburban Area in Ibadan, Western Nigeria. *Nigerian Journal of Economic and Social Studies* 9(3):351-374.

173   ----. 1968. Some Social Psychological Aspects of Fertility Among Married Women in an African City: Comments. *Nigerian Journal of Economic and Social Studies* 10(1):117-123.

174   ----. 1968. Urban Fertility Patterns in Western Nigeria: A Study of Reproductive Behavior and Some Factors Affecting it in Selected Yoruba Towns. Ph.D. Dissertation. University of London. London.

175   ----. 1969. Rural-Urban Fertility Differentials in Western Nigeria. *Population Studies* 23:363-378.

176   ----. 1971. The Problem of Multiple Causation in Population Analysis with Particular Reference to the Polygamy-Fertility Hypothesis. *The Sociological Review* 19:165-178.

177   ----. 1971. Status Differentials in Fertility Attitudes of Married Women in Two Communities in Western Nigeria. *Economic Development and Cultural Change* 19:641-651.

178   ----. 1974. Reduced Fertility and Associated Factors in the Western State of Nigeria. In *Sub-fertility and Infertility in Africa: Report of an International Workshop, Ibadan, Nigeria, 1973*, ed. B.K. Adadevoh, pp. 43-53. Ibadan: Caxton Press.

179   ----. 1978. Women's Changing Intra-Familial Role and Its Impact on Population Attitudes and Reproductive Behavior in a Nigerian Metropolis. Paper presented at the International Seminar on Integration of Theory and Policy in Population Studies. Legon.

180   Olusanya, Philip O. 1969. Moderization and the Level of Fertility in Western Nigeria Proceedings of the International Union for the Scientific Study of Populaton General Conferece, Vol. 1. pp. 812-825. London.

181   Oppong, C. 1982. Maternal Role Rewards, Opportunity Costs and Fertility. World Employment Programme. Population and Labour Policies Programme Working Paper No. 120. ILO. Geneva.

182   Oppong, C.; Adaba, G.; Bekombo-Priso, M.; and Mogey, J., Eds. 1978. *Marriage, Fertility and Parenthood in West Africa*. Canberra: Australian National University, Dept. of Demography, Changing African Family Monograph Series, No.4.

183   Oronsaye, A. U. 1979. The Outcome of Pregnancies Subsequent to Induced and Spontaneous Abortion. *International Journal of Gynaecology and Obstetrics* 17:274-277.

184   Orubuloye, I. O. 1977. Family Obligations and Fertility in Nigeria: The Case of the Yoruba of Western Nigeria. In *The Economic and Social Supports for High Fertility: Proceedings of the Conference held on Family and Fertility Change, November 16-18, 1976.*, pp. 203-217. Canberra: Austirlian National University, Department of Demography, Changing African Family Project Companion Series, No. 2.

185   ----. 1977. Fertility Differentials and Fertility Control Among the Yoruba of South Western Nigeria. Paper presented in the Department of Demography. Australian National University. Canberra.

186   ----. 1977. Fertility, Sexual Abstinence and Contraception Among the Yoruba of Western Nigeria: A Study of Selected Rural Communities in Ekiti and Ibadan Division. Ph.D. Dissertation. Australian National University. Canberra.

187   ----. 1977. High Fertility and the Rural Economy: A Study of Yoruba Society in Western Nigeria. In *The Persistence of High Fertility*, ed. John C. Caldwell, pp. 361-392. Canberra: Australian National University.

188   ----. 1979. Sexual Abstinence Patterns in Rural Western Nigeria- Evidence From a Survey of Yoruba Women. *Social Science and Medicine* 13A:667-672.

189   ----. 1981. *Abstinence as a Method of Birth Control: Fertility and Child-Spacing Among Rural Yoruba Women of Nigeria*. Canberra: Australian National University, Department of Demography, Changing African Family Monograph Series, No.8.

190   ----. 1981. Child-Spacing Among Rural Yoruba Women: Ekiti and Ibadan Divisions in Nigeria. In *Child Spacing in Tropical Africa: Traditions and Change*, ed. H. Page and R. Lesthaeghe, pp. 225-236. New York: Academic Press.

191   ----. 1981. Rural-Urban Fertility Differentials Among the Yoruba of Nigeria. In *Population and Economic Development in Nigeria in the 1980's*, ed. H. Chojnacka, P.O.Olusanya and F. Ojo, pp. 28-40. New York: United Nations Department of Technical Co-operation for Development.

192   ----. 1981. The Significance of Breast-Feeding on Fertility and Mortality in Africa. In *Population Dynamics: Fertility and Mortality in Africa*, pp. 499-512. Addis Ababa: United Nations Economic Commission for Africa (UNECA).

193   Ottong, G. J. 1978. Factors Affecting Marriage and Fertility in Shika, Zaria. Paper presented at the International Seminar on Integration of Theory and Policy in Population Studies. Legon.

194   Ottong, Joseph G. 1978. *Population Dynamics, Fertility and Family Planning in a Rural Community: A Study in Manchok, Southern Zaria, Nigeria*. Canberra: Australian National University, Department of Demography. Changing African Family Project Monograph Series, No. 4.

195   Owie, I. 1980. Opinions and Beliefs Regarding Family Size Among a Population of Nigerian Undergraduate Students. *Journal of American College Health Association* 28(5):287-289.

196   Oyemada, Adefunke, and Ogunmuyiwa, Taiwo A. 1981. Sociocultural Factors and Fertility in a Rural Nigerian Community. *Studies in Family Planning* 12:109-111.

197   Page, H. J. 1972. Fertility and Child Mortality South of the Sahara. In *Population Growth and Economic Development in Africa*, ed. S.H. Ominde and C.N. Ejiogu, pp. 51-66. London: Heinemann.

198   Page, H. J., and Lesthaeghe, R. 1981. *Child-Spacing in Tropical Africa: Traditions and Change*. London/New York: Academic Press.

199   Rehan, N., and Abashiya, A. K. 1981. Breastfeeding and Abstinence Among Hausa Women. *Studies in Family Planning* 12:233-237.

200   Romaniuk, A. 1968. Infertility in Tropical Africa. In *The Population of Tropical Africa*, ed. John C. Caldwell and C. Okonjo, pp. 214-224. New York: Columbia University Press.

201   Santow, Gigi. 1978. A Microsimulation of Yoruba Fertility. *Mathematical Biosciences* 42:93-117.

202   Santow, Gigi, and Bracher, M. 1981. Patterns of Postpartum Sexual Abstinence and their Implications for Fertility in Ibadan, Nigeria. In *Child-spacing in Tropical Africa: Traditions and Change*, ed. H.J. Page and R. Lesthaeghe, pp. 201-223. New York: Academic Press.

203   Saucier, J. F. 1972. Correlates of the Long Postpartum Taboo: A Cross Cultural Study. *Current Anthropology* 13:283-267.

204   Schoenmaeckers, R; Shah, I. H.; Lesthaeghe, R.; and Tambashe, O. 1981. The Child-Spacing Tradition and the Postpartum Taboo in Tropical Africa. In *Child-Spacing in Tropical Africa: Traditions and Change*, ed. H.J. Page and R. Lesthaeghe, pp. 25-71. London: Academic Press.

205   Sembajwe, Israel. 1979. Effect of Age at First Marriage, Number of Wives, and Type of Marital Union on Fertility. *Journal of Biosocial Science* 11:341-351.

206   ----. 1980. Religious Fertility Differentials Among the Yoruba of Western Nigeria. *Journal of Biosocial Science* 12:153-164.

207   ----. 1981. *Fertility and Infant Mortality Amongst the Yoruba in Western Nigeria*. Canberra: Australian National University, Department of Demography. Changing African Family Project Monograph Series No.6.

208   Stenning, Derrick J. 1966. Household Viability Among the Pastoral Fulani. In *The Development Cycle in Domestic Groups*, ed. Jack Goody, pp. 92-119. Cambridge: Cambridge University Press.

209   Talbot, P. A. 1927. *Some Nigerian Fertility Cults*. London: Humphrey Milford.

210   Tiffany, Sharon. 1982. *Women, Work and Motherhood: The Anthropological Perspective on Working Women*. New York: Prentice-Hall Spectrum Books.

211   Trevitt, Lorna. 1973. Attitudes and Customs in Childbirth Amongst the Hausa Women in Zaria City. *Savanna* 2(2):223-226.

212   Trevor, Jean. 1975. Family Change in Sokoto: A Traditional Moslem Fulani/Hausa City. In *Population Growth and Socioeconomic Change in West Africa*, ed. John C. Caldwell, pp. 236-253. New York/London: Columbia University Press.

213   Tshinyongolo, Mulunda. 1981. Fertility Differentials in Urban Nigeria. Ph.D. Dissertation. University of Michigan. Ann Arbor.

214   Ukaegbu, Alfred O. 1975. Marriage and Fertility in East Central Nigeria: A Case Study of Ngwa Igbo Women. Ph.D. Dissertation. University of London. London.

215   ----. 1976. The Role of Traditional Marriage Habits in Population Growth: The Case of Rural Eastern Nigeria. *Africa* 46:390-398.

216   ----. 1977. Fertility of Women in Polygynous Unions in Rural Eastern Nigeria. *Journal of Marriage and the Family* 39:397-404.

217   ----. 1977. Socio-cultural Determination of Fertility: A Case Study of Rural Eastern Nigeria. *Journal of Comparative Family Studies* 8:99-115.

218   ----. 1978. Family Size Preference of Spouses in Rural Eastern Nigeria. *Journal of Developmental Studies* 14:150-164.

219   UNECA. 1963. Fertility, Mortality, International Migration and Population Growth in Africa. Conference held in Cairo, October-November 1962. E/CN.14/ASPP/L.2, E/CN.9/CONF.3/L.2. New York.

220   ----. 1979. *Some Fertility Trends and Their Implications for Africa.* Addis Ababa: United Nations.

221   Uyanga, J. T. 1977. Socio-Economic Values in the Fertility Behavior of Nigerians. *Social Action* 4:379-398.

222   Uyanga, Joseph. 1977. Family Size, Family Income and Working Mothers in the Jos Plateau Area. *Savanna* 6:25-29.

223   ----. 1977. Socio-Economic Values in the Fertility Behavior of Nigerians. *Social Action* 4(27):379-398.

224   ----. 1979. Is Overcrowded Urban Living a Factor in Fertility Decisions? A Case Study of Metropolitan Calabar. *Social Action* 29:150-162.

225   ----. 1980. The Value of Children and Childbearing in Rural Southeastern Nigeria. *Rural Africana* 7:37-54.

226   ----. 1981. Correlates of Population Pressure in Rural Households: A Nigerian Case Study. *Journal of Comparative Family Studies* 12:219-232.

227   Van de Walle, Etienne. 1965. An Approach to the Study of Fertility in Nigeria. *Population Studies* 19:5-16.

228   ----. 1968. Fertility in Nigeria. In *The Demography of Tropical Africa*, ed. Brass W, A. Coale, P. Demeny, D. Heisel, F. Lorimer, A. Romaniuk and E. Van de Walle, pp. 515-527. Princeton: Princeton University Press.

229   Verma, O. P., and Singha, P. 1982. Fertility Pattern of Muslim Hausa Women in Northern Nigeria. *Nigerian Journal of Economic and Social Studies* 24(2):185-198.

230   Ware, Helen. 1974. Educational Differentials in Family Building Aspirations and Practice in Rural Nigeria. *Rural Demography* 1:129-171.

231   ----. 1975. The Limits of Acceptable Family Size in Western Nigeria. *Journal of Biosocial Science* 7:273-296.

232   ----. 1975. The Relevance of Changes in Women's Roles to Fertility Behavior: The African Experience. Paper presented at the Population Association of America Meeting. Seattle, WA.

233   ----. 1976. Security in the City: The Role of the Family in Urban West Africa. The Economic and Social Supports for High Fertility: Proceedings of the Conference held on Family and Fertility Change, November 16-18, 1976, pp. 385-408. Canberra: Australian National University. Dept. of Demography.

234   ----. 1977. Women's Work and Fertility in Africa. In *The Fertility of Working Women: A Synthesis of International Research*, ed. Stanley Kupinsky, pp. 1-34. New York: Praeger.

235   ----. 1981. *Women, Education and Modernization of the Family in West Africa*. Canberra: Australian National University, Dept. of Demography. Changing African Family Project Series Monograph No.7.

236   ----. 1983. Female and Male Life-Cycles. In *Female and Male in West Africa*, ed. C. Oppong, pp. 6-31. London: George Allen and Unwin.

237   Westfall, G. D. 1974. Nigerian Women: A Bibliographical Essay. *Africana Journal* 5:99-138.

238   World Health Organization. 1983. *Women and Breastfeeding*. Geneva: World Health Organization.

Ten
Family Planning

1   Abbott, Joan. 1974. The Employment of Women and the Reduction of Fertility: Implications for Development. *World Development* 2:23-26.

2   Acsadi, George T., and Johnson-Acsadi, Gwendolyn. 1983. Demand for Children and Spacing in Sub-Sahara Africa. Background paper for the report on Population Strategies for Sub-Saharan Africa. Washington, D.C.: The World Bank.

3   Acsadi, Gyorgy T. 1971. Some Problems of Yoruba Fertility and Its Regulation. Paper presented at the Faculty of Social Sciences Staff Seminar. University of Ife. Ile-Ife.

4   ----. 1972. Fertility Among the Yoruba. Presented to the Seminar on Family Planning in West Africa, pp. 7-12. University of Ibadan. Ibadan.

5   ----. 1974. Fertility Change and Stability in Sub-Saharan Africa: Toward a Working Hypothesis of Demographic Transition. Paper presented at the Meetings of the Population Association of America. New York.

6   ----. 1976. Traditional Birth Control Methods in Yorubaland. Culture, Natality and Family Planning. Chapel Hill, N.C.: Carolina Population Center.

7   Acsadi, Gyorgy T.; Igun, Adenola A.; and Johnson, Gwendolyn Z. 1972. Surveys of Fertility, Family, and Family Planning in Nigeria. Institute of Population and Manpower Studies (IPMS), Publication No.2. University of Ife. Ile-Ife.

8   Adaba, Gemma. 1978. *Rationality and Responsibility in Family Planning in Traditional African Society*. Canberra: Australian National University, Dept. of Demography. Changing African Family Monograph Series, Vol. 2 No.4.

9   Adegoye, O. A. 1973. Towards a Rational Population Policy in Nigeria. *Nigerian Opinion* 9(4):12-17.

10   Adeniyi-Jones, O. 1967. The Place of Family Planning in Community Integration and Development. In *Proceedings of the Eighth International Conference of IPPF*, pp. 92-96. Santiago, Chile.

11   Adenuga, E. A. B. 1971. Problems of Family Planning. Paper presented at the Seminar on Population Problems and Policy in Nigeria. University of Ife. Ile-Ife.

12   Adeokun, Lawrence A. 1971. Problems of a Family Planning Project in a Rural Area. Paper presented at the Seminar on Population Problems and Policy in Nigeria. University of Ife. Ile-Ife.

13   ----. 1978. Population Composition and Family Welfare in S.W. Nigeria. Paper presented at the National Workshop on the Introduction of Population Concepts into the Curricula of Agricultural Training Institutions. University of Ife. Ile-Ife.

14   ----. 1979. 1971-1975 National Survey of Fertility and Family Planning: Phase 1 Southwest Nigeria. Department of Demography and Social Statistics, DSS Monograph No.1. Faculty of Social Sciences, University of Ife. Ile-Ife.

15   ----. 1983. Marital Sexuality and Birth-Spacing Among the Yoruba. In *Female and Male in West Africa*, ed. C. Oppong, pp. 127-137. London: George Allen and Unwin.

16   Adeokun, Lawrence A., and Farooq, Ghazi M. 1974. Patterns of Fertility, Anti-Natal Knowledge and Practice: Impact of a Rural Family Planning Program. Ishan Division, Nigeria, 1969-1972. Institute of Population and Manpower Studies Report No.3. University of Ife. Ile-Ife.

17   Adeokun, Lawrence. 1981. Nigeria: Treading a Cautious Path. *People* 8(2):20-22.

18   Adepoju, Aderanti. 1975. Population Policies in Africa: Problems and Prospects. *African Affairs* 74:461-479.

19   Aderinto, Adeyemo. 1971. A Case For the Small Family. *Nigerian Opinion* 7(1):13-15.

20   African Population Newsletter. 1971. Nigeria: Two Fresh Approaches to the Problem of Population Control. *African Population Newsletter* 4:23-26.

21   Ajobor, L. N. 1976. Contraceptives and Abortions in Nigeria. *Nigerian Medical Journal* 6:367.

22   Akande, J. O. 1979. Law and the Status of Women in Nigeria. Economic Commision for Africa. (ECA/ATRCW/RE801/79). Addis Ababa: ATRCW.

23   Akingba, J. B. 1971. The Nigerian Attitude to Unwanted Pregnancies. *Nigerian Medical Journal* 1:179-183.

24   ----. 1971. *The Problem of Unwanted Pregnancies in Nigeria Today*. Lagos: Heinemann.

25   ----. 1977. Abortion, Maternity and Other Health Problems in Nigeria. *Nigerian Medical Journal* 7(4):465-471.

26   Akingba, J. B., and Gbajumo, S. A. 1970. Procured Abortion: Counting the Cost. *Journal of the Nigerian Medical Association* 7(2):17-28.

27   Akinkugbe, J. B., and Aderounmu, S. A. 1971. Response to Family Planning in Ile-Ife. Paper presented at the Seminar on Population Problems and Policy in Nigeria. University of Ife. Ile-Ife.

28   Akinla, Oladele, and Adadevoh, K. A. 1969. Abortion: A Medical-Social Problem. *Journal of the Nigerian Medical Association* 6(3):16-22.

29   Akinla, Oladele. 1968. The Problems of Abortion in Lagos, Nigeria. Paper presented at the Sixth World Congress on Fertility and Sterility. Tel Aviv.

30   ----. 1970. Abortion in Africa. In *Abortion in a Changing World, Vol.1*, ed. R.E. Hall. New York: Columbia University Press.

31   ----. 1971. Abortion in Tropical Africa. *Lagos Notes* 3:27-37.

32   ----. 1973. Africa, Abortion and the Law. *Nigerian Medical Journal* 3(3):128-130.

33   Arowolo, Oladele O. 1970. Preliminary Report on Rural Family Planning Evaluation Scheme 1969-70: Ishan Division, Mid-Western State of Nigeria.

34   ----. 1973. Abortion as a Factor in Fertility Regulation in Nigeria--A Proposal. Paper presented at the IPPF Conference on Medical and Social Aspects of Abortion. Accra, Ghana.

35   Aweda, David A. 1978. Educated Elite and Their Attitude Toward Family Planning and Fertility. *Odu* 17:64-84.

36   Ayangade, Samuel Okun. 1978. Birth Interval Study in a Culturally Stable Urban Population. *International Journal of Gynaecology and Obstetrics* 15:497-500.

37   Bakare, C. G. 1972. Instrumentation Problems in the Psychological Studies of Family Planning: A Nigeria Experience. In *Proceedings of the Conference of Psychology and Family Planning, Nairobi, Kenya, August 1-2, 1971*, ed. H.P. David, pp. 105-110. Washington, D.C.: Transactional Family Research Institute.

38   Bakare, C. G., and Lambo, T. A. 1971. An Experimental Study of the Effects of Persuasive Communications on the Acceptance of Family Planning in a Nigerian Rural Environment. Programme of Social Science and Legal Research of Population Policy. University of Ibadan. Ibadan.

39   Balogun, I. A. B. 1972. Islam, Polygamy and Family Planning in Nigeria. *Birthright* 7(1):35-42.

40   Bamisaiye, A.; De Sweemer, C.; and Ransome-Kuti, O. 1978. Developing a Clinic Strategy Appropriate to Community Family Planning Needs and Practices: An Experience in Lagos, Nigeria. *Studies in Family Planning* 9(2-3):44-48.

41   Baum, S.; Hay, C.; and Huguet, J. 1972. An Inventory of Fertility and Related Surveys Conducted or Planned Since 1968 (Part 1). International Demographic Statistics Center. International Statistical Programs Division. U.S. Bureau of the Census. Washington, D.C.

42   Berelson, Bernard. 1969. *Family Planning Programs: An International Study.* N.Y.: Basic Books.

43   Bernard, Roger; Kendall, Paul; Potts, Ellen M.; and Malcolm, David. 1980. Promotion of Postpartum Contraception Using MCM as a Tool of Management. In *Voluntary Sterilization: A Decade of Achievement*, ed. M.E. Schima and I. Lubell, pp. 197-205. New York: Association for Voluntary Sterilization.

44   Black, Timothy. 1972. *A Survey of Contraceptive Markets in Four African Countries.* Chapel Hill, NC.: Population Services, Inc.

45   Bongaarts, John; Frank, Odile; and Lesthaeghe, Ron. 1984. The Proximate Determinants of Fertility in Sub-Saharan Africa. *Population and Development Review* 10(3):511-537.

46   Caldwell, John C. 1968. The Control of Family Size in Tropical Africa. *Demography* 5(2):598-619.

47   ----. 1971. Anti-Natal Practice in Tropical Africa. In *International Population Conference, 1969, Vol.2*, pp. 1223-1239. Liege: IUSSP.

48   ----. 1971. Urbanization and Fertility Controls in Tropical Africa. *African Urban Notes* 6:33-43.

49   ----. 1975. Fertility Control. In *Population Growth and Socioeconomic Change in West Africa*, ed. John C. Caldwell, pp. 58-97. New York/London: Columbia University Press.

50   ----. 1976. Demographic and Contraceptive Innovators: A Study of Transitional African Society. *Journal of Biosocial Science* 8(4):347-365.

51   Caldwell, John C., and Caldwell, Pat. 1976. Demographic and Contraceptive Innovators: A Study of Transitional African Society. *Journal of Biosocial Science* 8:347-365.

52   ----. 1978. The Achieved Small Family: Early Fertility Transition in an African City. *Studies in Family Planning* 9:2-18.

53   Caldwell, John C., and Igun, A. 1970. The Spread of Anti-Natal Knowledge and Practice in Nigeria. *Population Studies* 24:21-34.

54   ----. 1972. Anti-Natal Knowledge and Practice in Nigeria. In *Population Growth and Economic Development in Africa*, ed. S.H. Ominde and C.M. Ejiogu, pp. 67-76. London /Ibadan /Nairobi: Heinemann.

55   Caldwell, John C., and Ware, H. 1977. The Evolution of Family Planning in an African City: Ibadan, Nigeria. *Population Studies* 31:487-507.

56   Chadike, Patrick. 1969. The Possibility of Fertility Change in Modern Africa: A West African Case. *African Social Change* 602-614.

57   Chukwuocha, C. C. 1975. An Appraisal of the Population Policy of Nigeria Since Independence: 1960-1975. Research paper. University of Ghana. Legon.

58   Daramola, T.; Wright, R. D.; Sofoluwe, G. O.; Adeniyi-Jones, A.; and Elliott, H. 1968. Attitudes in Nigeria Towards Family Planning. In *The Population of Tropical Africa*, ed. J.C. Caldwell and C. Okonjo, pp. 401-409. New York: Columbia University Press.

59   De Sweemer, C. C., and Lyons, T. 1975. Nigeria (Family Planning Programs). *Studies in Family Planning* 6(8):291-293.

60   Dow, Thomas E., Jr. 1977. Breastfeeding and Abstinence Among the Yoruba. *Studies in Family Planning* 8(8):209-214.

61   Durojaiye, M. O. 1970. Social-Psychological Considerations in Promoting Planned Parenthood in Nigeria. *Journal of the Society of Health* 5(1):21-24.

62   Eigbefoh, A. A. 1976. Population Problems, Policies and Programmes as They Relate to National Development in Nigeria. *African Population Newsletter* 21:13-15.

63   Ekanem, Ita I. 1979. Ways of Controlling Family Size: A Case Study of the Eastern States of Nigeria. In *Population Education Source Book for Sub-Saharan Africa*, ed. R.K. Udo, pp. 280-289. Nairobi: Heinemann.

64   Ekanem, Ita I., and Chukundum, Uche. 1978. Knowledge, Attitude and Practice of Family Planning in Eastern Nigeria: Implications and Prospects. *Odu* 17:36-63.

65   Ekanem, Ita I., and Farooq, G. M. 1977. The Dynamics of Population Change in Southern Nigeria. *Genus* 33:119-140.

66   Epstein, T. S., and Jackson, D. 1977. *The Feasibility of Fertility Planning: Micro Perspectives*. Elmsford, N.Y.: Pergamon Press.

67   Famplanco News. 1972. Supplement on 2nd Nationwide Family Planning Week. *Famplanco News* 1(4):4-5.

68   Farooq, Ghazi M., and Adeokun, Lawrence A. 1976. The Impact of Rural Family Planning Program in Ishan, Nigeria, 1969-72. *Studies in Family Planning* 7:158-169.

69   Grayson, J. 1981. Third World Policies and Realities. *Lancet* 3217(1):445-446.

70   Gwatkin, Davidson R. 1972. Policies Affecting Population in West Africa. *Studies in Family Planning* 3(9):214-221.

71   Haub, C. 1983. Nigeria. *Intercom* 11:11-12.

72   Hunponu-Wusu, O. O. et al. 1974. Demographic and Fertility Indicators Among Family Planning Acceptors in Kaduna, Northern Nigeria. *Savanna* 3:77-84.

73   Igun, A. A., and Acsadi, G. T. 1971. Evaluation of Rural Family Planning Project in Ishan: A Preliminary Report. Paper presented to Seminar on Population Problems and Policies in Nigeria. Demographic Research and Training Unit. University of Ife. Ile-Ife.

74   Ilori, F. A. 1981. Sex Differentials in Attitude to Family Size in Nigeria and Their Implications for Family Planning Programmes. In *Population and Economic Development in Nigeria in the 1980's*, ed. H. Chojnacka, P.O. Olusanya and F. Ojo, pp. 209-219. New York: United Nations Dept. of Technical Co-operation for Development.

75   Ilori, Felicia Adedoyin. 1979. Background Characteristics of Total and Sample Population. In *1971-75 National Survey of Fertility, Family and Family Planning Phase 1: S.W. Nigeria*, ed. L.A. Adeokun. Ile-Ife: University of Ife.

76   Ilori, Felicia Adedoyin, and Adeokun, L. A. 1976. Status of Women and the Knowledge, Attitude and Practice of Family Planning in Southwest Nigeria: An Empirical Investigation. Paper presented at the Conference of Nigerian Women and Development in Relation to Changing Family Structure. Ibadan.

77   Jeffreys, M. D. W. 1944. A Contraceptive Girdle From Calabar Province, Nigeria. *Man* 44:70-80.

78   Johnson, G. Z. 1972. Family Planning as a Population Policy Instrument for West African Countries. Paper presented to the Seminar on Family Planning in West Africa. University of Ibadan. Ibadan.

79   Lakeru, A. A. 1971. Problems of Family Planning. Paper presented at the Seminar on Population Problems and Policy in Nigeria. University of Ife. Ile-Ife.

80   Lambo, T. Adeoye, and Bakare, C. G. M. 1971. The Psychological Dimensions of Fertility: An Intensive Study in Western State, Nigeria. *Rural Africana, Current Research in the Social Sciences* 14:82-88.

81   Lucas, David; Sherlaimoff, Tania; Waddell-Wood, Peter; and Higman, Merle. 1985. *An Annotated Bibliography of the Nigerian Fertility and Family Planning Literature.* Canberra: Dept. of Demography, Australian National University.

82   McWilliam, J. A. 1982. Nigeria. In *International Encyclopedia of Population. Vol.2,* ed. J.A. Ross, pp. 471-476. New York: Free Press.

83   McWilliam, John. N. D. Preliminary Report of a Survey on Knowledge of Population and Attitudes Toward Family Formation and Family Planning of a Sample of Ahmadu Bello University Students. Zaria.

84   McWilliam, John, and Chukwudum, Uche. 1976. *Nigeria: Selected Studies in Social Science Research for Population and Family Planning Policies and Programmes.* London: International Planned Parenthood Federation.

85   Makinwa, Pauline K. 1976. Government Policies and Population Growth in Nigeria. Paper presented at the Annual Meeting of the Population Association of America. Montreal.

86   ----. 1980. The National Cost of Illegal Abortion: A Case for Family Planning Programmes. Paper presented at CenSCER. University of Benin. Benin.

87   Makinwa-Adebusoye, P. K.; Nichols, D. J.; and Kelly, S. E. 1982. 1980 Lagos Contraception and Breast-feeding Study. Final Report. CenSCER. Univeristy of Benin. Benin.

88   Mbanefoh, Gini F. 1981. Implications of the Threshold Fertility Hypothesis for Population Growth Control Policy in Nigeria: The Need for Public Action. In *Population and Economic Development in Nigeria in the 1980's,* ed. Helena Chojnacka, P.O. Olusanya and F. Ojo, pp. 68-77. New York: United Nations Dept. of Technical Co-operation for Development.

89   Mellbring, G. 1971. *Report on Family Planning and Demography in Five West African Countries.* Paris: Organisation for Economic Co-operation and Development.

90   Miller, K. A., and Inkeles, A. 1974. Modernity and Acceptances of Family Practice Programs of Developing Countries. *Journal of Social Issues* 30(4):167-188.

91   Morgan, R. W. 1971. Traditional Contraceptive Techniques in Nigeria. Paper presented at the First African Regional Population Conference. Accra.

92   ----. 1972. Family Planning Acceptors in Lagos, Nigeria. *Studies in Family Planning* 3(9):221-226.

93   ----. 1974. Traditional Contraceptive Techniques in Nigeria. In *Population in African Development. Vol.2.*, ed. P. Cantrelle, pp. 105-114. Liege, Belgium: International Union for the Scientific Study of Population.

94   ----. 1976. Yoruba Modernization and Fertility in Lagos. In *Interdisciplinary Communications Programs, New Perspectives on the Demographic Transition*, pp. 1-51. Washington, D.C.: Smithsonian Institution. Occasional Monograph Series No. 4.

95   ----. 1982. Distribution of Modern Contraceptive Use in a Medium Income Rural Population in Nigeria, in the Absence of an Adequate Health Care Delivery System: A Preliminary Determination of Relationships Between Modern Contraceptive Use and Levels of Nutrition, Child Mortality, and Fertility. Final report prepared for U.S. AID, Grant AID-DSPE-G-00008, Research Program by Boston University and the University of Ife, February 1979-1981.

96   Morgan, R. W., and Kannisto, V. 1973. A Population Dynamics Survey in Lagos, Nigeria. *Social Science and Medicine* 7(1):1-30.

97   Mosley, W. H.; Osteria, Y.; and Huffman, S. L. 1977. Fertility Regulation During Human Lactation- Interactions of Contraception and Breast-Feeding in Developing Countries. *Journal of Biosocial Science* 4:93-111.

98   Mott, Frank L. 1974. Demographic Change and Social Policy for a Nigerian Village. *Human Resources Research Bulletin* 5(1).

99   ----. 1976. Some Aspects of Health Care In Rural Nigeria. *Studies in Family Planning* 7(4):109-114.

100 National Seminar on Women. 1979. Laws and Customs Affecting Women. Resolutions issued by a National Seminar on Women. CenSCER. Benin.

101 Nigeria. Federal Government. 1968. Family Planning in Nigeria. In *Commonwealth Secretariat Report of the Second Commonwealth Medical Conference*. Kampala.

102 ----. 1971. Two Fresh Approaches to the Problem of Population Control. *African Population Newsletter* 4:23-26.

103 Nigeria. National Population Commission. 1983. Nigeria Fertility Survey 1981-1982, Preliminary Report (March). National Population Commission. Lagos, Nigeria and World Fertility Survey. London.

104   Oduntan, S. O. 1976. The Status of Women in Family Planning. Paper presented at the Conference on Nigerian Women and Development in Relation to Changing Family Structure, April 26-30. Department of Preventive and Social Medicine. University of Ibadan. Ibadan.

105   Ogunode, F. A. 1981. Guidelines for the Fourth Development Plan and Population Policy for the 1980's. In *Population and Economic Development in Nigeria in the 1980's*, ed. Helena Chojnacka, P.O. Olusanya and F. Ojo, pp. 193-208. New York: United Nations Dept. of Technical Co-operation for Development.

106   Ohadike, P. O. 1969. Normative and Attitudinal Transformation in Family Size Values and Birth Control in a Modernizing African Community. Proceedings of the 22nd Congress of the International Institute of Sociology. Rome.

107   Ojelade, Mukaila Adesina. 1982. The Socioeconomic Determinants of Fertility Behavior and Attitude in Southwest Nigeria, 1971-73. Ph.D. Dissertation. University of Pennsylvania. Philadelphia.

108   Ojo, O. A. 1971. The Problems of Family Planning in Nigeria. Paper presented at the Seminar on Population Problems and Policy in Nigeria. University of Ife. Ile-Ife.

109   Ojo, Olufemi. 1971. Social and Economic Implications of Rapid Population Growth in Nigeria. Paper presented at the Seminar on Population Problems and Policy in Nigeria. University of Ife. Ile-Ife.

110   Ojo, S. L. 1974. Need for Liberalisation of Laws Dealing With Abortion in Africa. Paper presented at the Inaugural Conference, Population Association of Africa. University of Ibadan. Ibadan.

111   Okediji, Francis Olu. 1967. Married Women in the City of Ibadan and Family Planning. *Nigerian Opinion* 3(3):177-179.

112   ----. 1967. Some Social Psychological Aspects of Fertility Among Married Women in an African City. *Nigerian Journal of Economic and Social Studies* 9(1):67-68.

113   ----. 1968. Attitudes, Knowledge and Practice of Family Planning Techniques Among Married Women in the City of Ibadan. *West African Medical Journal* 17(1):211-218.

114   ----. 1968. Some Social-psychological Aspects of Fertility Among Married Women in an African City: Rejoinder. *Nigerian Journal of Economic and Social Studies* 10(1):125-133.

115   ----. 1973. Theoretical and Methodological Critique of Surveys of Knowledge Attitude and Practice of Family Planning in Nigeria. *International Review of Modern Sociology* 3(1):1-11.

116   ----. 1978. *The Limitations of Family Planning Programs in the Developing Nations*. Canberra: Australian National University, Dept. of Demography. Changing African Family Project Monograph Series, No.4, Vol.2.

117   ----. 1979. Population Policy Programmes in Nigeria. In *Population Education Resouce Book for Sub-Saharan Africa*, ed. R.K Udo, pp. 271-279. Nairobi: Heinemann.

118   Okediji, Francis Olu; Caldwell, John C.; Caldwell, Pat; and Ware, Helen. 1976. The Changing African Family Project: A Report With Special Reference to the Nigeria Segment. *Studies in Family Planning* 7(5):126-136.

119   Okediji, Francis Olu; Caldwell, John; Caldwell, Pat; and Ware, Helen. 1978. *The Changing African Family Project: A Report With Special Reference to the Nigerian Segment*. Canberra: Australian National University, Dept. of Demography. Changing African Family Project Monograph Series, No.4, Vol.2.

120   Okediji, Peter Ade. 1972. Family Planning in Nigeria: A Psychologist's Contribution. Paper presented at the African Studies Association Meeting. Philadelphia.

121   ----. 1978. *The Status of the African Woman in Family Planning*. Canberra: Australian National University, Dept. of Demography. Changing African Family Project Monograph Series, No.4, Vol.2.

122   Okojie, Xto. 1971. The Use of Oral Contraceptive Pills as a Means of Fertility Control in a Rural Area of Nigeria. *Nigerian Medical Journal* 1(4):248-250.

123   Okojie, Xto, and Montague, Joel. 1975. Hospital Based Family Planning in Rural Africa: Some Lessons From the Midwestern Sate of Nigeria. *Transactions of the Royal Society of Tropical Medicine and Hygiene* 69:189-197.

124   Ola, D. K. 1975. A Statistical Analysis of the Diffusion of Family Planning in Lagos and Western States of Nigeria. *Nigerian Geographical Journal* 18(2):121-133.

125   Olusanya, P. O. 1968. The Case for a National Family Planning Programme in Nigeria. *Nigerian Opinion* 4(7-9):344-346.

126   ----. 1968. Some Social Psychological Aspects of Fertility Among Married Women in an African City: Comments. *Nigerian Journal of Economic and Social Studies* 10(1):117-123.

127   ----. 1969. Nigeria: Cultural Barriers to Family Planning Among the Yorubas. *Studies in Family Planning* 37:13-16.

128   Olusanya, Philip O. 1972. Urban-Rural Contacts and the Diffusion of Antinatal Attitudes Among a West African Peasant Group: The Case of Western Rural Nigeria. In *Symposium of Implications of Population Trends for Policy Measures in West Africa*, ed. N.O. Addo, pp. 147-156. Legon: University of Ghana, Dept. of Sociology.

129   ----. 1981. *Nursemaids and the Pill: A Study of Household Structure, Female Employment and the Small Family Ideal in a Nigerian Metropolis*. Legon: University of Ghana. Ghana Population Series No. 9.

130   Ominde, S. H., and Ejiogu, C. 1972. *Population Growth and Economic Development in Africa*. London: Heinemann.

131   Onifade, A. 1973. Knowledge, Attitude and Practice of Contraception in Ibadan. *Nigerian Medical Journal* 3(1):40-43.

132   ----. 1977. Attitudes Towards Abortion in Ibadan. *Nigerian Medical Journal* 7(7):461-464.

133   Onwuazor, S. N. 1977. Continuity and Change: Abortion and Family Size in a Nigerian Village. In *The Feasibility of Fertility Planning: Micro Perspectives*, ed. T.S. Epstein and D. Jackson, pp. 67-95. New York: Pergamon.

134   Oppong, C.; Adaba, G.; Bekombo-Priso, M.; and Mogey, J., Eds. 1978. *Marriage, Fertility and Parenthood in West Africa*. Canberra: Australian National University, Dept. of Demography, Changing African Family Monograph Series, No.4.

135   Oronsaye, A. U. 1979. The Outcome of Pregnancies Subsequent to Induced and Spontaneous Abortion. *International Journal of Gynaecology and Obstetrics* 17:274-277.

136   Orubuloye, I. O. 1977. Fertility, Sexual Abstinence and Contraception Among the Yoruba of Western Nigeria: A Study of Selected Rural Communities in Ekiti and Ibadan Division. Ph.D. Dissertation. Australian National University. Canberra.

137   Ottong, Joseph G. 1978. *Population Dynamics, Fertility and Family Planning in a Rural Community: A Study in Manchok, Southern Zaria, Nigeria*. Canberra: Australian National University, Department of Demography. Changing African Family Project Monograph Series, No. 4.

138   Oyediran, M. A. 1969. Family Planning in Nigeria. *Journal of Medical Education* 44(11):160-161.

139   ----. 1981. Maternal and Child Health and Family Planning in Nigeria. *Public Health* 95:344-346.

140   Oyediran, M. A., and Ewumi, E. O. 1976. A Profile of Family Planning Clients at the Family Health Clinic, Lagos, Nigeria. *Studies in Family Planning* 7:170-174.

141   Page, H. J., and Lesthaeghe, R. 1981. *Child-Spacing in Tropical Africa: Traditions and Change*. London/New York: Academic Press.

142   Population Bulletin. 1975. Family Planning in Africa. *Population Bulletin* 30(1):11-27.

143   Rehan, N. 1984. Knowledge, Attitude and Practice of Family Planning of Hausa Women. *Social Science and Medicine* 18:839-844.

144   Solanke, Folake. 1977. Abortion: A Legal Perspective. *Nigerian Medical Journal* 7-9.

145   Stepan, J., and Kellogg, E. H. 1972. *The World's Laws on Voluntary Sterilization For Family Planning Purposes*. Medford, MA.: The Fletcher School of Law and Diplomacy. Law and Population Monograph Series No.8.

146   Sullivan, J. H., and Chester, J. C. 1976. *U.S. Development Aid Programs in West Africa. 1.Population Planning Activities. 2.The Senegal River Basin Project 3.Reimbursable Development in Nigeria*. Washington, D.C.: U.S. Government Printing Office.

147   Traub, F. A. 1978. A Study of the Role of the Yoruba Husband in Family Planning: Implications for Family Planning Education. Master's Thesis. University of Ibadan. Ibadan.

148   Trevor, Jean. 1975. Family Change in Sokoto: A Traditional Moslem Fulani/Hausa City. In *Population Growth and Socioeconomic Change in West Africa*, ed. John C. Caldwell, pp. 236-253. New York/London: Columbia University Press.

149   Tshinyongolo, Mulunda. 1981. Fertility Differentials in Urban Nigeria. Ph.D. Dissertation. University of Michigan. Ann Arbor.

150   Uche, Chukwudum. 1978. *Opinion Leaders in an Information-Rich Environment: Some Suggestions for Family Planning Research in Nigeria*. Canberra: Australian National University, Dept. of Demography. Changing African Family Project Monograph Series, No.4, Vol.2.

151   Uche, Chukwudum, and Ekanem, Ita I. 1982. Knowledge, Attitude and Practice of Family Planning in Eastern Nigeria. *Sociologus* 32:97-126.

152   Udo, A. A., and Weiss, E. 1979. *The Calabar Rural MCH/FP Project 1975-1979: What We Have Learned About Family Planning*. New York: Population Council.

153   Ukaegbu, A. O. 1977. Family Planning Attitudes and Practices in Rural Eastern Nigeria. *Studies in Family Planning* 8(7):177-183.

154   Ukaegbu, Alfred O. 1977. Family Planning Attitudes and Practices in Rural Eastern Nigeria. *Studies in Family Planning* 8:177-183.

155   UN. 1972. *Measures, Policies, and Programmes Affecting Fertility, With Particular Reference to National Family Planning Programmes.* New York: United Nations.

156   Uyanga, Joseph. 1982. Child Mortality and Contraception Usage: A Study of Rural Acceptors in Nigeria. *Rural Africana* 14:61-68.

157   Ware, Helen. 1976. Motivations for the Use of Birth Control: Evidence from West Africa. *Demography* 13:479-493.

158   Weidemann, W. C. 1977. Attitudes Towards Family Planning in Southern Nigeria. In *Family Welfare and Development in Africa, Proceedings of the IPPF Regional Conference, Ibadan, Nigeria, August 29- September 3, 1976,* ed. F.T. Sai, pp. 66-73. London: International Planned Parenthood Federation.

159   Weiss, E.; Udofia, G.; and Madunagu, B. 1981. The Use of Modern Family Planning in Rural Nigeria. Paper presented at American Public Health Association Annual Meeting. Center for Population and Family Health, Columbia University. New York.

160   Weiss, Eugene, and Udo, A. A. 1981. The Calabar Rural Maternal and Child Health/Family Planning Project. *Studies in Family Planning* 12:47-57.

161   White, J. J. 1968. Some Shortcomings of a National Family Planning Program. *Nigerian Opinion* 4(10-11):370-371.

162   Williamson, J. B. 1970. Subjective Efficacy and Ideal Family Size as Predictors of Favorability Toward Birth Control. *Demography* 7(3):329-339.

163   Wright, R. D. 1968. A Family Planning Programme for Nigeria. *West African Medical Journal* 17(6):227-229.

Chapter Eleven
Migration and Development

1   Abbott, Joan. 1974. The Employment of Women and the Reduction of Fertility: Implications for Development. *World Development* 2:23-26.

2   Acsadi, Gyorgy T. 1971. Population Policy and the Second Nigerian National Development Plan. Paper presented at the Seminar on Population Problems and Policy in Nigeria. University of Ife. Ile-Ife.

3   Adedeji, Adebayo, and Rowland, L. 1973. *Management Problems of Rapid Urbanization in Nigeria; The Challenge to Government and Local Authorities*. Ile-Ife: University of Ife Press for the Institute of Administration.

4   Adegbola, O. 1975. An Approach to the Study of the Impact of Rural-Urban Migration on the Rural Economy. Paper presented at the Internal Migration Conference. University of Ife. Ile-Ife.

5   ----. 1981. Demographic Changes, Labour Supply and Land Resources in a Modernizing Economy: Nigeria in the 1980's and Beyond. In *Population and Economic Development in Nigeria in the 1980's*, ed. Helena Chojnacka, P.O. Olusanya and F. Ojo, pp. 89-103. New York: United Nations Dept. of Technical Co-operation for Development.

6   Adegoye, O. A. 1973. Towards a Rational Population Policy in Nigeria. *Nigerian Opinion* 9(4):12-17.

7   Adejuyigbe, O., and Helleniner, F. M., eds. 1977. *Environmental and Spatial Factors in Rural Development in Nigeria*. Ile-Ife: University of Ife Press.

8   Adekanye, Tomilayo O. 1984. The Ownership of Agricultural Products: Some Considerations for Integrating Women Into Rural Development in Africa. Presented at the Workshop on Women in Agriculture in West Africa, May 1984. International Livestock Centre for Africa. ITTA. Ibadan.

9   Adekoya, M. A. 1977. Barriers to an Effective Organization of Women's Work: The Women's Programme Section in Nigeria. *Les Carnets de l'enfance/Assignment Children* 38:80-83.

10   Adeniyi-Jones, O. 1967. The Place of Family Planning in Community Integration and Development. In *Proceedings of the Eighth International Conference of IPPF*, pp. 92-96. Santiago, Chile.

11   Adepoju, Aderanti. Urbanization and Migration in West Africa. Unpublished manuscript. University of Ife. Ile-Ife.

145

12   ----. 1974. Rural-Urban Socio-Economic Links: The Example of Migrants in South-West Nigeria. In *Modern Migrations in Western Africa*, ed. Samir Amin, pp. 127-137. London: Oxford University Press.

13   ----. 1975. Dynamics of Urban Population Growth in Nigeria: The Role of Repeated Migration. In *Papers presented at the Seminar on Internal Migration in Nigeria held at the University of Ife, May 5-8, 1975*, pp. 45-70. Ile-Ife: University of Ife, Institute of Population and Manpower Studies.

14   ----. 1975. Some Aspects of Migration and Family Relationships in South-West Nigeria. In *Changing Family Studies*, ed. C. Oppong, pp. 148-156. Legon: University of Ghana, Institute of African Studies.

15   ----. 1975. Urban Migration Differentials and Selectivity: The Example of Western Nigeria. *African Urban Notes* 2:1-24.

16   ----. 1976. Dynamics of Urban Population Growth in Nigeria: The Role of Repeated Migration. *Jimlar Mutane* 1:124-138.

17   ----. 1976. Internal Migration in Southwest Nigeria: A Demographic and Socio-economic Study of Recent In-migrations into the Towns of Ife and Oshogbo. Ph.D. Dissertation. University of London. London.

18   ----. 1976. Internal Migration of Nigeria. Unpublished manuscript. University of Ife. Ile-Ife.

19   ----. 1977. Migration, Economic Opportunities and Occupational Mobility: A Case Study in Western Nigeria. *Quarterly Journal of Administration* 11:167-183.

20   ----. 1977. Policy Implications of Migration Into Medium-Sized Towns: The Case of Abeokuta, Nigeria. Department of Demography and Social Statistics. University of Ife. Ile-Ife.

21   ----. 1978. Migration and Development in Nigeria. Department of Demography and Social Statistics. University of Ife. Ile-Ife.

22   ----. 1978. *Migration and Fertility: A Case Study in South-West Nigeria*. Canberra: Australian National University, Dept. of Demography. Changing African Family Project Monograph Series, No. 4, Vol.2.

23   ----. 1978. Migration and Rural Development in Nigeria. *African Perspectives* 1:79-92.

24   ----. 1980. Migration and Development: The Case of Medium-Sized Towns in Nigeria. Project report. Research Programme on Socio-Demographic Studies on Population Trends in Relation to Development. UNESCO Population Division. Paris.

25   ----. 1980. Rural Migration and Development in Nigeria. Project report. Population and Development Research on Migration in Developing Countries. Ford Foundation. New York.

26   ----. 1982. *Medium-Sized Towns in Nigeria: Research and Policy Prospects*. Paris: UNESCO.

27   ----. 1983. Patterns of Migration by Sex. In *Female and Male in West Africa*, ed. C. Oppong, pp. 54-66. London: George Allen and Unwin.

28   Adepoju, Aderanti, and Ekanem, Ita I. 1975. Interdisciplinary Approach to the Study of Migration and Related Variables. In *Papers presented at the Seminar on Internal Migration in Nigeria held at the University of Ife, May 5-8, 1975*, pp. 71-94. Ile-Ife: University of Ife, Institute of Population and Manpower Studies.

29   Adesina, Segun. 1977. *Planning and Educational Development in Nigeria*. Lagos: Educational Industries Nigeria Ltd.

30   Adewuyi, A. O. 1973. The Need for Home Economics in Nigerian Development. Master's Thesis. Texas Women's University. Denton, TX.

31   Adewuyi, Alfred A. 1978. Population Growth and Economic Development. *Nigerian Behavioural Sciences Journal* 1(1):39-47.

32   Adeyemi, A. 1973. Rural-Urban Migration in Isanlu, Kabba Division of Kwara State. Research essay. Ahmadu Bello University. Zaria.

33   Adeyokunnu, Tomilayo. 1981. *Women and Agriculture in Nigeria*. Addis Ababa: ATRCW, UNECA.

34   Agusiobo, O. N. 1981. African Women in Rural Development. *Africa Insight* 11(1):40-43.

35   Ajaegbu, H. I. 1972. Population Growth and Economic Development in Nigeria. In *Population Growth and Economic Development in Africa*, ed. S.H. Ominde and C.N. Ejiogu, pp. 262-269. London: Heinemann.

36   ----. 1975. Migrants and the Rural Economy in Nigeria. Paper presented at the Internal Migration Conference. University of Ife. Ile-Ife.

37   ----. 1976. The Increasing Elite Group in Nigeria's Population: Their Demographic-Economic Role and Their Implications for Development Planning. *Jimlar Mutane* 1(1):113-123.

38   ----. 1976. *Urban and Rural Development in Nigeria*. London: Heinemann.

39   Ajaegbu, H. I., and Mann, C. E. 1975. Human Population and the Disease Factor in the Development of Nigeria. In *The Population Factor in African Studies*, ed. R.P. Moss et al, pp. 123-138. London: University of London Press.

40   Akande, J. O. 1978. Development, Law and the Status of Women. *Journal of the Nigerian Society of International Law* 2(1).

41   Akeredolu-Ale, E. A. 1975. *The Underdevelopment of Indigenous Entrepreneurship in Nigeria*. Ibadan: Ibadan University Press.

42   Akinola, R. A. 1967. Problems of Urban Development in Nigeria- An Example of Ibadan. *Bulletin of the Ghana Geographical Association* 12:7-22.

43   Aluko, Olajide. 1970. The United Nations Development Programme in Nigeria. *Administration* 301-334.

44   Aluko, S. A. 1971. Population Growth and the Level of Income in Nigeria. Paper presented at the Seminar of Population Problems and Policy in Nigeria. University of Ife. Ile-Ife.

45   Amin, S. 1974. *Modern Migrations in Western Africa*. London: Oxford University Press for International African Institute.

46   Anyanwu, C. N. 1981. *Principles and Practice of Adult Education and Community Development*. Ibadan: Abiprint Publishing Co.

47   Arikpo, Okoi. 1967. *The Development of Modern Nigeria*. Baltimore: Penguin Books.

48   Aronson, D. R. 1978. *The City is Our Farm: Seven Migrant Ijebu Yoruba Families*. Boston, MA.: Schenkman.

49   Arowolo, Oladele O. 1981. Fertility and Mortality Trends: Implications for Education, Health and Housing Expenditures in Nigeria. In *Population and Economic Development in Nigeria in the 1980's*, ed. H. Chojnacka, P.O. Olusanya and F. Ojo, pp. 77-89. New York: United Nations Dept. of Technical Co-operation for Development.

50   Audu, I. S. 1975. Higher Education for Development: Case Study, Ahmadu Bello University. New York International Council for Educational Development. New York.

51   Awoliyi, E. A. 1967. Role of Women and Women's Organizations in the Solution of Problems of Environmental Hygiene in Nigeria. *Journal of the Society of Health* 2(2):7-8.

52   Awosika, Keziah. 1976. Nigerian Women in the Labour Force: Implications for National Economic Planning. Paper presented at the National Conference on Women and Development in Relation to Changing Family Structure. University of Ibadan. Ibadan.

53   Awosika, Keziah; DiDomenico, Catherine; Dennis, Carolyn; and Ogunsheye, Adetorn. 1982. *Nigerian Women in Development--Their Changing Roles in Family and Society. Papers and Proceedings of an International Conference, University of Ibadan, 1976.* Ibadan: Limited Mimeo Edition.

54   Baker, Tanya. 1959. Women's Role in the Development of Tropical Africa and Sub-Tropical Countries. Report of the 31st Session of the International Institute of Differing Civilizations (INCIDI), pp. 73-83. Brussels.

55   Ballay, Ute B. 1983. Women in Nigeria: Aspects of Social Transformation. *Africana Marburgensia* 16(2):33-59.

56   Bamidele, C. A. 1973. Rural-Urban Migration Among the People of Odo-Owa, Igbomina-Ekiti Division, Kwara State. Research essay. Ahmadu Bello University. Zaria.

57   Barbour, K. M., and Prothero, R. M. 1961. *Essays on African Population.* London: Routledge and Kegan Paul.

58   Barnes, Sandra T. 1974. Becoming a Lagosian. Ph.D. Thesis. University of Wisconsin. Madison.

59   ----. 1975. Social Involvement of Migrants in Lagos, Nigeria. Paper presented at the Internal Migration Conference. University of Ife. Ile-Ife.

60   Beneria, Lourdes. 1982. *Women and Development: The Sexual Division of Labour in Rural Societies.* New York: Praeger.

61   Berry, S. 1983. Work, Migration, and Class in Western Nigeria: A Reinterpretation. In *Struggle for the City: Migrant Labour, Capital, and the State in Urban Africa,* ed. Frederick Cooper, pp. 247-273. Beverly Hills: Sage.

62   Boserup, Esther. 1970. *Woman's Roles in Economic Development.* London: George Allen and Unwin, Ltd.

63   ----. 1977. *Women and National Development: The Complexities of Change.* Chicago: Chicago University Press.

64   Brown, C. K. 1979. The Participation of Women in Rural Development in Kaduna State of Nigeria. Centre for Social and Economic Research. Ahmadu Bello University. Zaria.

149

65   Bulengo, Martha. 1975. Women in Rural Development. *African Women* 21(1).

66   Burfisher, Mary, and Horenstein, Nadine. 1983. *Sex Roles in the Nigerian Tiv Farm Household and the Differential Impacts of Development Projects*. New York: Population Council.

67   Buvinic, Mayra et al. 1975. Women in Development: Preliminary Annotated Bibliography. Office of International Science, American Association for the Advancement of Science. Washington, D.C.

68   ----. 1976. *Women and World Development: An Annotated Bibliography*. Washington, D.C.: Overseas Development Council.

69   ----. 1978. Women-Headed Households: The Ignored Factor in Development Planning. Report Submitted to AID/WID. International Center for Research on Women. Washington, D.C.

70   Caldwell, John C. 1975. *Population Growth and Socioeconomic Change in West Africa*. New York/London: Columbia University Press.

71   Caldwell, John C.; Netting, Robert; Norman, D. W.; Hill, Polly; Weil, Peter; and Johnson, Robert. 1969. Population and Rural Development Research in West Africa. *Rural Africana* 8:5-60.

72   Carew, Jay Gleason. 1981. A Note on Women and Agricultural Technology in the Third World. *Labour and Society* 6(3):279-285.

73   Casal, Lourdes et al. 1977. *Women and Development*. Racine, WI.: Johnson Foundation.

74   Charlick, Robert. 1974. Power and Participation in the Modernization of Rural Hausa Communities. Ph.D. Dissertation. University of California at Los Angeles. Los Angeles.

75   Cho, L. J. 1964. Estimated Refined Measures of Fertility for All Major Countries of the World. *Demography* 1(1):359-374.

76   Chojnacka, Helena; Olusanya, P. O.; and Ojo, F., Eds. 1981. *Population and Economic Development in Nigeria in the 1980's. Proceedings of a National Workshop held at the University of Lagos, 12-14 September 1979*. New York: U.N. Department of Technical Co-operation for Development.

77   Chukwuocha, C. C. 1975. An Appraisal of the Population Policy of Nigeria Since Independence: 1960-1975. Research paper. University of Ghana. Legon.

78   Cohen, Abner. 1969. *Custom and Politics in Urban Africa: A Study of Hausa Migrants in Yoruba Towns*. Berkeley: University of California Press.

79   Dalli, A. L. 1973. Migration and Spatial Change: A Bachama Example. Research essay. Ahmadu Bello University. Zaria.

80   Damachi, U. G. 1972. *Nigerian Modernization*. New York: The Third Press.

81   Damachi, U. G., and Seibel, H. D. 1973. *Social Change and Economic Development in Nigeria*. New York: Praeger.

82   Di Domenico, Catherine M. 1980. Women in Development: A Case Study of Their Labor Force Participation in Ibadan and Its Implications for Differential Role Performance. CenSCER Conference. University of Ibadan. Ibadan.

83   Diejomaoh, V. P. 1965. *Economic Development in Nigeria: Its Problems, Challenge and Prospects*. Princeton, N.J.: Princeton University, Industrial Relations Section. Research Report Series No. 107.

84   Doxiadis Associates International. 1973. Nigeria: Development Problems and Future Needs of Major Urban Centres. Report prepared for Federal Ministry of Economic Development. Nigeria.

85   Due, Jean M. 1982. Constraints to Women and Development in Africa. *Journal of Modern African Studies* 20(1):155-166.

86   Ebigbola, J. A. 1981. Population and Education in the Third National Development Plan and Recommendations for the Next Plan Period: A Case Study of the UPE Scheme in Nigeria. In *Population and Economic Development in Nigeria in the 1980's*, ed. Helena Chojnacka, P.O. Olusanya and F. Ojo, pp. 117-127. New York: United Nations Dept. of Technical Cooperation for Development.

87   Ejiogu, C. N. African Migrants in Lagos Suburbs. Ph.D. Dissertation. Australian National Univerisity. Canberra.

88   ----. 1968. African Rural-Urban Migrants in the Main Migrant Areas of the Lagos Federal Territory. In *The Population of Tropical Africa*, ed. J.C. Caldwell and C. Okonjo, pp. 320-330. New York: Columbia University Press.

89   ----. 1975. Metropolitanization: The Growth of Lagos. In *Population Growth and Socioeconomic Change in West Africa*, ed. John Caldwell, pp. 308-320. New York: Columbia University Press.

90   Ekanem, Ita I., and Adepoju, Aderanti. 1977. Directing Migration to Medium-Sized Cities. *Ekistics* 44:213-215.

91   Eke, I. I. U. 1966. Population of Nigeria: 1952-1965. *Nigerian Journal of Economic and Social Studies* 8(2):289-309.

92   Ekundare, Olufemi Richard. 1974. The Impact of Economic Development on Customary Marriages in Nigeria. Paper presented at the seminar New Directions in African Family Law. Leiden.

93   Entwisle, Barbara, and Coles, Catherine. 1985. Methodology in the Study of Female Roles: Demographic Surveys and Nigerian Women. Presented at the Annual Meeting of the African Studies Association. New Orleans.

94   Essang, S. M., and Mabawonku, A. F. 1974. Determinants of Impact of Rural-Urban Migration: A Case Study of Selected Communities in Western Nigeria. African Rural Employment Research Network Paper No.10. East Lansing.

95   ----. 1975. Impact of Urban Migration on Rural Development: Theoretical Considerations and Empirical Evidence from Southern Nigeria. *Developing Economies* 13:137-149.

96   Etukudu, A. T. U. 1978. Rural and Urban Household Incomes and Expenditures in Nigeria. *Human Resources Research Bulletin* 78(6).

97   Fadayomi, Theophilus O. 1979. Rural Outmigration in Nigeria: Its Determinants and Policy Implications. *Rural Africana* 6:47-61.

98   Fallers, L. A. 1967. *Immigrants and Associations*. The Hague: Mouton.

99   Fapohunda, Eleanor R. 1978. Women at Work in Nigeria: Factors Affecting Modern Sector Employment. In *Human Resources and African Development*, ed. U.G. Damachi and V.P. Diejomaoh, pp. 220-241. New York/London: Praeger.

100   Fapohunda, O. J. 1978. Characteristics of the Informal Sector of Lagos. *Human Resources Research Bulletin* 78(1).

101   ----. 1981. Human Resources and the Lagos Informal Sector. In *The Urban Informal Sector in Developing Countries*, ed. S.V. Sethuraman, pp. 70-82. Geneva: International Labour Office.

102   Fatunde, S. S. 1972. Adult Education for Social Development: Women's Programme in the Western State of Nigeria. Federal Ministry of Education. Lagos.

103   Gbodi, E. B. 1973. Migration into Gombe in the North Eastern State of Nigeria. Research essay. Ahmadu Bello University. Zaria.

104   George, M. V., and Eigbefoh, A. A. 1973. *Population Growth and Migration in Lagos*. Cairo: Research Monograph Series, Cairo Demographic Series, No.4.

105   Goddard, A. D.; Mortimore, M. J.; and Norman, D. W. 1975. Some Social and Economic Implications of Population Growth in Rural Hausaland. In *Population Growth and Socioeconomic Change in West Africa*, ed. John C. Caldwell, pp. 321-336. New York/London: Columbia University Press.

106   Green, Leslie. 1974. Migration, Urbanization and National Development in Nigeria. In *Modern Migrations in Western Africa*, ed. Samir Amin, pp. 281-304. London: Oxford University Press.

107   Gwatkin, Davidson R. 1972. Policies Affecting Population in West Africa. *Studies in Family Planning* 3(9):214-221.

108   Hafkin, Nancy J. 1977. *Women and Development in Africa: An Annotated Bibliography*. Addis Ababa: U.N. Economic Commission for Africa, Bibliographic Series No.1.

109   Hafkin, Nancy J., and Bay, E. G. 1976. *Women in Africa: Studies in Social and Economic Change*. Stanford: Stanford University Press.

110   Hance, W. A. 1970. *Population, Migration and Urbanization in Africa*. New York: Columbia University Press.

111   Hasken, Fran P. 1976. *Sites and Services Program in Africa and the Integration of Women in Their Development*. The author (187 Grant St., Lexington, MA., 02173).

112   Hay, Margaret Jean, and Stichter, Sharon. 1984. *African Women South of the Sahara*. London, New York: Longman.

113   Heyer, Judith; Roberts, Pepe; and Williams, Gavin. 1981. *Rural Development in Tropical Africa*. London: Macmillan.

114   Hill, Polly. 1977. *Population, Prosperity and Poverty: Rural Kano 1900 and 1970*. Cambridge: Cambridge University Press.

115   Igun, A. A. 1972. The Collection of Demographic Statistics for Reconstruction and Development in Nigeria. In *Demographic Statistics in Nigeria*, ed. A.A. Igun and G.T. Acsadi, pp. 23-46. Ile-Ife: Universtiy of Ife.

116   Ilori, Felicia Adedoyin. 1976. Determinants of Urban Growth in Western Nigeria, 1952-1963. *Odu* 13:60-79.

117   ----. 1976. Human Fertility as a Variable in Employment Development in Nigeria. Paper presented at the Conference on Employment Generation and Economic Development in Nigeria. Ibadan.

118   ----. 1977. The Role and Status of Women in Development and Population Issues. Paper presented at the International Seminar on Population, Employment and Development in Nigeria. University of Ibadan. Ibadan.

119   Imam, Ayesha, and Pittin, Renee. 1984. The Identification of Successful Women's Projects: Kaduna State, Nigeria. ILO Report. Geneva.

120   Imoagene, S. O. 1978. Migrating Into Unemployment and Poverty: Some Consequences of the Urban Revolution in Nigeria. *African Development* 3:53-64.

121   International Institute of Differing Civilizations. 1959. *Women's Role in the Development of Tropical and Sub-Tropical Countries.* Brussels: International Institute of Differing Civilizations.

122   Iro, M. I. 1980. Migration of Igbo to Metropolitan Lagos: The Post-War Experience 1970-74. In *National Ethnic Movements,* ed. J. Dofny and A. Akiwowo, pp. 183-191. Beverly Hills/London: Sage.

123   Janelid, Ingrid. 1974. The Need for Developing Social Indicators. Paper presented at the National Seminar on Home Economics Development Planning held at the International Institute of Tropical Agriculture, 8-14, December 1974. Ibadan.

124   Kassem, W. 1973. Rural-Urban Migration in Pakshin District. Research essay. Ahmadu Bello University. Zaria.

125   Kayode, F. 1972. The [Second Nigerian National] Development Plan and the Control of the Private Sector. *Quarterly Journal of Administration* 6:323-332.

126   Kisekka, Mere Nakateregga. 1980. The Identification and Use of Indicators of Women's Participation in Socio-economic Development in the Context of Nigeria and Uganda. UNESCO Meeting on Women's Participation in Socio-economic Development. SS.80/CONF.620/2. Rome.

127   ----. 1981. The Role of Women in Socioeconomic Development: Indicators as Instruments of Social Analysis--The Case of Nigeria and Uganda. In *Women and Development,* pp. 33-47. Paris: UNESCO.

128   ----. 1981. *Women and Development in Nigeria: An Annotated Bibliography.* Addis Abbada: UNECA, ATRCW/ Ford Foundation. Bibliographic Series No. 4.

129   Kuper, Hilda. 1965. *Urbanization and Migration in West Africa.* Los Angeles: University of California Press.

130   Lacey, Linda. 1981. Urban Migration in Developing Countries: A Case Study of Three Cities in Nigeria. Ph.D. Dissertation. Cornell University. Ithaca.

131   Liman, Alhaji M. 1974. Home Economics in the Third National Development Plan, 1975-1980. Paper presented at the National Seminar on Home Economics Development Planning held at the International Institute of Tropical Agriculture, Ibadan, 8-14, December 1974. Federal Department of Agriculture. Lagos.

132   Little, Kenneth. 1957. The Role of Voluntary Associations in West African Urbanization. *American Anthropologist* 59:579-596.

133   ----. 1960. The West African Town: Its Social Basis. *Diogenes* 29:16-31.

134   Lloyd, Peter C. 1975. Perceptions of Class and Social Inequality Among the Yoruba of Western Nigeria. In *Migration and Development: Implications for Ethnic Identity and Political Conflict*, ed. H.I. Safa and B.M. duToit. Paris: Mouton.

135   Longhurst, Richard. 1980. Rural Development Planning and the Sexual Division of Labour: A Case Study of a Moslem Hausa Village in Northern Nigeria. World Employment Programme Research Working Papers, WEP/10/WP/10. ILO. Geneva.

136   Lucas, David. 1974. Notes on Research in Progress: Ibibio/Kwale Survey. *Lagos Notes and Records* 5:65-67.

137   ----. 1974. Occupation, Marriage and Fertility Among Nigerian Women in Lagos. Human Resources Research Unit. Research Bulletin No.3/001. University of Lagos. Lagos.

138   ----. 1974. Some Aspects of Marriage, Fertility and Migration Among Women in Lagos. University of Lagos Research Bulletin. Lagos.

139   Lucas, David, and Williams, G. 1973. Nigeria. In *Country Profiles*. New York: Population Council.

140   Mabogunje, A. L. 1977. The Urban Situation in Nigeria. In *Patterns of Urbanization: Comparative Country Studies*, ed. S. Goldstein and D.F. Sly, pp. 569-641. Dolhain: Ordina Editions.

141   Mabogunje, A. L., and Filani, M. O. 1981. The Informal Sector in a Small City: The Case of Kano. In *The Urban Informal Sector in Developing Countries*, ed. S.V. Sethuraman, pp. 83-89. Geneva: International Labour Office.

142   McWilliam, J. A. 1982. Nigeria. In *International Encyclopedia of Population. Vol.2*, ed. J.A. Ross, pp. 471-476. New York: Free Press.

143   Makinwa, Paulina Kofoworola. 1981. *Internal Migration and Rural Development in Nigeria: Lessons from Bendel State*. Ibadan: Heinemann.

144   Makinwa, Pauline K. 1976. Government Policies and Population Growth in Nigeria. Paper presented at the Annual Meeting of the Population Association of America. Montreal.

145   ----. 1980. The Role of Women in Nigerian Socio-Economic Development. Paper presented at CenSCER Conference. University of Benin. Benin.

146   Makinwa-Adebusoye, P. K.; Ozo, A. O.; and Abudu, F., eds. 1984. Proceedings of the National Conference. The Urban Poor in Nigeria, April 1984. CenSCER, University of Benin. Benin City.

147   Matsepe, Ivy. 1977. Underdevelopment and African Women. *Journal of Southern African Affairs* 2:135-143.

148   Mayo, Marjorie. 1969. Two Steps Forward, One Step Back: An Account of Some of the Difficulties That Can Plague Work Among Women. *Community Development Journal* 4(2):93-98.

149   Michelwait, D. R.; Reigelman, M. A.; and Sweet, C. F. 1976. *Women in Rural Development - Survey of the Roles of Women in Ghana, Lesotho, Kenya, Nigeria, Bolivia, Paraguay, and Peru.* Boulder, Co: Westview Press.

150   Moody, Elize. 1979. Women and Development: A Selected Bibliography. Occasional Paper No. 43. Africa Institute of South Africa. Pretoria.

151   Moore, J. Aduke. 1960. The Sphere and Influence of Women in Africa. *Journal of Human Relations* 8(3-4):709-717.

152   Morgan, R. W. 1973. Migration as a Factor in the Acceptance of Medical Care. *Social Science and Medicine* 7(11):865-873.

153   Morrill, W. T. 1963. Immigrants and Associations: The Ibo in Twentieth Century Calabar. *Comparative Studies in Society and History* 5(4):424-448.

154   Moude, H. N. 1973. The Causes and Consequences of Rural-Urban Migration in Kwoi. Research essay. Ahmadu Bello University. Zaria.

155   National Council of Women's Societies, Nigeria. 1985. The UN Decade for Women 1975-1985: The Nigerian Situation. Presented at the NGO Forum, UN Conference on Women, Nairobi, Kenya, July 1985. Ikeja: Literamed Publications (Nig.) Ltd.

156   New Africa. 1978. Aid and the Male Chauvinist. *New Africa* 12:75.

157   New Internationationalist. 1980. The Hundred Hour Week. *New Internationalist* 26.

158   Newman, Jeanne S. 1984. *Women of the World: Sub-Saharan Africa.* Washington, D.C.: WID-USAID and U.S. Department of Commerce, Bureau of the Census.

159   Nigeria. 1970. Second National Development Plan 1970-74. Programme of Post-War Reconstruction and Development. Lagos: Federal Ministry of Information; Printing Division.

160   ----. 1980. *Outline of the Fourth National Development Plan 1981-85.* Lagos: Federal Ministry of Planning.

161   Nigeria. East-Central State. 1974. Ministry of Economic Development and Reconstruction. Statistics Division.

162   Nigeria. Federal Department of Agriculture. 1974. Report of the National Seminar on Home Economics Development Planning. Institute of Tropical Agriculture, 8-14 December, 1974. Ibadan.

163   Nigeria. Federal Government. 1971. *Survey of Working Women with Family Responsibilities.* Federal Ministry of Labour.

164   ----. 1973. *Guidelines for the Third National Development Plan 1975-1980.* Lagos: Ministry of Economic Development and Reconstruction, Central Planning Office.

165   Nigeria. Federal Government. 1975. *Third National Development Plan, 1975-1980, Vol. 1.* Lagos: Federal Ministry of Economic Development, Central Planning Office.

166   Nigeria. Federal Government. 1975. *Third National Development Plan, 1975-1980, Vol.1 and 2 Project Summary.* Lagos: Federal Ministry of Economic Development; Central Planning Office.

167   Nigeria. Federal Ministry of Social Development, Youth Sports And Culture. 1979. Nigeria Country Statement to the Second Regional Conference on the Integration of Women in Development. Lusaka.

168   Nigeria. Federal Republic. 1974. Second National Development Plan 1970-74:. Second Progress Report. Central Planning Office, Federal Ministry of Economic Development. Lagos.

169   ----. 1980. Guidelines for the Fourth National Development Plan 1981-85. The Federal Ministry of Planning. Lagos.

170   Nigeria. Kaduna State Government. 1977. Population Census of Kaduna State 1963 and Projections from 1976 to 1980 by Local Government Councils and Districts. Statistics Division. Ministry of Economic Development. Kaduna.

171   Nigeria. North Central State. 1975. *Third National Development Plan 1975-80. North Central State Programme.* Kaduna, Nigeria: Government Printer.

172   Norman, David W.; Simmons, E. B; and Hays, Henry M. 1982. *Farming Systems in the Nigerian Savanna: Research and Strategies for Development.* Boulder, CO.: Westview Press.

173   O'Barr, Jean F. 1977. *Third World Women--Factors in Their Changing Status.* Durham, N.C.: Center For International Studies, Duke University.

174   Ogunode, F. A. 1981. Guidelines for the Fourth Development Plan and Population Policy for the 1980's. In *Population and Economic Development in Nigeria in the 1980's,* ed. Helena Chojnacka, P.O. Olusanya and F. Ojo, pp. 193-208. New York: United Nations Dept. of Technical Co-operation for Development.

175   Ohadike, P. O. 1968. Urbanization: Growth, Transition and Problems of a Premier West African City. *Urban African Quarterly* 3(4):69-90.

176   Ohaji, Gregory C. 1976. Rural-Urban Migration in the Anambra and Imo States of Nigeria: Basic Economic Implications. Ph.D. Dissertation. Saint Louis University. Saint Louis.

177   Ojo, Olufemi. 1971. Social and Economic Implications of Rapid Population Growth in Nigeria. Paper presented at the Seminar on Population Problems and Policy in Nigeria. University of Ife. Ile-Ife.

178   Okediji, Francis Olu. 1974. Population Dynamics Research in Nigeria: Achievements and New Horizons. In *Population Dynamics Research in Africa,* ed. F.O. Okediji, pp. 3-18. Washington,D.C.: Smithsonian Institute, Interdisciplinary Communications Program.

179   Okediji, O. O. 1975. On Voluntary Associations as Adaptive Mechanisms in West African Urbanization: Another Perspective. *African Urban Notes* B(2):51-73.

180   Okonjo, Isabel Kamene. 1975. The Role of Women in Development of Culture in Nigeria. In *Women Cross-Culturally: Change and Challenge,* ed. R. Rohrlich-Leavitt, pp. 31-40. The Hague: Mouton.

181   ----. 1976. The Role of Women in Social Change Among the Igbo of Southeastern Nigeria Living West of the River Niger. Ph.D. Dissertation. Boston University. Boston.

182   Olayemi, Olusegun A. 1979. Movements of Population from Urban to Rural Areas of Yoruba Towns, Nigeria: A Case Study of Ibadan. *Geneve-Afrique* 17:65-81.

183 Olowolaiyemo, Michael. Urban Petty Producers in Nigeria and Programmes for Assisting Them. Vol. V. Center for Developmental Studies. University College of Swansea. Swansea.

184 Olusanya, P. O. 1969. Socio-economic Aspects of Rural-Urban Migration in Western Nigeria. NISER. University of Ibadan. Ibadan.

185 ----. 1975. In-Migration and the Development of Absentee Farming in the Forest Zone of South-West Nigeria. Paper presented at the Internal Migration Conference. Ile-Ife.

186 Olusanya, Philip O. 1981. The Demographic Situation in Nigeria and its Implication for National Development Policy in the Next Decennium. In *Population and Economic Development in Nigeria in the 1980s*, ed. H. Chojnacka, P.O. Olusanyo and and F. Ojo. New York: UN Department of Technical Cooperation for Development.

187 Ominde, S. H., and Ejiogu, C. 1972. *Population Growth and Economic Development in Africa*. London: Heinemann.

188 Omu, Fred I. A.; Makinwa, Paulina K.; and Ozo, A. O., eds. 1980. *Proceedings of the National Conference on Integrated Rural Development and Women in Development. 2 vols*. Benin City: University of Benin, CenSCER.

189 Onah, J. Onuora, and Iwuji, E. C. 1976. Urban Poverty in Nigeria. *South African Journal of Economics* 44(2):185-193.

190 Oppong, C. 1983. *Female and Male in West Africa*. London: George Allen and Unwin.

191 Orubuloye, I. O. 1977. High Fertility and the Rural Economy: A Study of Yoruba Society in Western Nigeria. In *The Persistence of High Fertility*, ed. John C. Caldwell, pp. 361-392. Canberra: Australian National University.

192 Osunade, M. A. 1978. A Descriptive Profile of the Non-farm Factor: A Case Study of Ipetu Ijesa, Oyo State, Nigeria. *South African Journal of African Affairs* 8(1):44-52.

193 Ottenberg, Phoebe, and Ottenberg, Simon. 1964. Ibo Education and Social Change. In *Education and Politics in Nigeria*, ed. H.N. Weiler, pp. 25-63. Freiburg: Rombach.

194 Parson, K. H. 1970. The Land Tenure Problem in Nigeria. *AID Spring Review* 9.

195 Patel, A. U., and Anthonio, O. B. 1973. Farmers' Wives in Agricultural Development: The Nigerian Case. Presented at the 15th International Congress of Agricultural Economics. Sao Paulo.

196 Paulme, Denise. 1963. *Women's Role in Economic Development*. Berkeley: University of California.

197   Peel, J. D. Y. 1978. Olaju: A Yoruba Concept of Development. *Journal of Development Studies* 14(2):139.

198   Peil, Margaret. 1975. Migration and Labour Force Participation: A Study of Four Towns. Paper presented at the Internal Migration Conference. Ile-Ife.

199   Pettis, S. T. 1971. Social Consequences of Rural Urban Youth Migration in Two African Countries: Nigeria and Kenya. Ph.D. Dissertation. Brandeis University. Waltham, MA.

200   Prothero, M. R. 1975. Mobility in North Western Nigeria: Perspectives and Prospects. Paper presented at the Internal Migration Conference. Ile-Ife.

201   Quinlan, M.; Madeley, J.; and Otobo, D. 1983. Nigerian Survey. *African Business* 55:29.

202   Ransome-Kuti, F. 1961. The Status of Women in Nigeria. *Journal of Human Relations* 10(1):67-72.

203   Remy, Dorothy. 1975. Underdevelopment and the Experience of Women: A Nigerian Case Study. In *Toward an Anthropology of Women*, ed. R.R. Reiter, pp. 358-71. New York, London: Monthly Review Press.

204   Riggs, Mrs. Stanley. 1956. Community Development in Eastern Region. *Nigeria* 52:2-9.

205   Rihani, May. 1978. *Development as if Women Mattered: An Annotated Bibliography with a Third World Focus*. Washington, D.C.: Overseas Development Council.

206   Roder, Wolf. 1971. Economic Development Problems in a Remote Region of Nigeria: The Kainji Lake Case. Paper presented at the African Studies Association Meeting. Denver.

207   Sada, P. O. 1970. The Rural Urban Fringe of Lagos: Growth and Planning Problems. *Nigeria Magazine* 40-45.

208   Sada, P. O., and Oguntoyinbo, J. S. 1978. *Urbanization Processes and Problems in Nigeria*. Ibadan: Ibadan University Press.

209   Safa, H. I. 1982. *Toward a Political Economy of Urbanization in Third World Countries*. Delhi: Oxford University Press.

210   Schubert, P.; Iroh, E.; and Moroney, S. 1983. Nigerian Survey. *African Business* 59:29.

211   Seers, Dudley. 1981. What Needs Are Really Basic in Nigeria: Some Thoughts Prompted by an ILO Mission. *International Labour Review* 120(6):741-750.

212   Sethuraman, S. V. 1981. *The Urban Informal Sector in Developing Countries*. Geneva: International Labour Organization.

213   Shenton, R. W., and Lennihan, Louise. Capital and class: peasant differentiation in N. Nigeria. *Journal of Peasant Studies* 9,1:47-70.

214   Simmons, E. B. 1976. Economic Research on Women in Rural Development in Northern Nigeria. American Council on Education, Paper 10. Overseas Liaison Committtee. Washington, D.C.

215   Sudarkasa, Niara. 1975. National Development Planning for the Promotion and Protection of the Family. Paper presented at the Conference on Social Research and National Development in Nigeria. University of Ibadan. Ibadan.

216   Tinker, Irene, and Michelle Bo Bramsen. 1976. *Women and World Development*. Washington, D.C.: Overseas Development Council.

217   Uba, S.; Nwankwo, G. O.; and Umoh, J. 1977. Nigeria Survey. *New African Development* 11(6):499.

218   Udo, Reuben K. 1975. Migration and Urbanization in Nigeria. In *Population Growth and Socioeconomic Growth in West Africa*, ed. John C. Caldwell, pp. 298-307. New York/London: Columbia University Press.

219   UN. 1970. *Participation of Women in the Economic and Social Development of Their Countries. Report of the Secretary General. E/CN.6/513/REV.1*. New York: United Nations.

220   ----. 1977. *Women, Population and Development*. New York: United Nations Fund For Population Activities.

221   UN Commission on the Status of Women. 1967. *The Participation of Women in Community Development Programmes*. New York: United Nations.

222   ----. 1968. *The Role of Women in the Economic and Social Development of Their Countries*. New York: United Nations.

223   UNECA. The Role of Women in New Nigeria. Regional Meeting on the Role of Women in National Development, Addis Ababa, March 17-26, 1969, Collected Papers. Prepared by the U.N. Economic and Social Council. E/CN.14/SW/INF/16. New York.

224   ----. 1963. Fertility, Mortality, International Migration and Population Growth in Africa. Conference held in Cairo, October-November 1962. E/CN.14/ASPP/L.2, E/CN.9/CONF.3/L.2. New York.

225   ----. 1975. *Recommendations of Regional Meetings for Africa on the Role of Women in Development*. Addis Ababa: UNECA.

226   ----. 1975. *Women of Africa: Today and Tomorrow*. Addis Ababa: Women's Programme.

227   ----. 1976. Workshop for Planners and Trainers in Programmes to Improve the Quality of Rural Life. Ibadan, May 1975. Economic Commision for Africa. Addis Ababa.

228   ----. 1977. The New International Economic Order: What Roles for Women?. E/CN.14/ATRCW/77/WD3. Addis Ababa.

229   UNECA. Human Resources Development Division. 1972. Women: The Neglected Human Resource for African Development. *Canadian Journal of African Studies* 6(2):359-370.

230   UNESCO. 1968. Problems of Plan Implementation: Development Planning and Economic Integration in Africa. New York.

231   UNFAO. 1965. *Agricultural Organization in Nigeria*. Rome: United Nations Food and Agricultural Organization.

232   USAID. 1974. *A Seven Country Survey on the Roles of Women in Rural Development*. Washington, D.C.: USAID.

233   US Dept. of Commerce. Bureau of the Census. 1980. Social Statistics in Nigeria. Federal Office of Statistics. Washington, D.C.

234   Wellesley Editorial Committee. 1977. *Women and National Development: The Complexities of Change*. Chicago: University of Chicago Press.

235   Williams, Gavin. 1976. *Nigeria: Economy and Society*. London: Rex Collings, Ltd.

236   Women In Nigeria. 1985. The Conditions of Women in Nigeria and Policy Recommendations up to 2000 A.D. Presented at the NGO Forum, UN Conference on Women, Nairobi, Kenya. Zaria, Nigeria.

237   World Bank. 1974. *Nigeria: Options for Long-Term Development. Report of A Mission Sent to Nigeria by the World Bank*. Baltimore: The Johns Hopkins University Press.

238   Youssef, Nadia. 1974. *Women and Work in Developing Societies*. Berkeley: University of California, Institute of International Studies. Population Monograph Series No.15.

239   ----. 1976. Women in Development: Urban Life and Labour. In *Women and World Development*, ed. Irene Tinker and Michele Bo Bramsen, pp. 70-77. Washington, D.C.: Overseas Development Council.

240   Zollner, Joy. 1970. Roles of Women in National Development in African Countries. *International Labour Review* 101:399-401.

241   ----. 1971. African Conference on the Role of Women in National Development. *International Labour Review* 104:555-557.

242   ----. 1972. African Seminar on the Participation of Women in Economic Life. *International Labour Review* 105:175-177.

243   ----. 1975. Women's Role in Future Development. *Literacy Work* 15:24-25.

Chapter Twelve
General Works

1   Abraham, Roy Clive. 1940. *The Tiv People (2nd. ed.)*. London: Crown Agents.

2   Ajisafe, A. K. 1924. *Laws and Customs of the Yoruba People*. London: Routledge and Kegan Paul.

3   Akinola, R. A. 1967. Urban Tradition in Yorubaland. *Nigeria Magazine* 95:344-350.

4   Armstrong, R. 1955. *The Idoma-Speaking Peoples. Ethnographic Survey of West Africa, Part 10*. London: International African Institute.

5   ----. 1955. *The Igala. Ethnographic Survey of West Africa, Part 10*. London: International Africa Institute.

6   Baker, Tanya. 1954. The Social Organization of the Birom People. Ph.D. Dissertation. University of London. London.

7   Bascom, William. 1958. Yoruba Urbanism: A Summary. *Man* 58(253):190-191.

8   ----. 1969. *The Yoruba of South-Western Nigeria*. New York: Holt, Rinehart, and Winston, Inc.

9   ----. 1962. Some Aspects of Yoruba Urbanization. *American Anthropologist* 55(4):699-709.

10   Basden, G. T. 1966. *Among the Ibo of Nigeria*. London: Cass.

11   Biobaku, S. O. 1957. *The Egba and Their Neighbors*. Oxford: Clarendon Press.

12   Bohannan, Laura. 1951. A Comparative Study of Social Differentiation in Primitive Society. Ph.D. Dissertation. Oxford University. Oxford.

13   Bohannan, Laura, and Bohannan, Paul. 1953. *The Tiv of Central Nigeria*. London: International African Institute.

14   Bohannan, Paul. 1965. The Tiv of Nigeria. In *Peoples of Africa*, ed. J.L. Gibbs, pp. 513-546. New York: Holt, Rinehart, and Winston, Inc.

15   Bohannan, Paul, and Bohannan, Laura. 1958. *Three Source Notebooks on Tiv Ethnography*. New Haven, CT.: Human Relations Area Files.

16   ----. 1968. *Tiv Economy*. Evanston, IL.: Northwestern University Press.

17   Boston, J. S. 1969. *The Igala Kingdom*. Ibadan: Oxford University Press.

18   Bradbury, R., and Lloyd, Peter C. 1957. *The Benin Kingdom and Edo Speaking People of South-Western Nigeria. Ethnographic Survey of West Africa, Part 13*. London: International African Institute.

19   Brotherton, J. G. H. 1969. The Nomadic Fulani of Northern Nigeria. *Nigerian Field* XXXIV:126-136.

20   Brown, Paula. 1955. *The Igbira. Ethnographic Survey of West Africa, Part 10*. London: International African Institute.

21   Buchanan, Keith M., and Pugh, J. C. 1955. *Land and People of Nigeria*. London: University of London Press Ltd.

22   Chukwu, Oliver C. 1977. The Igbo of Nigeria: An Analytical Description of Selected Cultural Factors. Ph.D. Dissertation. United States International University. San Diego.

23   Clapperton, Hugh. 1829. *Journal of a Second Expedition into the Interior of Africa*. London: Murray.

24   Clifford, Miles. 1944. Notes on the Bassar-Komo Tribe in the Igala Division. *Man* 44:107-116.

25   Cobbald, Elizabeth. 1983. Muslim Hausa Women in Northern Nigeria: An Annotated Bibliography. *African Research and Documentation* 32:22-29.

26   Cohen, Ronald. 1960. The Structure of Kanuri Society. Ph.D. Dissertation. University of Wisconsin. Madison.

27   ----. 1967. *The Kanuri of Bornu*. New York: Holt, Rinehart, and Winston, Inc.

28   Cordwell, Justine M. 1952. Some Aesthetic Aspects of Yoruba and Benin Culture. Ph.D. Dissertation. Northwestern University. Evanston.

29   De St. Croix, F. W. 1944. *The Fulani of Northern Nigeria*. Lagos: Government Printer.

30   Dike, Azuka. 1975. The Resiliance of Igbo Culture: A Case Study of Akwa Town. Ph.D. Dissertation. New School for Social Research. New York.

31   Downes, R. M. 1969. *The Tiv Tribe*. Farnborough: Gregg.

32   ----. 1971. *Tiv Religion*. Ibadan: University Press.

33   Eades, J. S. 1980. *The Yoruba Today*. London: Cambridge University Press.

34   East, Rupert Trans. 1965. *Akigba's Story: The Tiv Tribe as Seen by One of Its Members*. London: Oxford University Press.

35   Elakhe, Peter. 1963. Ekue Rites. *Nigeria* 76:45-56.

36   Fadipe, N. A. 1970. *The Sociology of the Yoruba*. Ibadan: Ibadan University Press.

37   Fagan, Ethel S. 1930. Some Notes on the Bachama Tribe, Adamawa Province, Northern Nigeria. *Journal of the African Society* 29(115-116):269-279.

38   Fagg, W., and Willet, F. 1960. Ancient Ife, An Ethnographic Survey. *Odu* 8.

39   Ferguson, John. 1970. *The Yorubas of Nigeria*. Bletchley, Bucks: Open University.

40   Folarin, Adebisi. 1939. *The Laws and Customs of Egbaland*. Abeokuta: Egba Native Administration Press.

41   Forde, Daryll. 1955. *The Nupe. Ethnographic Survey of West Africa, Part 10*. London: International African Institute.

42   ----. 1962. *The Yoruba-Speaking Peoples of South-Western Nigeria*. London: International African Institute.

43   Forde, Daryll, and Jones, G. I. 1950. *The Ibo- and Ibibio-Speaking Peoples of South-Eastern Nigeria. Ethnographic Survey of West Africa, Part 3*. London: International African Institute.

44   Frantz, Charles. 1978. Ecology and Social Organization Among Nigerian Fulbe. In *The Nomadic Alternative: Modes and Models of Interaction in the African-Asian Deserts and Steppes*, ed. Wolfgang Weissleder, pp. 97-118. The Hague: Mouton.

45   Frobenius, Leo. 1913. *The Voice of Africa*. 2 vols. London: Hutchinson.

46   Green, M. 1964. *Igbo Village Affairs*. London: Frank Cass.

47   Gunn, Harold D., and Conant, F. P. 1960. *Peoples in the Middle Niger Region, Northern Nigeria. Ethnographic Survey of West Africa, Part 15*. London: International African Institute.

48   Gunn, Harold D., and F.P. Conant. 1953. *Peoples of the Plateau Area of Northern Nigeria. Ethnographic Surveys of West Africa, Part 7*. London: International African Institute.

49 Hopen, C. Edward. 1958. *The Pastoral Fulbe Family in Gwandu*. London: Oxford University Press.

50 Hopkins, A. G. 1969. A Report on the Yoruba. *Journal of the Historical Society of Nigeria* 5:67-100.

51 Ibrahim, Y. A. 1976. Igbirra Traditional Institutions. *Nigeria Magazine* 119/120:51-66.

52 Jones, G. I. 1961. Ecology and Social Structure Among the North-Eastern Ibo. *Africa* 31(2):117-134.

53 Kaberry, Phyllis. 1952. *Women of the Grassfields*. London: Colonial Research Publication No. 14, H.M. Stationery Office.

54 Kato, M. N. 1974. A Study of Traditional Social Organization Among the Kaje With Reference to Social Change During the Recent Past. M.Sc. Thesis. Ahmadu Bello University. Zaria.

55 Kraph-Askari, Eva. 1969. *Yoruba Towns and Cities*. Oxford: Clarendon Press.

56 Leith-Ross, Sylvia. 1939. *African Women: A Study of the Ibo of Nigeria*. London: Faber and Faber.

57 ----. 1944. *African Conversation Piece*. London: Hutchinson.

58 ----. 1951. *Beyond the Niger*. London: Butterworth.

59 ----. 1965. *African Women*. London: Routledge and Kegan Paul.

60 Lieber, J. W. 1971. Efik and Ibibio Villages. Occasional Paper No.13. Institute of Education. University of Ibadan. Ibadan.

61 ----. 1971. Ibo Village Communities. Occasional Paper No.12. Institute of Education. University of Ibadan. Ibadan.

62 Lloyd, Peter C. 1965. The Yoruba of Nigeria. In *Peoples of Africa*, ed. J.L. Gibbs Jr., pp. 549-582. New York: Holt, Rinehart, and Winston, Inc.

63 ----. 1974. *Power and Independence: Urban Africans' Perception of Social Inequality*. London: Routledge and Kegan Paul.

64 Lloyd, Peter C.; Mabogunje, A. L.; and Awe, B. 1967. *The City of Ibadan*. London: Cambridge University Press.

65   Mabogunje, A. L. 1962. *Yoruba Towns*. Ibadan: Ibadan University Press.

66   ----. 1968. *Urbanization in Nigeria*. London: University of London Press.

67   Madauci, Ibrahim et al. 1968. *Hausa Customs*. Zaria: Northern Nigeria Publishing Corporation.

68   Meek, Charles Kingsley. 1931. *Tribal Studies in Northern Nigeria*. London: Oxford University Press.

69   ----. 1957. *Law and Authority in a Nigerian Tribe*. London: Oxford University Press.

70   ----. 1971. *The Northern Tribes of Nigeria: An Ethnographical Account of the Northern Provinces of Nigeria Together with a Report on the 1921 Decennial Census*. London: Cass.

71   Morrill, W. T. 1961. Two Urban Cultures of Calabar, Nigeria. Ph.D. Dissertation. University of Chicago. Chicago.

72   Nadel, S. F. 1942. *A Black Byzantium: The Kingdom of Nupe in Nigeria*. London: Oxford University Press.

73   Na'ibi, Mallam S. et al. 1969. *The Gwari, Gade and Koro Tibes of the Abuja Emirate*. Ibadan: Ibadan University Press (Africana Publishing Corp.).

74   National Council of Women's Societies, Nigeria. 1985. The UN Decade for Women 1975-1985: The Nigerian Situation. Presented at the NGO Forum, UN Conference on Women, Nairobi, Kenya, July 1985. Ikeja: Literamed Publications (Nig.) Ltd.

75   Nigeria. Federal Government. 1956. The Nupe of Pategi. *Nigeria* 50:260-279.

76   Nigeria. National Library. 1969. *Social Life and Customs in Nigeria: A Selective Bibliography*. Lagos: National Library Publication, 12.

77   Njoku, O. 1974. The Dibia Secret Society in Iboland. *Review of Ethnology* 4:66-70.

78   Nsughe, P. O. 1974. *Ohafia: A Matrilineal Ibo People*. London: Oxford University Press.

79   Offonry, H. Kanu. 1947. The Ibo People. *West African Review* 18:167-168.

80   Ojike, Mbonu. 1955. *My Africa*. London: Blanford Press.

81   Ojo, G. J. A. 1967. *Yoruba Culture*. Ibadan: University of Ife and University of London Press, Ltd.

82   Ojo, G. J. Afolabi. 1966. *Yoruba Culture*. Ibadan: The Caxton Press (West Africa) Ltd.

83   Okediji, Francis Olu, and Okediji, O. O. 1970. *The Sociology of the Yoruba*. Ibadan: Ibadan University Press.

84   Okojie, C. G. 1960. *Ishan Native Laws and Customs*. Yaba: John Okwesa & Co. and the Nigeria National Press.

85   Okoli, Joe. 1964. The People of Anambra: Anambra Women. *African Historian* 1(2):41-46.

86   Olapade, J. O. 1980. Osun People in Oyo State. *Nigerian Field* 45:26-33.

87   Osborne, Oliver H. 1968. The Egbado of Egbaland. Ph.D. Dissertation. Michigan State University. East Lansing.

88   Ottenberg, Phoebe. 1965. The Afikpo Ibo of Eastern Nigeria. In *Peoples of Africa*, ed. J.L. Gibbs Jr., pp. 1-37. New York: Holt, Rinehart, and Winston, Inc.

89   Paulme, Denise. 1963. *Women of Tropical Africa, trans. by H.M. Wright*. London: Routledge and Kegan Paul.

90   Schwab, W. B. 1951. Some Problems of Acculturation in Nigeria. *Philadelphia Anthropological Society Bulletin* 4(3):3-4.

91   Seton, Ralph S. 1929. Notes on the Igala Tribe, Northern Nigeria. *Journal of African Society* 29:42-52.

92   Smith, M. G. 1965. The Hausa of Northern Nigeria. In *Peoples of Africa*, ed. L. Gibbs, pp. 119-55. New York: Holt, Rinehart, and Winston, Inc.

93   Stenning, Derrick J. 1959. *Savannah Nomads: A Study of the Wodaabe Pastoral Fulani of Western Bornu Province, Northern Nigeria*. London: Oxford University Press.

94   ----. 1965. The Pastoral Fulani of Northern Nigeria. In *Peoples of Africa*, ed. J.L. Gibbs Jr., pp. 361-401. New York: Holt, Rinehart, and Winston, Inc.

95   Talbot, D. Amaury. 1915. *Woman's Mysteries of A Primitive People*. London: Frank Cass and Co. Ltd. Reprinted 1968.

96   Talbot, P. A. 1926. *Life in Southern Nigeria*. London: MacMillan.

97   ----. 1926. *The Peoples of Southern Nigeria*. London: Humphrey Milford.

98   Temple, Olive. 1965. *Notes on the Tribes, Provinces, Emirates and States of the Northern Province of Nigeria*. London: Cass.

99   Uchendu, Victor C. 1963. Status and Hierarchy Among the Southeastern Igbo. Master's Thesis. Northwestern University. Evanston.

100   ----. 1965. *The Igbo of Southeastern Nigeria*. New York: Holt, Rinehart and Winston.

101   USAID. 1983. *Africa: Nigeria--Selected Statistical Data by Sex*. Washington D.C.: US Bureau of the Census, AID.

102   Westfall, G. D. 1974. Nigerian Women: A Bibliographical Essay. *Africana Journal* 5:99-138.

103   Women In Nigeria. 1985. The Conditions of Women in Nigeria and Policy Recommendations up to 2000 A.D. Presented at the NGO Forum, UN Conference on Women, Nairobi, Kenya. Zaria, Nigeria.

104   Yeld, Rachael E. 1960. A Study of the Social Position of Women in Kebbi (Northern Nigeria). Masters Thesis. London University. London.